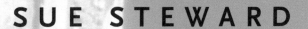

SUE STEWARD

Salsa

Musical Heartbeat
of Latin America

FOREWORD BY WILLIE COLON

with 228 illustrations, 74 in colour

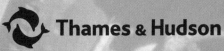

Thames & Hudson

Contents

For Greg Neale

Designed by Norman Reynolds

First published in the United Kingdom in 1999 by Thames & Hudson Ltd, 181A High Holborn, London WC1V 7QX

© 1999 Thames & Hudson Ltd, London

British Library Cataloguing-in-Publication Data A catalogue record for this book is available from the British Library

ISBN 0-500-28153-X

Printed in Hong Kong by H & Y Printing Limited

Foreword
Willie Colón

Salsa's magic has always been transmitted from skin to skin – in a silent, seductive dance clinch, and through a sheet of dried goat skin – the voice of the drum.

IT'S GOING TO BE hard to really explain what salsa is. The French say, 'Ça se sent, ça ne s'explique'; you have to feel it. As a founding salsero I'd like to give you my personal cosmic opinion of what salsa is to me.

Salsa is more than just a good time, wiggling your butt and working up a sweat. It is all that but it is also much more. To many displaced young Latinos all over the world salsa is a validation – it is home, a flag, and grandma. Kids who are constantly told that they are different because they are Latinos, despite being first-, second- or even third-generation US or whatever born, will cling to this music for answers. It is a cultural place where they can belong, a socio-political movement, a platform to tell our stories and communicate across the broad expanses that we inhabit. It is a chronicle and a testimony that we were here on this planet, a showcase to display our talent to the world. It is an economic phenomenon that has allowed many lucky Latinos (like yours truly) to travel, be educated and live well. Salsa was the force that unified diverse Latino and other non-Latino racial and ethnic groups. It was our church prayer, town meeting, singles group and political rally, all at the same time.

Salsa continues the ancient traditions of aural learning, of cleansing your sorrows in dance as your body is carried away by the beat. It is the reconciliation of the three roots that make up our Latino culture: the African, European and native Caribbean roots.

Salsa is a social, musical, cultural, hybrid force that has embraced jazz, folklore, pop and everything else that is relevant or could stand in its evolutionary path. It is the basis for rap/hiphop, house and dance (disco). It is the groundwork that made Gloria Estefán and Antonio Banderas palatable to the world.

As I grew up the pride I got from playing my music allowed me to tell stories in order to continue the thread that bound us across the world. Quite by accident, I started my little sidewalk group of diverse nationalities. My eclectic social and music education ranged from Rafael Hernández to The Beatles to Gran Combo, to Carlos Gardel (tango), to Ramito (jíbaro), Herb Alpert, James Bond and James Brown. And when I decided to write and make music, that's what

came out, a swinging musical Jabberwocky that the oldtimers heatedly refuted and condemned for being a blasphemous, ignorant concept. And that is what has always been my point. Salsa is not a *rhythm*. It is a *concept*. An open, ever-evolving musical, cultural, socio-political CONCEPT.

The average ages of the fans singing my songs? About seventeen. At any salsa concert or dance you will find an age range from teenagers to grand-mothers. We've got septuagenarians like Tito Puente and Celia Cruz and at the other end teenyboppers, filling venues together. Salsa is not a fad. There are Mexican, Venezuelan, Peruvian, Spanish, Cuban, Puerto Rican, Canary Island, Hawaiian, Dominican, Colombian, New York, Los Angelino, even British, French, German, Japanese and New Zealander salsa groups. A few years ago I played in the Colombian jungle town of Quibdó, where some people turned up in canoes. My very next gig was at a US presidential inaugu-ration (they were a much harder audience).

On behalf of myself and my salsero colleagues, many of whom are no longer with us, I want to thank Sue Steward for documenting those phantoms of Swing that we have come to know and love musically. I myself never met everyone I would have liked to. In too many cases it's too late, but this book has helped put a face on some of my heroes.

ABOVE LEFT: **Accordions have been popular in Latin America since the mid-19th century. At a Colombian vallenato festival like the one shown here, accordionists are kings.**
ABOVE RIGHT: **As this Cuban mother and daughter reveal, age has no meaning in a culture where children can beat out the crucial clave rhythm before they can talk.**

Introduction
The world of salsa

Anibal (Andy) Vásquez was one half of the Mambo Aces dance duo. At the Palladium ballroom in Manhattan in the 1950s, circles of admirers and imitators gathered every night to watch him cutting lindy-hop and jitter-bug steps with traditional Cuban and Puerto Rican folk routines.

'SALSA IS WHAT YOU EAT; mambo is what you dance' is Tito Puente's pained response to the word salsa. Unfortunately for him, the term is here to stay. Like 'jazz' and 'blues', it is one of those musical catch-alls – totally confusing and thoroughly useful. And for record stores, a godsend. Tell someone you're going to a salsa club and you reveal the language, the geography, the high-heeled dress code, and the fact that you're about to have an energetic, endorphin-loaded night out.

Using the language of the kitchen for music is already well established in jazz in expletives like 'cooking!' and 'tasty!', and there are as many theories about the origin of the word 'salsa' as there are styles of music included in the category. The top Cuban son group in the 1930s, Sexteto Habanero, recorded a song still performed today called 'Echale salsita!' – literally, 'Put the sauce on it!' – and the Cuban superstar Beny Moré signed off his explosive shows in the forties and fifties with a sparky catchphrase, 'Hola, salsa!', which translates limply as 'Hey, sauce!'

The first self-conscious use of 'salsa' to describe modernized Cuban dance music came in 1966, when a Venezuelan radio DJ, Danilo Phidiad Escalona, launched a show called 'La hora del sabor, la salsa y el bembe', an untranslatable phrase, but literally 'The hour of flavour, spiciness and liturgy' – music for body and soul. By the end of the 1970s, the word was synonymous with the sound of Latin New York, as created by Fania Records. One of Fania's trademarks was its use of distinctive and brilliantly graphic album covers, designed by a cocky young Puerto Rican New Yorker called Izzy Sanabria who also doubled up as MC to the legendary Fania All Stars supergroup. All through their shows he would bark 'Salsa!', first to introduce soloists and then to drive them on. Throughout the seventies, in his pioneering magazine *Latin NY*, Sanabria used the word 'salsa' to describe the music he covered: Latin New York's take on Cuban dance music, played mostly by Puerto Rican New York musicians. Fania's salsa set the standards for the rest of Latin America.

Today the term 'salsa' covers most kinds of Latin dance music, not just its immediate Cuban ancestors (son, guaracha, mambo, guajira – see Chapter 1 for their stories). Even the very different Dominican merengues and Colombian cumbias are included in its embrace, for the convenience of record shops and review pages (and this book). The unsexy term 'Latin Music' is an alternative, but is confusing because it also includes the myriad different styles coming out of Brazil and the explosion of Latin pop and rock being produced in South America, particularly in Argentina.

So this is the story of salsa. It begins among its tangled root system in Cuba, careens through the Spanish-speaking islands of Puerto Rico and the Dominican Republic, and travels to Miami and New York, where an entirely different slant has been put on the root stock through neighbourly contact with African-American music. Different styles like merengue and bomba, mambo and plena, all reflect the details of their local history, because even though they share common ancestors in Spain and Africa, neither the Spanish nor the Africans were one homogeneous group: the 'Spanish' included descendants of the Moors (North African Arabs), who colonized them for more than four hundred years, as well as Africanized Canary Islanders; the 'Africans' had been shipped in as slaves from regions more different from each other than Spain and England. That magnificent gene pool created this most exhilarating and influential music.

Uniting the various styles is an underlying rhythmic frame known as the clave, clapped out enthusiastically by the audiences in sinuous 1-2-3, 1-2 phrases. Like the Spanish language – the language of salsa – clave means different things in different places. The New York composer/pianist Isidro Infante hears the clave drifting like a ghost through flamencos; Cuban percussionist Daniel Ponce hears it in Jimi Hendrix solos. But everybody hears it in salsa: according to the veteran conga player Joe Cuba, 'Clave makes the (Latin music) world go round.'

The continental Latin countries tell a different story. Colombia represents the continent here – not just because of my personal passion for its music, but also because of its tremendous impact on the rest of salsa since the eighties, when Joe Arroyo's Caribbean-flavoured songs, known as 'tropical salsa' swept through the charts. In the late nineties another Colombian – an ex-TV soap star called Carlos Vives – was the talking point with his accordion-led vallenato-salsa, which inspired copies from both Gloria Estefán and Julio Iglesias. Focusing on Colombia leaves some glaring omissions, but these are logically accommodated elsewhere. Venezuela's top-league singer, songwriter and bandleader Oscar D'León, one of the great soneros of this time, built his career on a passion for Cuba's heroic singer Beny Moré and the mighty mambo bands of fifties Havana. The prolific Panamanian songwriter Omar Alfanno belongs here because he makes a career from selling hit songs to a generation of Puerto Rican singers. His own early inspiration was his fellow Panamanian singer–songwriter Rubén Blades, who fits into the salsa tale through his key role in the Fania story and his own international success as a crossover singer.

No such dramatic development took place in Europe, but the UK's sixty-year love affair with Latin music needs honouring – from Edmundo Ros's supper-club band to Roberto Pla's Latin Jazz Ensemble, via Blue Rondo a la Turk and the Spice Girls; from the Embassy Club to A Night in Havana. Some infectious Latin pop fusions have had an impact on the charts. A recent and significant triumph has huge international consequences: the 1998 Latin Grammy award went to the London offices of World Circuit Records for its modern Anglo-Cuban-American collaboration between Ry Cooder and a group of veteran Cuban musicians on the *Buena Vista Social Club* album. The award also acknowledged the other independent risk-takers in the UK who, since the eighties, have put salsa on the world music map. Not forgetting the Cuban and Colombian dance teachers in the UK who rose to the monumental challenge of teaching salsa steps to English audiences.

The charanga is one of Cuba's most enduring and adaptable styles. Musicians in overcrowded Havana rehearse wherever they can, often in the open, giving neighbours a free taste of the night's performance.

Carnival derives from the
Catholic holy days when
slaves were allowed to
dance through the streets to
their own music. In modern
Cuba (left) carnival has been
a training ground for many
great musicians, particularly
drummers.
In the Puerto Rican town
of Loiza Aldea, the legacy
of the Africans is preserved
in the bomba dance
(above right), driven by
a line of drummers.

The foundations of salsa are unarguably in Cuba and the capital of modern salsa is New York, with Miami as its satellite town. But wherever American Latins settle, a salsa scene will spring up. The West Coast is represented here by San Francisco, with its Latino population of Cubans and Puerto Ricans as well as Chicanos and Mexican-Americans, and a nightlife revolving around a handful of significant bands.

The second part of the book swings away from the familiar salsa locations and spins off into some of the offshoots of the Afro-Hispanic musical breeding ground. Latin Jazz, invented in 1943 by the Cuban musicians Mario Bauzá and Machito, grew from a fusion of traditional Afro-Cuban rhythms with the complex horn arrangements of the great dance bands led by Chick Webb, Cab Calloway and Duke Ellington. Today's Latin Jazz has reinvigorated the flagging jazz scene and has acquired a league of influential soloists and composers who occupy a niche between the dancehall and the concert hall. They also have their own Grammy award. The honourable King of Latin Jazz, Tito Puente, with over half a century of crackling timbales solos, continues to produce music for the latest generation. Much Latin Jazz is still dancing music as it was in Puente's heyday, when his solos transfixed hundreds of mamboniks at the Palladium ballroom in Manhattan.

Family trees play a major part in this story but none is more potent or poignant than the branch that connects salsa to African music. This significant aside tells the story of salsa's return to its point of origin: to West and Central Africa. A thriving trade in exported salsa has been influential in those same regions of the continent which surrendered so many millions of people hundreds of years ago. The response was African salsa – a mixture of local guitar-based brews and traditional music, heavily influenced by records imported from the top bands of Cuba and New York. In the nineties, the process was reversed yet again, when the forward-thinking guitarist Juan Luis Guerra employed African rumbas and the Senegalese producer Ibrahim Sylla founded the 'Africando' project, bringing together African and Latin New York musicians.

My first contact with the real live thing in 1981 was straight in at the deep end at a Labour Day salsa extravaganza in Madison Square Gardens, when the Fania All Stars performed to a screaming, dancing audience of 18,000 Latin New Yorkers. This is the kind of book I wanted to read when I got home that night with a thousand questions buzzing in my brain – about the extraordinary musicians I'd shaken hands with, drooled over, danced to and been dazzled by; and about the music that had kept the audience on its feet for more than three hours. After my first equally stirring trip to Cuba, in 1985, I needed a book to help fill in the gaps after meeting the legends and struggling with interviews. So – plug in the CD, and match the chapter to the tune.

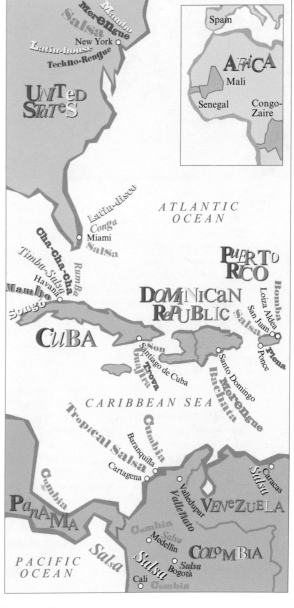

Salsa's ancestral home: Africa and Spain, the former Spanish Caribbean islands and Colombia, and the umbilically connected salsa capitals, New York and Miami.

Salsa: The music, the dance

THE SALSA ORCHESTRA has its origins in the wandering guitar and percussion trios who played the first popular 'son' songs in turn-of-the-century Cuba. These have evolved into today's formidable show bands in which percussion is centre stage, with the horns, bass and piano fanning out around them and the singers up front.

Salsa instruments often work in blocks: the cowbell paired with congas; bass (electric or double) with piano. Rhythm is the heart of the music. Most percussion instruments – congas, bongos, tamboras, batás – are played in pairs or have twin heads, allowing players to converse not only with each other but also between their left and right hands. One head is higher pitched, thinner skinned, female, and the other deeper, male. Songs unfold in a series of conversations and ad-libbed solos, most typically in a solo-and-chorus, call-and-response structure descended from African song. This is most obvious between the singer and the band, but also takes place between soloing instruments. Singers are the most promiscuous – they play to their coro (backing) singers and also to the other instruments. In partnerships based on years of working together, it's like watching lifelong tango partners in full flight.

Threaded through salsa is the fundamental rhythm called clave. Children clap its 1-2-3, 1-2 pattern almost before they can speak. Feelings run high on the subject. 'Clave is your basic rhythm pattern,' declares New York conga player Joe Cuba. 'If you're off clave, you're off rhythm.' He cites the formidable pianist Eddie Palmieri: 'Eddie's left hand is always in clave, it gives him his base, then his right hand can jump all over the world.' Cuban trumpeter Jesús Alémany is adamant, 'Clave is the vertebra of my musical feeling, the crucial way that the bass line, percussion and chorus, and of course the dance itself, link together.' The biggest sin for such purists is to play out of clave, though that has never bothered mavericks like Willie Colón, who started breaking the rules in the 1970s, or today's leading salsa producer, Sergio George, who delights in reversing clave and changing its accent. Colombia's salsa musicians have their own sense of clave which stops and starts and changes mid-song, and the dancers match it. Cutting-edge musicians all over Latin America are today mixing rap rhymes and electronic beats into its patterns.

Latin percussion can be baffling to outsiders. A London promoter grumbled at having to pay for 'some guy to bang a pair of wooden sticks' and another for 'just shaking a pair of maracas'. 'If you put all those bits together,' he moaned, 'the timbales, the cowbell and the wood-blocks, you'd have a drum kit – and one wage to pay.'

Latin instruments often perform rhythm, harmony and melody all at once. Pianists are percussionists; conga players play melodies. Many modern pianists incorporate percussionists' techniques into their solos, leaping up to bang the keys with their arms or heels, like Jerry Lee Lewis, or twanging the strings like John Cage. The double bass player Israel 'Cachao' López, father of the mambo, drums the bass's polished wood with his knuckles between bowing or plucking the strings. Percussion sections can operate like an orchestra; a single drummer can play both rhythms and tunes.

Each musician *appears* to play to a different rhythm with no connection to the rest, though in fact they are instinctively, precisely related. The main problem facing newcomers to salsa is how to disentangle the seemingly impenetrable cross-rhythms, and then – how to start dancing. And, remember, to paraphrase New York dance teacher Denis Symmons: Salsa is a macho dance, done to macho music, played by macho musicians!

Making the Music: The instruments

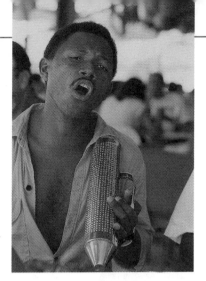

CLAVES

Salsa's basic tool, a pair of smooth wooden cylindrical blocks which, when banged together, fill the air with a clear, bell-like tone. Cuban soldiers carried claves in their pockets during the 1898 War of Independence with Spain, ready to accompany guitarists' songs.

MARACAS

The ancient legacy of the Caribbean Indians, these small, round, dried gourds with handles attached are a greatly underestimated instrument. When shaken by a virtuoso, the seeds or pellets inside smash against the head in a single sharp note, as precise as any electronic pulse.

GUIRO, GUIRA

The other legacy of the Caribbean Indians, these rhythmic 'scrapers' add a regular hissing, scratchy pulse to many styles of Latin music. Their shapes and sizes vary, from the Cuban güiro, made of shiny, serrated, long, woody gourds and scratched with a stick, to the Dominican guayo, a pointed metal cylinder designed to grate vegetables but transformed into an upbeat timepiece when vigorously scraped with a metal stick or Afro haircomb in merengue groups.

QUIJANO (donkey's or horse's jawbone)

Only folkloric or real old-timey son bands in eastern Cuba still use these intriguing early instruments made out of the dried jawbone of a donkey or horse. The loose back teeth create a soft shuffling sound when shaken.

BONGO

Developed in Eastern Cuba's first son groups, the uniquely Cuban bongo drums are made of cedar wood to give a bright, light, pinging sound. The two drum heads are of different sizes – the larger, deeper macho and the smaller, higher hembra. Bongo techniques include a sighing glissando effect made by running the heel of the hand across the head. Other sounds are drawn through the changing angles and weights of fingers, nails and hands – like a masseur working the skin.

CONGA

The most commonplace drum in music other than salsa. It was originally a single, large, portable instrument played in carnival parades and religious ceremonies. Modern versions work in 'sets' or 'nests' of up to six differently tuned drums, each requiring a different technique to coax its voice. Techniques have changed since the 1940s when Latin New Yorker Joe Cuba first played: 'There were no tuning keys then, you had to heat the skin with a little paraffin stove to get the right pitch. Nowadays, the keys give you the pitch in minutes.' Congas signify Africa; they were first introduced to the dancehall in the 1940s by Cuban guitarist Arsenio Rodríguez, and were a shocking reminder of the African presence.

BATA

Until 1930, when the composer Gilberto Valdés wrote a piece involving them, batá drums appeared only in the private ceremonies of the Afro-Cuban santería religion. They are talking drums which 'sing' the esoteric songs of the ancient Yoruba languages of the slaves. They were traditionally wrapped with scarves in the colours of the santería saints, and bound with leather straps hung with beads and bells which created a soft jingle behind the main rhythms. Batá are played in threes, each with a different voice and gender. Some are hundreds of years old, protected in temples like holy relics and played only by the babalao (priest) who feeds them and sings their ancient chants. Traditionally, women were kept away from them, but the taboo has been gradually broken and today several talented female drummers work in Cuban bands.

CENCERRO (COWBELL)

Metal cowbells were originally welded together in pairs. When hit with a stick or by a pedal attached to the timbales kit, today's single cattle bells yield two distinctive metallic tones – a high note near the handle and a deeper note from the open bell. 'Pacheco bells', invented by salsa icon Johnny Pacheco in the 1960s, are scored with a groove across the surface to give extra tones. Cowbells are a favourite accompaniment in Puerto Rican salsa, adding a regular, tick-tocking, cantering beat.

Continued on page 16

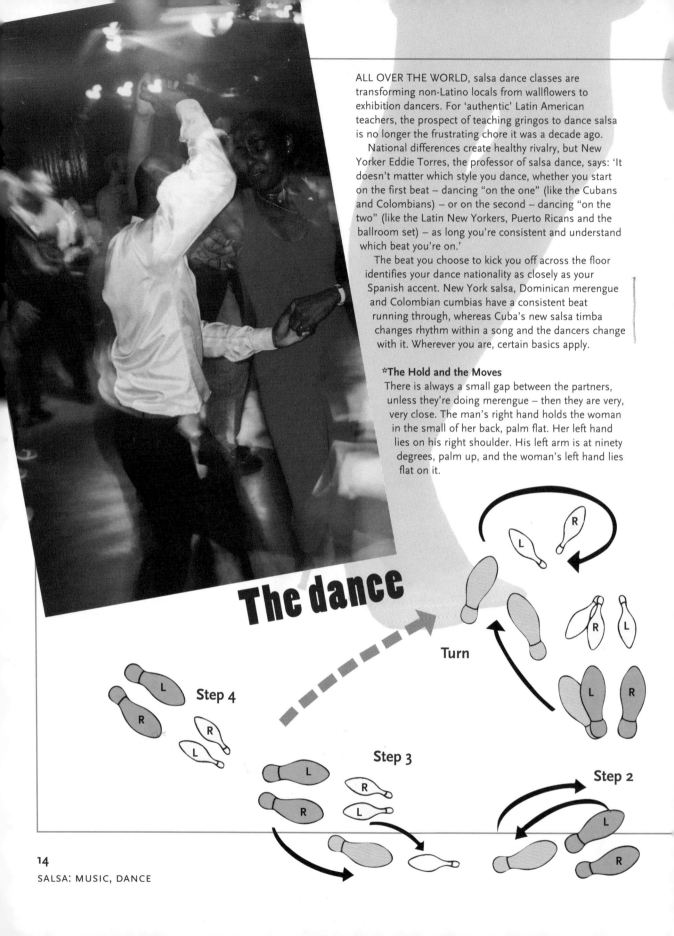

ALL OVER THE WORLD, salsa dance classes are transforming non-Latino locals from wallflowers to exhibition dancers. For 'authentic' Latin American teachers, the prospect of teaching gringos to dance salsa is no longer the frustrating chore it was a decade ago.

National differences create healthy rivalry, but New Yorker Eddie Torres, the professor of salsa dance, says: 'It doesn't matter which style you dance, whether you start on the first beat – dancing "on the one" (like the Cubans and Colombians) – or on the second – dancing "on the two" (like the Latin New Yorkers, Puerto Ricans and the ballroom set) – as long you're consistent and understand which beat you're on.'

The beat you choose to kick you off across the floor identifies your dance nationality as closely as your Spanish accent. New York salsa, Dominican merengue and Colombian cumbias have a consistent beat running through, whereas Cuba's new salsa timba changes rhythm within a song and the dancers change with it. Wherever you are, certain basics apply.

*The Hold and the Moves

There is always a small gap between the partners, unless they're doing merengue – then they are very, very close. The man's right hand holds the woman in the small of her back, palm flat. Her left hand lies on his right shoulder. His left arm is at ninety degrees, palm up, and the woman's left hand lies flat on it.

The dance

Turn

Step 4

Step 3

Step 2

The upper body hardly moves, no swinging shoulders, they just flow. All the signalling and rapport comes through the arms. The hips move automatically as a result of the shift of body weight from one side to the other with the knee bent.

*Basic Salsa Steps

The pattern is eight steps, four to each foot, regardless of the dance style. The woman stands in front of the man – always a mirror image of him. The first step is on the spot, a tap or a pause, 'on the one', then the nationalities divide at 'the break' on the second beat.

　　*Cubans pause, then move backwards away from each other, pushing away by the palms of their hands.

　　*Colombians do a kick or skip.

　　*New Yorkers move forward.

Step 1: The man's left foot (LF) and the woman's right foot (RF) both move backwards.

Step 2: Use the same foot as for Step 1 and move back to original position, transferring weight back.

Step 3: The heel of RF (man's) and LF (woman's) pushes down, leg bends, and that moves the hips.

Step 4: Man's RF flat on the floor, LF back to neutral in new position.

Spins and Turns

The man literally puts the woman in a spin and she has no choice – either she turns or she falls.

The spins take place between Step 3 and 4. On Step 2, the man pushes the woman's right arm out sideways as a signal to turn. On Step 3, he pulls her arm in and spins her by swinging her arm while she's on the ball of her foot, heel up. On Step 4, she lands back in the original position.

*Merengue

Merengue moves at a tremendous speed with a lot more movement than in salsa. It's a sideways dance – left, right, left, right – with just two basic steps to match the rigid 2/4 beat, but that can be interrupted with forward moves.

*Cumbia

The couples hold each other's hands out to the side, around waist level, and there is a lot of hip movement, with the upper body stiff. Cumbias have three steps, two with one leg, one with the other. The solid 2/4 beat is repeated like merengue. It is a fleet-footed, skipping dance.

Step 1
Tap, kick or pause

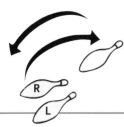 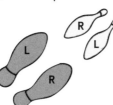

TAMBORA

The essential merengue drum is a double-ended wooden barrel held together by metal hoops and covered at each end with goatskin. A driving, thrumming triple rhythm is stoked by the left hand's palm and fingers while the right hand produces a backing beat with a stick. Tambora and saxophones set up a darting call-and-response relationship which drives on the dancers.

TIMBALES

This descendant of the round-bottomed kettle drum (tympani) brought by Italian opera companies to Cuba in the nineteenth century was adopted by military brass bands and commandeered by the charanga orchestras which played danzóns. As they became more portable the techniques got richer. Their crisp, metallic tone is a perfect foil for the sweeter fiddles-and-flute leads which dominate the charanga sound.

ABOVE: An all-woman batá group and their dancer – unheard-of until the 1990s, when women first began to play these formerly holy drums. LEFT: A silent rhythm section on a Havana sidewalk: beaded shaker, batá drums and set of congas.

Modern timbales masters such as Tito Puente use the sticks on every surface – for rim shots, side shots and top shots, and to ring the cowbell suspended above. Puente explains its function: 'The timbales marks the breaks and fills in with a different sound from the other percussion – sharper, higher pitched, metallic. It carries the basic beat, the timing, and of course is used for solos too.'

PANDERETA

A frame drum tambourine with no jangles – brought to the Caribbean by the Spanish and Canary Islanders who inherited it from the Arab musicians – is central in the Puerto Rican plena style where it traditionally accompanies the guitar and vocalists.

VIBRAPHONE

This sophisticated xylophone sits on a stand like an ironing board and is operated by a foot pedal. The sticks are fluffy at one end, for a soft, muted ring, and wooden at the other, for a sharper note. Vibraphones lend a mellow, cool texture to Latin Jazz.

MARIMBA, MARIMBULA

The first bass notes in Cuban son songs were blown from a hole in the side of the big round earthenware bottles used to store cooking oil. The more powerful marímbula, with its marvellous, deep, earthy voice, replaced these. The marímbula is a cedar wood box with metal tongues bolted to one side and a sound-hole cut above the prongs. It derives from the thumb pianos known as mbiras and sanzas, found all over Africa, and can be slung round the player's neck like a cigarette girl's tray, or sat on while the musician plucks the prongs with a leather thong. It was eventually replaced by the more versatile double bass.

BASS

The story of the bass in salsa is one of increasing syncopation and complexity. The Grand Master of the Latin bass is Israel 'Cachao' López, a Cuban whose infinitely inventive double bass style has inspired every generation's bass players since the 1930s.

GUITAR

The most obvious Spanish legacy in Latin music is the guitar. Guitars are the basic country peasant instrument, the evocative voice of Cuban and Puerto Rican country

dwellers, who Creolized the Spanish styles to suit their Caribbean lives. New instruments evolved in both places: the Cuban tres with three double strings carried the son style, and the Puerto Rican cuatro with four then five strings is associated with plenas. A small Cuban lute – the laoud – features in the country music (guajira) tradition.

VIOLIN
Violins were introduced to Cuba by European classical musicians and became a focus of the modern charanga style, where they soar and sway in a block behind the solo flute and singers. The experimental Cuban violinist Alfredo de la Fé added a fifth string to his violin and an array of electronic gadgets to create searing, improvised rock-style solos, which he called 'techno salsa'.

PIANO
Piano solos arrived in Latin dance music through the improvisations woven into courtly Cuban danzóns in the late nineteenth century. By the 1930s they replaced the quieter tres guitar used in the son sextets and septets. Pianist Charlie Palmieri remembered the piano's original anchoring bass function in bands in 1930s New York: 'I had to play a boring tuba beat – oom-pah, oom-pah all through,' he groaned. New York's Fania All Stars pianist, Larry Harlow, introduced the first electric piano into salsa in the 1970s, and a decade later Bonny Cepeda launched the electronic merengue era with his synthesizer playing.

ACCORDION
The German button accordion first reached the Dominican Republic around 1870, rapidly replacing the guitars and banjos in merengue groups. In Colombia, wild careening accordion solos are a feature of both the valley music known as vallenato and the traditional cumbia dances.

Open-air session: bongos, laoud (lute), marímbula.

CHINESE CORNET
This metallic, oboe-like instrument was traditionally a mainstay of Cuba's carnival parades – its wild, hysterically high voice could cut through the noise of massed drummers and singers. Its strident call is still occasionally heard in folkloric son sextets in Eastern Cuba.

FLUTE
The five-hole, black wooden flute was taken to Cuba by French families fleeing the eighteenth-century Haitian revolution. Many musicians switched to a metal concert flute because wood is too sensitive to Cuba's climate and metal offers more volume and versatility; others prefer the wooden flute's warm, breathy tone to the crystal perfection of the metal. In charanga styles, the flute is the focal point – its strong, high trilling notes blast across the violins and percussion.

TRUMPET, TROMBONE & SAXOPHONE
The trumpet's bright and trilling tone was introduced into Cuban son bands in the 1930s, instantly transforming the songs' rural sweetness to fit the city's brashness. The greatest son trumpeter, Félix Chappotín, created a template of high-pitched, searing solos which every trumpeter since has aspired to.

Dominican child with tambora drum.

The thirties American Swing music influenced most Caribbean music, from son and cumbia to calypso. Its fast, complex and exhilarating arrangements for saxophones and trumpets were imitated by the horn sections of the great mambo bands of the forties and fifties which are the basis of today's salsa orchestras. A solo tenor saxophone was a key melody instrument in traditional merengue; in today's dancebands, layers of saxophones play short, snappy phrases which dart across each other with mathematical precision.

From the time of their arrival in the Spanish Caribbean's military bands in the nineteenth century, trombonists always moonlighted in dancebands. The instrument fits neatly in salsa between the trumpet's highs and the saxophone's blues. Its melancholy tones were a key texture in Cuba's contradanse and danzón orchestras, while the son groups preferred the sharper trumpet tone.

1 The roots of salsa

Chapter 1 CUBA: The roots of salsa

FOR THOUSANDS of American tourists in the decades between Prohibition and the Cuban revolution of 1959, entering the narrow port of Havana must have been like passing through the gates of heaven. As the port loomed into view, the colonnades and verandahs of the colonial houses came into focus, and the first strains of music from the bars and cafés which line the narrow streets stirred holiday-makers with the taste of pleasures ahead. This was the capital city with the reputation for the sexiest dance music in the world.

The first part of the salsa story focuses on the Cuban styles that make up salsa. But it is impossible to understand either salsa itself or the various styles of music under the salsa umbrella without knowing something of the alliances between the Africans and the Europeans in Cuba.

The same stretch of crowded river that carried American tourists into pre-revolutionary Havana greeted a very different cargo over the three hundred years prior to the full abolition of slavery in Cuba in 1873. During that time, nearly one million Africans were delivered to the island to be sold as slaves. Their input into salsa's history is as significant as that of the Spanish settlers who bought them.

The first slaves, who came from Mozambique and the Congo, were sent to work in gold-mines, replacing the native Indians who had failed to survive the Spanish brutality. They went on to work the small farms where sugarcane and tobacco crops were being established and cattle raised. The rapid growth of these industries in the seventeenth century increased the need for workers, and the catchment area in West Africa expanded to an arc including what is now Nigeria, Ghana, Togo, Benin and Cameroun.

The majority of slaves came from the ancient Yoruba kingdom (now Nigeria), which had a sophisticated culture and a complex religious system. But there was another major group, the Congos, who came from what is now the Federation of Congo and Angola. Their culture was different from the Yoruba, and introduced new elements into the music evolving in Cuba. Even today, Afro-Cubans still identify with their ancestral groups, in music, dancing and their religious lives, down to the coloured beads around their wrists and the colours of clothes worn on certain days of the week.

Once in Cuba, the slaves were originally divided into mixed tribal groups, to prevent communication and plotting, but this created such debility and depression and, more importantly for their owners, the loss of so much labour, that the system was rearranged along ethnic lines, enabling the slaves to preserve some of their traditional music and religions. The survival in Cuba of African religions – santería, abakwa and palo – is largely due to the fact that slaves were able to retain the languages of the sacred drums concealed in

Planting and harvesting the 'white gold' (sugarcane) was the relentless task of the plantation slaves. Only on their Sunday holidays could they create in their barracks a semblance of their African home, dressing up and dancing to music.

PRECEDING PAGES:
The port of Havana, shown in an early 19th-century lithograph.

their religious ceremonies. The drum music and singing associated with each of these cults has trickled into popular music and forms a significant strand in the salsa story.

In consultation with the Church, the Spanish government established mutual-benefit societies known as cabildos (chapter houses) or naciones (nations) which were founded on ethnic lines. These community centres enabled the slaves to maintain their religious rituals and also helped them to buy their freedom. For freed citizens, life in the towns and cities was increasingly autonomous and a sense of community developed. By the eighteenth century, meeting places, dancehalls, bars and places of worship had been set up and the cabildos had also opened their doors to poor Spanish and mulatto workers.

The deal which enabled the Africans to maintain their religious music depended on their being baptized as Christians. But they did not entirely renounce their old faiths – the remarkable similarity between the Catholic saints and the Yoruba pantheon of saints/gods, known as orishas, allowed the Christian saints to be twinned to African gods, so permitting Africans to pay homage to their own deities while also involved in the Catholic service. This Afro-Cuban religion became known as santería (or lucumi).

Santería ceremonies (bembés) involve sacrifice, healing, invocation and possession. Orishas are summoned using several types of drum, but most important are the three egg-timer-shaped batá drums, strung with jangling bells. Each orisha has a complex set of rhythms associated with him or her called toques, which the drums play out to call the god down. At this point, one of the dancers in the room is possessed by the orisha's spirit and responds by walking, dancing and making gestures associated with that god, and singing or speaking in the appropriate tongue. The congregation knows instantly which orisha has come down and responds with appropriate songs.

Preparing a santería ceremony (bembé) in a Havana back-yard. The woman drives unwholesome spirits away from offerings to the orishas (gods) with a smoking bunch of sanctified herbs.

Until the early part of the twentieth century, santería was a close secret in the African community. But gradually the island's great percussionists and singers emerged from the neighbourhoods with the strongest santería and abakwa traditions, and brought their musical skills with them.

In 1936 the musicologist and writer Dr Fernando Ortiz went on a lecture tour of Cuba, demonstrating the Afro-Cuban music and bringing the drums out of hiding. He made contact with several musicians, including a glamorous young Afro-Cuban singer called Mercedita Valdés, who became popular as a singer of quasi-religious songs, including her hit song 'Babalú' (a distortion of babalao, or priest). Valdés's first album, *Toques de santos*, released in 1946, introduced the sacred rhythms to the dancehall. It contributed to santería's exotic respectability and inspired a wave of songs based on the chants.

Gradually, even the most sacred instruments found their way into the dancehalls. The guitarist Arsenio Rodríguez revolutionized dancebands when he added a conga drum in 1938, and Dizzy Gillespie stirred New York audiences to a frenzy by introducing the Afro-Cuban drummer Chano Pozo into his band. Pozo accompanied his conga-playing with fragmented abakwa chants. In the 1960s Celia Cruz released two classic albums based on songs to the orishas – *Homenaje a los santos* (Homage to the Saints) – though she denies being an initiate.

In the abakwa religion, an assortment of sacred drums, rattles and bells are used. Abakwa is the most secretive of the Afro-Cuban religions; women are still kept at a distance from it. The holiest drum, the ekue, is never seen, only heard howling its holy messages from behind a curtain. Abakwa dances involve frightening masked figures known as diabolitos (little devils) who represent the gods and whose costume looks like a flamboyant version of Ku Klux Klan dress.

Latin music is littered with abakwa clues, as it is with hints of santería. The diabolitos gave their name to a new rhythm invented by Arsenio Rodríguez in the late 1930s (he called it diabolo – it was later renamed mambo). Santería's batá drums have been incorporated into dance groups. In New York in the early 1980s, the newly arrived Cuban percussionist Daniel Ponce hooked up with the venerated percussionist and initiated santero Milton Cardona in batá drum jam-sessions, and in nineties Havana the ultimate taboo was broken when several all-women batá groups were established.

The older generation of salsa singers still incorporate gestures and dance steps derived from santería dancing – a flick of the hand, a swish of a white handkerchief, a shudder of the shoulders, or a thrust of the pelvis. After the revolution, Havana's tourist-oriented cabaret shows presented 'authentic' Afro-Cuban vignettes featuring leading singers and percussionists associated with santería. In the dollar-starved nineties, santería was put on official tourist itineraries; for an inflated fee, visitors can be guided through a genuine bembé, though parts of the ceremony remain secret.

The Efik people from Africa's Niger delta retain connections in Havana and Matanzas through the abakwa religion, a secretive, sinister cult once linked to gangsters and protection rackets. Abakwa dances are performed openly today at festivals and carnivals by spooky characters called diabolitos – little devils.

A key to the most significant orishas

BABALU-AYE the god of illness, equivalent to St Lazarus, walks with a crutch and bears open wounds on his legs. Casts infectious diseases when offended. His colours are lavender, beige and black.

CHANGO symbol of fire and thunderbolts, passion and lust. A great warrior, he lives in the tops of palm trees, talks through batá drums, and is paired with St Barbara. His colours are red and white.

ELEGGUA Obatala's son, also known as Elegba. He represents good and evil. Eleggua's shrine, kept behind the front door of family homes, is a grey stone studded with cowrie shell eyes and mouth. He dances like a hopping monkey, with outstretched fingers and arms. His colours are red and black. Twinned with St Anthony.

OBATALA symbol of peace and justice, associated with creation, death and dreams. Dressed in white and represented as a bent old man, Obatala is the father of the orishas. His dance is a shuffle.

OCHUN loves children, protects marriages and is responsible for arts and rivers. Married to wild macho Chango and paired with La Caridad del Cobre, Cuba's patron saint. Colours are yellow and gold.

OGUN powerful warrior god, associated with accidents, bloodshed, surgery. Colours are green and black.

OLOKUN the original owner of the earth; also represents the depths of the oceans. Olokún appears as a mermaid or a merman in sea blues and greens.

ORUNMILA commutes between heaven and earth but never takes possession. He works more subtly and in a different form from the other orishas. Paired with St Francis of Assisi.

OYA guards the gates of death and governs the winds and storms (essential to placate in these hurricane territories). Also the keeper of cemeteries. Oya's colours are gaudy floral patterns.

YEMAYA symbol of motherhood, and protector of women. Mother of the orishas, and queen of the seas, she dances fast, twirling and flicking the blue frills of her skirt like the curling foam on the waves. Her colours are blue and white.

'Las Siete Potencias' (The Seven Powers) – the most potent of the orishas, with their matching, equivalent Catholic saints. Many Cuban homes contain a shrine, from a discreet statue or poster of the orisha or its Catholic saint equivalent, to a kitsch life-size model. Around its feet offerings are placed according to its tastes: holy stones, bowls of food, bottles of rum, candy bars, loose dollars and pesos.

'Salsa is son'

The music of salsa is directly descended from the tradition of 'son', born and nurtured on the Eastern end of the island during the period of its liberation from Spain at the end of the nineteenth century. Son is the first truly homegrown, Afro-Cuban style, a rolling syncopated song and dance music, a collision of African rhythms with the poetry and guitars of Spain. It lives on in many guises – traditional and modern, and everything in between – and is continuously being reinvented with every new twist of history. 'Salsa is son' is a mantra repeated all over the salsa world.

The original son strongholds in the Eastern towns still resound with the names of the pioneers and the rhythms and instruments associated with them. At their son festivals one can sample the full spectrum of son nuances and see first-hand some of the original instruments – the quaint horses' jawbone rhythm-shakers, the cumbersome marímbula thumb piano basses, the hurdy-gurdy organs and various customized Spanish guitars and Arabic lutes, sometimes overshadowed by the electrified salsa-son big bands.

As with most styles of music, experts fail to agree on son's origins. Many trace it to 'Má Teodora', a song about a slave called Teodora and her sister Micaela, who sang around Santiago in the 1550s. But the style of son played today can be traced to the time of Cuba's triumph in its War of Independence with Spain in 1868, when people streamed into Havana from all over the island. Soldiers who had served there drifted to the capital and are thought to have taken son with them, carrying its basic instruments – claves, maracas and guitars – in their pockets and on their backs. The bass was easily improvised with an empty oil jug (botija), similar to those used by blues singers in American jugbands.

The simplest, and for many the perfect, embodiment of son was Trío Matamoros, founded in Santiago in 1912 by the guitarist Miguel Matamoros, with Rafael Cueto (guitar and voice) and the virtuoso maracas player Siro Rodríguez. They set the standard for guitar trios all around the world and became one of Cuba's greatest musical exports, touring Latin America and Europe and recording in New York.

In Havana, the early son trios expanded to cater for larger, more sophisticated audiences. In 1925 the popular Trío Oriental upgraded to Cuarteto Oriental, drawing in a bongo player. Bongos, until then, were played only in Afro-Cuban rumba sessions; their tight, bubbling tone added extra capital-city zip to the son. The expansion continued as quartets grew to sextets, establishing a standard line-up of guitar, tres, marímbula or upright double bass (contrabass) and bongos, as well as claves and maracas played by the first (primero) and second (segundo) singers. The last arrival was the trumpet, which transformed the band into a septet, a combination that brought greater volume in parks, beer gardens and other outdoor venues.

At son's core is the motivating lurch provided by the bass playing a pattern

ABOVE: **Miguel Matamoros's Trío Matamoros** established the template for son's lyrical guitars-and-voices harmonies, in immortal songs like 'Son de la loma'.
BELOW: Ignacio Pineiro (1889–1969), one of son's best-loved composers.

known as 'anticipated bass' which pushes dancers into movement. The original jug-bass was initially replaced by the cumbersome wooden box bass, the marímbula, which broadcast fuzzy, booming notes. This wonderfully archaic African instrument is still played by some remote country bands, and adds authenticity to a recent wave of neo-traditionalists. It was superseded by the more sophisticated and versatile upright double bass (contrabass), which was better suited to more sophisticated, indoor venues.

The sharp-and-sweet, catchy tunes are played on guitar and tres, both of which double as rhythm instruments. Initially they were strummed in time with the leading rhythm, but by the 1920s they were plucked and picked and used for improvised solos. Several guitarists, including Compay Segundo, the leading light in the Buena Vista Social Club, customized their guitars, adding extra strings to give more harmonic possibilities and volume. In the trios, two guitarists and a tres player or three guitarists harmonized and worked against each other. The lead singer needed a powerful tenor voice and skill at ad-libbing the fast-rapped verses about local goings-on, political intrigues, dreamy love sagas. Compay Segundo's cigar-smoked baritone was a second (segundo) voice. The two singers worked against each other's chorus (coro) in the African call-and-response pattern. The harsh swish of the third singer's maracas and the bubbling of the bongo further complicated the rhythms, while the claves kept them on course with the piping 1-2-3, 1-2 beat.

The perfect sextet line-up, Sexteto Habanero, with lead singer and claves player Abelardo Barroso (second from left), in front of a thatched bohío, symbol of the Cuban countryside. In 1927, Barroso added a trumpet to the line-up, soon to be occupied by Cuba's supreme trumpet stylist, Félix Chappotín.

A timeless scene from the Eastern countryside as Grupo Changui de Guantánamo perform the antiquated precursor to the son: the changui. Their instruments typically include the original son bass, the African marímbula, Cuban tres guitar, maracas and bongos, with the addition of a metallic scraper güiro.

The last – and optional – instrument in a line-up was the raucous Chinese cornet (corneta China) which played the lead tunes in the comparsas, the carnival bands. This was soon almost entirely replaced by the more powerful and versatile trumpet. The bass player Cachao insists that his brother Orestes introduced the first trumpet into a son group in 1926, when he was running Sexteto Apollo, and around that time a trumpet solo was built into the son repertoire. The story of son is a legacy of formidable trumpeters, all of whom pay tribute to the most significant, 'The Cuban Louis Armstrong', Félix Chappotín. Following him was Alfredo 'Chocolate' Armenteros, who played lead with the premier singer Beny Moré before moving to New York.

The son proved to be one of the most versatile styles: derivatives called sucu-sucu, guajira-son, pregon-son, son-rumba, afro-son, son-montuno and guaracha all had moments of glory, and have been rehabilitated by young Cuban bands. The guaracha emerged in the twenties and thirties from Havana's raucous music halls, many of them men-only venues. It was performed on guitars, percussion and Cuban lute (laoud), and its sly, bawdy lyrics encouraged the most skilful vocal improvisers. In the 1940s and 1950s Celia Cruz and Beny Moré both sang guarachas in the dancehalls, to knowing, rapturous applause.

Son is the basis of modern salsa, but almost unrecognizably transformed from the original trios. Right from the beginning, the guajira guitar music of the Spanish peasant farmers and the Afro-religious music of the former slaves enriched the son and brought in new instruments. Once in Havana, foreign influences were absorbed, particularly from American jazz and popular music heard on the radio.

Throughout the twenties, the son septets and trios were involved in a frenzy of recording sessions. The American record companies, led by RCA Victor, talent-scouted South America and the Spanish Caribbean as thoroughly as any ethnomusicologist. In Havana they set up studios in radio stations and nightclubs. Record-players, known as 'Victrolas' (after RCA Victor), became an essential piece of furniture, and records spread the capital's music all around the island, and back to the exiled communities in New York.

Radio talent contests became a way in for impoverished and untrained performers. Both Celia Cruz and Beny Moré were 'discovered' through winning a slot on radio. The arrival of radio also took son and its related styles across social boundaries, and changes became necessary to suit the larger dance-halls and meet the requirements of middle-class venues. Pressure was put on bandleaders to tone down the skin colour of their players. Rubén González remembers playing piano for Los Hermanos Castro (The Castro Brothers – no relation) in the 1930s: 'They always tried to have white musicians, but they had to accept us because of the way we played.' Sexteto Habanero were among the first to cross the racial divide. In 1926 President Machado (a mulatto) invited the group to play at the Presidential Palace in Havana, after which son was soon accepted into high society.

General Machado – 'The President of a Thousand Murders' – had taken control of Cuba in 1924 and clamped down on any opposition. When students rioted, he closed the university. His reign coincided with Prohibition in the US and was linked to American crime syndicates who used Cuba as an offshore money-making resort for American tourists. Prohibition (until 1933, the year of Machado's assassination) boosted trade and produced a crop of new hotels, nightclubs and casinos, owned and run by the Mob.

Hollywood got in on the act, with a host of musical films in which Cuban musicians – light-skinned, and not too 'authentic' – provided the soundtrack. Tinseltown's favourite Latin musician was the Spanish-born and Cuban-bred composer and bandleader, Xavier Cugat, who introduced America to a rhythmically simpler big-band version of son which became known as rhumba or rumba – and which had little connection with the deep roots rumba performed in the black neighbourhoods of Cuba's towns and cities (see below).

In 1931 bandleader Don Azpiazu rearranged one of the most enduring son songs, 'El Manicero' (The Peanut Vendor) – a hybrid son-pregon based on a streetseller's call, 'Ma-Ní!' (Peanuts!) – written by the young Havana pianist Moises Simón. In the process, Azpiazu also turned the son into a 'rhumba' to suit American tastes. His arrangement exploded onto Broadway and unleashed a global passion for Cuban music. The turbulent thirties saw many dramatic changes as Havana became known to a world that had gone rhumba crazy. But in Cuba the musicians looked to New York for inspiration. A wave of new bands with Americanized names like Happy Happy and Swing Havana filled nightclubs and casinos. Jazz and the new Swing bands wielded the strongest influence. 'New York was the place we all wanted to be, because of jazz. Chick Webb and Ella and Cab Calloway and all them Swing bands

RITA MONTANER

CENTENARIO DEL CINE

CUBA CORREOS 1995 75

Soprano Rita Montaner (1900–58) made her first rebellious appearances in the twenties, in Havana's beer gardens, at that time normally closed to women performers. Her first hit, 'Mama Inés' (in 1927), was a bawdy Afro-Cuban son, which she performed energetically, in defiance of rules that decreed that women should sing virtually motionless. In 1930 Montaner joined Josephine Baker's more enlightened *Revue* in Paris, and in 1931 performed in Al Jolson's Broadway musical, *The Wonder Bar*. In between, she recorded the first version of 'El Manicero' (The Peanut Vendor), written for her by Moises Simón. She then moved to Mexico City to make musical films. There, she embarked on a raunchy partnership with the flamboyant Afro-Cuban pianist and singer Ignacio Villa, whom she nicknamed 'Bola de Nieve' (Snowball). Their risqué act became a favourite at Havana's Tropicana cabaret from 1949 and on Cuban television throughout the fifties. She is shown here on a 1995 Cuban stamp commemorating the centenary of the cinema.

pouring off the radio back home,' the singer Miguelito 'Mr Babalú' Valdés told *Latin NY* magazine in the 1970s.

Valdés earned his reputation and nickname in the US with an act built around the success of his raunchy Afro-song, 'Babalú' – accompanying his ad-libbed chanting with conga drums. Unfortunately for him, Desi Arnaz took the same ingredients to New York's dancefloors and became a worldwide household name (he had the advantage of being married to America's favourite comedienne, Lucille Ball).

Many of the Cuban bands which had grown up as sextets or septets had by the 1940s ditched their tres players in favour of a pianist, thus ridding themselves of the folksy, ethnic tag, and deriving the greater power volume of the keyboards. Tres virtuoso Arsenio Rodríguez held out; he also transformed his band with extra trumpets but kept the tres. The expanded son groups were referred to as conjuntos, big brassy bands, led by up to four trumpets, piano, stand-up bass, guitar, three singers, bongo and congas. The model was already closer to today's salsa bands.

Son has proved its versatility throughout the century. In the 1970s, it was revolutionized by the singer/songwriter Adalberto Alvarez's band, Son 14, and La Original de Manzanillo, which features one of the great modern son improvisers, Cándido Fabre. In 1976 a group of Havana students set up a son preservation group called Sierra Maestra, complete with donkey's jawbone percussion, which contributed to a new wave of interest in the old masterpieces. In the late 1990s an utterly unprecedented interest in son suddenly erupted in the wake of the million-selling *Buena Vista Social Club* album and its companion-piece, *Afro-Cuban All Stars*, produced by former Sierra Maestra tres player Juan de Marcos González. These magical records and many that followed in their wake relaunched scores of musicians whose careers had begun with the acoustic, traditional version of son in the first half of the twentieth century and were ending in nightclubs and concert halls with a modernized big-band version of the same thing.

The elaborate sexual choreography of the rumba guaguancó unfolds as the male dancer attempts to approach and 'vaccinate' the woman. Her long, layered skirts are incorporated into the steps – to aid her playful defence of the man's lunges. Old-time dancers like Manuela Alonso object to young women dancing in trousers. Alonso complains: 'When women dance in trousers and they get "vaccinated" by the man, they have to cover themselves with their hands.

CUBA: THE ROOTS OF SALSA

Rumba – dancing with the drums

Of all the non-religious dances and music performed in Cuba today, rumba is the closest to the slaves' legacy, and many respected rumberos are direct descendants of slaves. When Celia Cruz waves a white handkerchief, hikes up her skirts, and dips and swoops like a bird; when her song dissolves into an Afro-scat, she is recreating something deeply encoded, almost genetic. Such references can unify a crowd as they did when music and dance first brought together dispersed slaves and freed Africans. The rumba's dance steps, rhythms and instruments are the secular relics of the slaves' religious rituals. Rumba was once the sole source of entertainment on the slaves' Sunday off, and even today, after any social event in the Afro-Cuban community – a funeral, a birthday, a saint's day – the religious segues into the secular, everybody gets down and the evening ends in a rumba.

Rumba is music played on a set of tuned wooden boxes or conga drums, accompanied by hand percussion (güiros, claves), and singers led by the akpwón, the lead singer. Dancers also play a significant part – their moves affecting the rhythms, the rhythms governing their moves. The origins of rumba lie in the ports of Havana and Matanzas, among the African dockers. Many African rhythms formed the repertoire, but today it has been distilled down to three – guaguancó, yambú and columbia – each with its own music and choreography. Traditionally, rumba was played on packing cases because slaves were allowed to use drums only on Sundays and holy days. Conveniently, codfish (bacalao) cases (easily available to the ports' workers) yielded just the right bass tone, and a particular brand of candle box could be tuned to the perfect high pitch. Today, however, even traditionalists use manufactured boxes (cajones). The drummer sits astride the bigger boxes and drums with both hands; the smaller boxes he holds between his knees. In some numbers, packing cases are replaced by differently sized conga drums – the largest, the male tumbadora, has the bass voice; the second, segunda, has the middle

'In the original rumba, they folded the hem of their skirt over themselves. You played conjuring tricks with your hands.' With the right partner, Alonso could extend the risqué antics almost indefinitely. Nothing today could ever repeat such excitement, or the brilliant improvisations that used to take place between drummers and dancers, but the 'Sábado de Rumba' (Rumba Saturdays) sessions in Havana are an exciting attempt at re-creation.

size and tone, and the smallest, the female quinto, has the highest pitch. The key drum is the quinto, said to carry the soul of rumba.

The GUAGUANCO rhythm accompanies a fast, erotic couple-dance of seduction (see pages 28–29), acted out through the antics of a rooster and a hen. The man dances gracefully around the woman, determined to provoke and challenge her. She ducks and swoops to avoid any contact, particularly his lunges and pelvic thrusts, wrapping the hems of her skirt around her belly to protect herself. The moment of climax – which varies according to skill and imagination – occurs with 'El Vacunao' (The Vaccination), when the man manages symbolically to 'vaccinate' her.

In guaguancó-salsa, the singer's improvisations can be stretched indefinitely and demand great vocal skill. Celia Cruz can go on for twenty minutes, during which time she will praise her band, compliment the audience, share gossip, even talk about her husband, Pedro, while the conga and bongo players thunder behind her, her chants darting in and out of their rhythms.

The YAMBU rhythm provides a slower, smoother couple-dance. It is the most Spanish of the rumbas and is sung in 4-line verses which trade news, insults and praises. The sexual elements are toned down because the dancers imitate old people, with a set of shuffly moves. (Today most dancers *are* in fact old, and the yambu is disappearing.) Two musicians play the codfish and candle cajones, while a third keeps time by tapping a metal coin against a glass bottle.

Eighty-something rumbera Manuela Alonso has lived in Cayo Hueso since her childhood. She danced as a young woman with Chano Pozo, who took his conga drum and a headful of barrio rhythms to New York in the forties. Alonso still delights in strutting with one of the brassy young men of her block when a rumba is called. She explains the dynamic between men and women in this rhythm with relish: 'You don't "vaccinate" in Yambú; the woman enjoys herself and the man suffers! She takes revenge, she has a good time – and he can't do anything!'

The COLUMBIA rhythm is the most African of the rumbas, derived from the diabolitos of the abakwa religion. It is the fastest and most exciting rumba dance, a showcase for a single male performer, who makes intricate patterns and complex acrobatic moves, and who works through a series of competitive and argumentative dialogues with the quinto drummer. Columbias have no lyrics, but the dancer or drummers occasionally break into a chant. Orlando Santa Cruz, a professional rumbero, explains: 'The columbia is the most eccentric of rumbas. Some men dance it with two knives, others with a glass on their heads. But in the old days it was more elegant, the men danced with a straw sombrero, and with a stick.' This was the inspiration for Beny Moré, who was rarely seen without either accessory.

A rumba starts when the lead singer, the akpwón, sets the pitch. With one hand over his ear, he establishes the key, sings a few unaccompanied opening lines of nonsense, known as 'la diana', then pauses. Because there is no piano, trumpet or guitar to give the key, he serves as the tonista – the pitch man. The claves player clacks out the crucial 1-2-3, 1-2 rhythm, and the rumba rolls. Singers trade cross rhythms with drummers, sometimes accompanying themselves with a pair of claves, or small sticks called pallitos, or by banging spoons against the sides of the drums. The singing follows the pattern found all over West Africa – an alternated solo and chorus, call and response. It is in both Spanish and African languages, but the words also break up into scats,

CUBA: THE ROOTS OF SALSA

as in the most articulate bebop songs. The complex dance steps are choreographed according to traditional themes based on religious ritual dances, and direct the drummers' playing.

It requires determination to track down an 'authentic' rumba. In the old days, they were held in the communal patios of crowded tenements (solares). Today they can still be found in the patios of tenements such as Jesús María, Cayo Hueso, Los Sitios and Africa, where washing is hung out and neighbours meet for a gossip and a beer. When a rumba is about to take place, drums are hauled out; people begin to appear; the first rum is splashed onto the ground – for the saints – and kitchens are raided for spoons, bottles, frying pans and sticks to build the charge of the beats.

To appreciate the Matanzas rumba, you have to drive along the coast to the old port, and catch a local group. Most famous are Los Muñequitos de Matanzas, founded in 1952. The original line-up, known as Guaguancó Matancero, performed a number called 'Los muñequitos' (The Little Dolls), which became their signature tune and inspired a breakaway troupe. Today, they spend most of the year touring, and their place back home has been filled by Afro-Cuba de Matanzas, whose style is more earthy and whose rumba is more aggressive, based on palo music, the religious music of the Congo slaves.

For decades rumba has been incorporated into nightclub routines in Havana, and several Cuban singers have built their careers singing rumba and other Afro-Cuban religious music in commercial settings. Merceditas Valdés, who died in 1996, was one of the most adored interpreters of songs to the orishas, and of rumba. Celeste Mendoza, known as 'The Queen of Guaguancó', still performs on radio, television and at Afro-Cuban theme-nights in Havana's nightclubs. Dressed in an African-style headwrap and a long dress, she accompanies her fruity contralto voice on conga drums in some performances. Her voice lacks the rough edge of the solar but she is respected for her loyalty to the tradition.

RHUMBA AND CONGA

There is often a confusion between rumba and rhumba. The forties dance craze known as rhumba, which today is strictly ballroom, was never a true rumba at all. The first rhumba hit – 'El Manicero' (The Peanut Vendor) – was, as already mentioned, actually a son. The 1939 song 'La Cucaracha' (The Cockroach), also a rhumba, originated in Havana and, like its subject, has spread all over the world. The conga is a rhumba with a double-beat which still throws audiences into a frenzy of side-kicks. American tourists took memories of it home from Havana and paved the way for Xavier Cugat and his one-time vocalist Desi Arnaz to popularize both dances – rhumba and conga, respectively – in the States. By that time, 'rhumba' in America meant any kind of Cuban music – just as 'salsa' does today.

In the early forties many Latin musicians objected to the bastardization of their music. Xavier Cugat wrote in *Esquire* in 1942 that the phoney rhumba was encouraged by President Roosevelt. He described it as 'A good neighbour scheme to make Yankees love Latins and vice versa.'

The conga, on the other hand, was born in Cuba's carnival parades, where the musicians who led the procession were grouped together in schools called comparsas. When the conga came onto the dancefloor, couples would alternately separate and reform in a human chain; the double-beat side-kick came later. Desi Arnaz introduced the conga to America through Miami and

Beny Moré

Cubans disagree about most
things when it comes to music,
but the one thing they all agree
on is that Beny Moré was the
greatest performer their country
ever saw. With his pure voice
and his electrifying stage
manner, he more than lived up
to his nickname, 'El Bárbaro del Ritmo' –The Wizard of
Rhythm.

Born in 1919 in the Eastern sugarcane-growing region of
Cuba, Bartolomé, as he was christened, was immersed in
the local rural music – the Spanish-influenced música
campesina and Afro-Cuban son and guaracha – and also
absorbed ideas from Afro-Cuban ceremonies. His intricate
dance steps and semaphore-like hand gestures, even his
walking stick, are all borrowed from rumba.

At twenty-one, the gawky Moré moved to Havana and
joined the many trovadores busking outside cafés and
bars and occasionally singing on the radio. In 1945 he was
hired as lead voice for a Mexican tour with Conjunto
Matamoros on condition that he change his name: in
Mexico only donkeys are called 'Bartolomé' (local slang for
'stupid'). With Matamoros, Beny's vocal style began to
emerge; it blossomed fully when he joined another exiled
Cuban bandleader, Pérez Prado, in his experiments with
the new mambo rhythm. These two brilliant and fearless
eccentrics in baggy zoot suits and gaudy ties gelled
perfectly; Prado's wildly imaginative piano playing and
blasting horn arrangements and Moré's clear, soaring
voice catapulted Prado – and the mambo – onto the
world's music and movie circuits.

The greatest Cuban singer,
Beny Moré (left), holding
sheet music that he could
not read, with Félix
Chappotín, 'The Cuban
Louis Armstrong'.

Moré returned to Cuba in 1951
without sharing Prado's international
success, though his voice rings through
many recordings. Back home, he
formed his own eighteen-piece La Banda Gigante, with the
assistance of trumpeter Alfredo 'Chocolate' Armenteros.
Beny called them his 'Tribe' – 'Mi Tribu'. The musically
illiterate singer relied on perfect pitch, intuition and the
Tribe's interpretations of his ideas to create masterpieces
like 'Santa Isabel de las Lajas', a cha-cha-cha tribute to his
hometown, and 'Bonito y sabroso', said to have been on
every jukebox in Cuba in 1953.

By the late fifties, Moré's legendary appetite for rum,
cigarettes and reefers caught up with him and he died of
cirrhosis of the liver in 1963, aged forty-four. Cuba was
plunged into mourning. Fidel Castro sent a wreath and a
team of soldiers to carry the coffin and one hundred
thousand mourners filled the streets of Santa Isabel de las
Lajas as the Tribe bore his body through the final Afro-
Cuban rituals.

BELOW: **Beny Moré in full
flight with the light-skinned
band which replaced his
Afro-Cuban Banda Gigante
for some television shows.**
RIGHT: **The customary
props: rumbero's hat and
straight walking-stick.**

New York, weaving through the audience as he had done as a kid in the Santiago de Cuba carnivals. In a pleasing piece of symmetry, Gloria Estefán and the Miami Sound Machine's Latin-disco version of 'Conga' in 1988 was the theme of Miami's Cuban Carnival that year, when 119,986 snaking Latin Americans – and a few tourists – kicked their way into the *Guinness Book of Records*, through the streets of Little Havana.

From salons to salsa clubs

The story of the transformation of Cuban music from the salon to the street follows several routes, one of the most defined being from the contradanza and danzón to the mambo and cha-cha-cha.

The contradanza derives from the French contredanse. The latter arrived in 1791, when Saint Domingue (now Haiti/Santo Domingo) erupted in revolution, and French noble families, together with their servants, fled to the south east coast of Cuba. The contredanse, the favourite music and dance of the French, had begun in the English courts but had been souped up with African flavours in Saint Domingue. The Cubans renamed it 'contradanza cubana', then simply contradanza.

Contradanzas were performed at formal occasions, usually to slow the pace at the end of an evening, after the minuets, rigadoons, lancers and quadrilles. The dancers, in crinolines and formal suits, lined up facing each other and wove under arcs of flowers.

Contradanzas are instrumentals, played originally by an 'orquesta típica', a recreational version of a military band. The dominant texture came from the violins and the brass (a small trumpet called a cornetín, with trombones, clarinet and bassoon). The rhythm was measured by a pair of round-bottomed timpani which let out muffled, thunderous notes. Occasionally, a güiro scraped with a wooden stick spiced up the line-up. From the contradanza emerged the danza, one of the first Creole forms – faster and more tuneful, with niftier steps and a tendency for couples to dance by themselves.

On 1 January 1879, Cuban bandleader Miguel Failde, a twenty-seven-year-old cornettinist from Matanzas, surprised his audience at a New Year party with a tune called 'Las Alturas de Simpson' (Simpson's Heights – a hip district in Matanzas at that time), which he announced as a 'danzón'. Failde had slowed the danza and broken it into three parts, separated by an all-important pause, which is the erotic heart of the danzón. He introduced both a clarinet and a brass solo, as well as a more upbeat rhythm. The line-dance had become a couple-dance, with the pair close enough during the pause to feel one another's breath, but away from the chaperone's glare.

The danzón was little changed until 1910, when a clarinettist called José Urfe, who had worked in several popular orchestras in Havana, wrote a tribute to the bowler hat worn by his friend Julián Baretto, the danzón violinist. In 'El bombín de Baretto', Urfe added two extra sections: a cornet solo and a vocal solo-and-chorus banter, both ideas taken from son. He also created a fresher, racier pace.

Twenty years later, the pianist and composer Antonio María Romeu was at a party in Havana as a guest of his friends from the Orquesta of Leopoldo Cervantes. During a danzón, Romeu joined in – 'to liven it up a bit', he said. From then on, piano became an essential ingredient in the line-up. Romeu founded

The original Mambo Kings – Arsenio Rodríguez (left, 1911–70) and Antonio Arcano (right, born 1911) – could both lay claim to the mambo style. Arcano's band Las Maravillas del Siglo dealt the elegant danzón a blow by introducing a conga drum and an African twist to the danzón rhythm; Rodríguez built mambo from the 'diablo' rhythm of the Congolese abakwa religion – taught him by his grandfather, a former slave. His career as a tres guitarist began in twenties son groups; in the 1930s, he provided the popular Orquesta Casino de la Playa with hit songs but couldn't perform with them because he was black. The 1937 song 'So caballo!' (Whoa, Horse!) heralded the mambo, which he perfected in his brassy conjunto (band). The 1987 tribute album, *Mano a mano* (Hand to Hand), sweetly illustrates the original Mambo Kings' differences.

his own orquesta, and softened the format by removing the brass and adding violins and the French-imported wooden flute. He called the line-up a 'charanga francesa', and this has been the formula for charangas ever since. In the 1940s and 1950s, the great cha-cha-cha bands of Havana – Orquestas Riverside and Aragón and Fajardo's Estrellas – were charangas; later, the format was electrified and boosted with new horn formations by Ritmo Oriental. (To clarify a confusing point: the charanga is neither a dance nor a rhythm; the word refers to the formation of the band.)

Though danzóns were still instrumentals, with no lyrics, it became fashionable to give them titles with musical, social, political or even sporting themes. The Cuban musicologist Argeliers León described them as 'newspapers and thermometers'. Titles like 'El carroferril central' (The Central Railway), 'El teléfono de larga distancia' (The Long-distance Telephone) and 'El Cometa Halley' (Halley's Comet) recorded significant events in Cuba.

In 1929 the saxophonist Aniceto Díaz revolutionized the dancehalls with his song 'Rompiendo la rutina' (Breaking the Routine). He had broken the first rule of danzón – by introducing a vocalist. Having heard a young singer called Paulina Alvarez on the radio, he asked her to do the vocals for him. The song launched a danzonete craze and earned the dynamic young soprano from Cienfuegos the title 'La Emperatriz del Danzonete' (a nod to the Empress of the Blues, Bessie Smith). Diaz had boosted the rhythms by introducing claves and maracas – he also added a piano solo.

WHO INVENTED THE MAMBO?

The issue of who invented the mambo is one of Cuba's favourite musical controversies. Today, people still divide into camps, captained by the flute player Antonio Arcano and tres guitarist Arsenio Rodríguez, with pianist Pérez Prado in third position. In the hit song 'Locas por el mambo' (Mad about the Mambo), the singer Beny Moré, who joined Prado's band in Mexico City in 1948, gives the credit to his boss:

> Who invented the mambo that suffocates me?
> Who invented the mambo that drives women mad?
> Who invented this thing?
> A short, stocky guy with a face like a seal's.

Antonio Arcano has a major claim as the mambo's inventor. In the late 1930s his Las Maravillas del Siglo (The Miracles of the Century) was one of the most popular danzón orchestras in Cuba. Its success revolved in part around the rhythm axis anchored by the three López brothers – Jesús on cello, Orestes on piano and Israel ('Cachao') on double bass. According to Cachao and Orestes, they formed a breathless production line: 'We wrote an average of 28 danzóns a week, 14 each, 2 a day. I wrote in the house, in the café, the street, even the bathroom!'

In 1938 Orestes came up with 'Mambo', a tune driven by a new, funky, African-accented rhythm from Cachao's bass, tagged on to the end of a danzón. Cachao called it 'sabrosuro' (tasty) and Arcano referred to it simply as the 'nuevo ritmo' (new rhythm). Within five years, the dance would be a global obsession, but at first it was too African for the danzón crowd in Havana's salons, and the radio stations banned it for six months. The New York musicologist René López, who compiled an album of the earliest examples of mambo, commented, 'It took months to persuade the public what the band already knew: "Danzón plus Mambo equals Excitement!"'

Arcano transformed the charanga line-up to match the new beat. His percussionist, Ulpiano Díaz, introduced timbales drums and hooked a cowbell to the stand. Arcano boosted the bass with extra strings – cello, viola and double bass – and soaring over the top was his trilling flute solo. Jesús López's staccato, syncopated piano solos completed the magic. Arcano also hired a conga drummer for the first recording of 'Mambo', and interlocked the rhythm patterns (tumbaos), connecting the piano to the basses and congas. They repeated them over and over, building the excitement to what one commentator called 'a dangerous climax'. The danzón was now opened up to improvisation – a jazz idea which Cachao carried with him into his recordings of descargas (jam sessions) over the next decade. The wildly original pianist Pérez Prado adopted the name 'Mambo' and from his base in Mexico City, teamed up with Beny Moré, he released a string of hit songs which switched the world to mambo mode.

Despite the fact that the great mamboniks Beny Moré, Pérez Prado, Machito, Mario Bauzá and Cachao were Cuban, mambo mania was never as dramatic an obsession in Cuba as it was elsewhere. What stole the glory in Havana was mambo's sweeter and more romantic daughter, the cha-cha-cha.

CHA-CHA-CHA

In 1948 a couple of renegade violinists, Enrique Jorrín and Félix Reyna, left Arcano's band to join the more commercial Orquesta América, where Jorrín was able to create his own sound. He started by doctoring a Mexican song 'Nunca' (Never), but made his mark in 1953 when he wrote a song about a woman he had watched on the streets near the Star Club. He put his lyrics to a more sensual version of the mambo. The song, 'La engañadora' (The Deceiver), immortalized both the streets and the woman:

Enrique Jorrín (1926–87) invented Cuba's most successful dance export, the cha-cha-cha, and perfected it with Orquesta América. Imitators emerged worldwide, but Jorrín remained unknown to the millions who danced his revolutionary rhythm.

The men just couldn't keep their eyes off
the young woman sauntering down Prado and Neptune.

She was voluptuous, shapely, charming
and, well, just magnificent.

But the truth always comes out eventually
Often without even checking.

Her shapely curves
turned out to be nothing but padding.
Those women who try and deceive us are so silly –
but I can't say you didn't warn me!

Now nobody looks at her,
Nobody sighs longingly
and nobody admires
her little cushions.

'La engañadora' slowed the mambo and simplified its rhythm. Most importantly, the musicians all sang the chorus – 'Cha-cha-cha is a dance like no

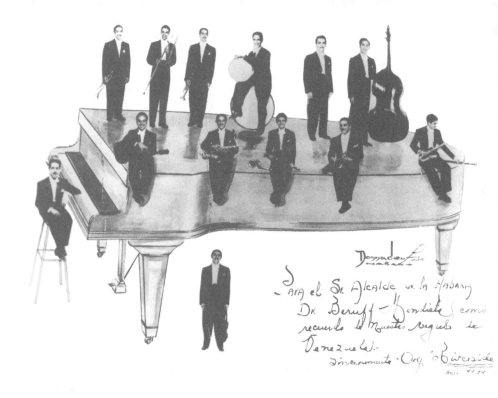

A Busby Berkeley-esque publicity photograph of Orquesta Riverside, the closest rivals to Enrique Jorrín's Orquesta América in the cha-cha-cha stakes. Riverside's secret weapon from 1942 was the husky-voiced singer Tito Gómez, a renowned improviser whose career began in shows promoting flights between Miami and Havana.

Orquesta Aragón – from Cienfuegos – with their tour bus in the 1950s, at the height of their popularity as the world's top cha-cha-cha band.

other' – in unison, which made it irresistibly catchy. Jorrín dropped in a double-beat and emphasized the last beat in a breathy 'CHA'. He says he got the idea for the name from the sound of the dancers' feet swishing across the floor. The New York dance instructor Denis Symmons explained the cha-cha-cha's global appeal to *Latin Beat* magazine: 'If mambo is slowed, the transitions are replaced by two quick steps, the result is the beautiful and sensual cha-cha-cha... it affords the dancer a more comfortable pace than the blistering tempo of a typical mambo, and it's by far easier to find the first beat in cha-cha-cha than in a mambo.'

Of the many bands to emerge during the forties and fifties, the most sublime and long-lasting was Havana's Orquesta Aragón, founded in Cienfuegos in 1939 by the noted violinist Orestes Aragón. Famous in the 1950s as a cha-cha-cha band, its unique identity really took shape after 1946, when Aragón handed the band over to his young lead violinist, Rafael Lay, and in 1955 the arrival of the flautist Richard Egues cemented its suave, smooth style. Orquesta Aragón had a wider influence in Latin music than any other pre-revolutionary band; its hit songs, particularly Egues's 'El bodeguero' (The Grocery Man) and others like 'Cachita', 'Suavecito' (Little Sweet One) and 'Tres lindas Cubanas' (Three Beautiful Cuban Girls), remain in the salsa repertoires today.

One spin-off from the cha-cha-cha was the casino – an Americanized version of the dance created by Orquesta Casino de la Playa in 1953. In the late nineties, a version of the casino was resurrected at Miami's fashionable Starfish Restaurant and for a few months was the town's cult dance. At this time Orquesta Aragón were still paying regular visits to the United States, and one of the leading danzón pianists, Guillermo Rubalcaba, then in his seventies, was touring the world with his charanga band. When not playing in the concert halls of Europe, Rubalcaba and his long-time bass-playing partner, Cachaoito – son of the great mambo pianist Orestes López – would drive along the coast to the crumbling Palace of Danzón in Matanzas, to entertain their contemporaries with the most elegant and shamelessly romantic Cuban dance music of the twentieth century.

Musica campesina – Cuba's country music

While Havana buzzed with the ceaseless rhythms of scores of slick and polished dancebands, and thousands of American tourists and local socialites swanned around the casinos and dancefloors of some of the world's most glamorous nightspots, an entirely different story unfolded in the country towns and villages all over the island where the majority of the population still lived in close connection with the land.

Cuba's country-dwellers always had their own stories to tell, different from the urban soneros or the suave danzoneros. Their 'música campesina' – country music – is told in poetic songs, which share a Spanish ancestry and romanticize the essence of old rural Cuba. Campesinos traditionally live in the

El Zapateado (the zapateo dancer), painted in 1847 by Frederic Niahle, shows the Spanish peasant dance performed in rural Cuba by a group of African and Spanish-Cuban guajiros. The tradition of country music developed from such cross-cultural encounters.

countryside and work the land. They include the cane-cutters and sugarcane factory workers who were originally brought from Africa; tobacco growers and rollers, many of whom came from the Canary Islands; gauchos in ten-gallon hats who herd cattle on horseback, and guajiros and guajiras, the small-time peasant farmers who are descended from the Spanish settlers. The guajiros are sharecroppers, their lives still hard and unmechanized. In Puerto Rico they are known as 'jíbaros' (their music is 'música jíbara'). Both guajiros and jíbaros share many features with the bluesmen of the American South and the poor whites who created US country music. Guajira music can move through minor keys, but it is generally an exuberant, escapist style, a celebration of the beauties of nature and of women, coaxed along by a liberal flow of rum and cigars.

Guajira music has sweet, emotive tunes and gentle rhythms. Its essential accompaniment is a guitar paired with one of several stringed instruments brought over by the Spanish – the Cuban version of the Arabic *oud*, called the

When Celina González, the doyen of Cuban Country Music, sings 'Yo soy el punto Cubano' (I *am* Cuban song), you believe her – though the polished nails and high-heeled mules are a far cry from the raw country life encapsulated in her songs.

'laoud'; a six-stringed tres guitar (with three double strings) or a small mandolin-like bandurria. Three guitarists who have specialized in collecting Eastern styles – guajiras, sons, guarachas and trovas, the original music of country people – are the great Beny Moré, who spent his childhood cutting cane at harvest time; Compay Segundo, who worked in the tobacco fields in his teenage years and rolled cigars for much of his adult life, and Eliades Ochoa, a younger musician who is never seen without his ten-gallon hat.

The country voice is high-pitched and open-throated, a descendant of flamenco. Songs tend to be long and anecdotal: some relate tales of history or fantasy; others are funny stories or political criticism; some simply rave about the beauty of a particular Cuban landscape or woman. They are written as a solo (verse) and chorus, in décimas (ten-line verses) and cuartetos (four-line verses made up of rhyming pairs), and rarely have the Afro-Cuban call-and-response structure of the son repertoire.

Though guajira music is thoroughly Cuban, it is the closest to the Spanish tradition. The songs draw heavily on European literary traditions; singers are referred to as 'poetas' and their subjects are landscapes filled with welcoming bohíos, symbolic trees and flowers, and, of course, love. They can also serve as patriotic odes to Cuba and its people. Fondly reworked versions of the classics have been performed by super-groups in the guajira, guaracha and son styles.

The original guajiros' festivities were regulated by natural events, in particular by the sugarcane harvest – the zafra. For the rest of the year, entertainment was casual and domestic, usually taking place on the porch with friends and family, guitars, hand percussion, familiar songs and rum-fuelled improvisations – scenes which vary little from those portrayed in many nineteenth-century paintings, in which couples are shown dancing the zapateo, a kind of tap-flamenco dance which is still performed today to a fast 2/4 beat.

Guajira songs have some of the most sophisticated lyrics in Cuban music, and rely on the singers' skills at improvisation within a tight musical structure. A closely related traditional country style is controversia, performed as sung challenges between two singers (originally between two teams) who trade improvised taunts and insults (these can be especially entertaining when the participants are husband and wife). Controversia is a dying art today and the skill of improvisation has been diverted into singing salsa – though there too it has become less of a requirement.

Although guajiras are associated with the Cuban countryside, several musicians adapted them to city standards. One of the earliest such composers in the twentieth century was Guillermo Portabales, who wrote painfully beautiful, timeless songs. A printer from Santiago de Cuba, Portabales developed a style called 'guajira de salón' – adding an elegant and more sensual coating to country themes. His greatest hits include 'El carretero', a guitar song about an ox-cart driver.

The archetypal image of a guajiro – the man in pleated guayabera shirt, big straw sombrero with upturned brim, machete stuck in belt, pulling on a cigar; the woman in long, layered skirt with lacy petticoat and flowers in her hair – was particularly shaped by two celebrated singers, Joseíto Fernández and Celina González. Both are urban guajiros: Celina González moved to Havana in her twenties; Joseíto Fernández, who wrote the world's most famous guajira song, 'Guantanamera', was born within sight of Havana's Capitol building. In their different ways, they popularized country music, with its

Joseíto Fernández was born
in central Havana, near the
Capitol building, but made
his name with a song about
a country girl from
Guantánamo. He worked as
a shoemaker and busked to
American tourists until his
break came through the
radio series which spawned
'Guajira Guantanamera'.

lovely tunes and languid rhythms, and contributed to this style's eventual association with the very essence of Cuba.

Celina González has done more than any other artist to bring guajira music into towns and cities. But, ironically, her early successes in a duo with her late husband, Reutilio, were not with classic guajira songs about the countryside but with homages to the Afro-Cuban saints, sung in the guajira style. In the typical campesina décima format, the first song she wrote – 'A Santa Bárbara' – was a huge hit and is still at the centre of her repertoire today.

Joseíto Fernández was Cuba's professional guajiro. His reputation was built on romantic songs which glorified the country people, but he also contributed to political campaigns. He dressed like a country porch singer throughout most of his career and even at the peak of his fame still walked through the streets of Havana, on his way to radio or television studios, or to work in the city's nightclubs, greeting people who recognized his embroidered guayabera shirt and wide-brimmed straw hat.

Fernández's name will always be associated with 'Guantanamera', not the slushy, kitsch, tourist versions, but the original – a heart-rending piece of nostalgia and nationalism that tears at the throat of every exile. 'Guantanamera' grew out of a 1935 series on Radio CMCD. Fernández was contracted to write songs for a soap opera which consisted of sketches about the feuds and love dramas in a family. The sketches were linked by musicians who sang the storyline. One theme, called 'La guajira Guantanamera', described the adventures of a country girl from Guantánamo. Joseíto Fernández recorded hundreds of versions of the song, each with a different storyline; the song's versatility was part of the reason for its success. At one show with guest Beny Moré, Fernández asked the bandleader to direct his big band in a version of

'Guantanamera'. The two magnificent Cuban voices told the tale, and, in the telling, the country girl from Guantánamo was whisked from the peace of the Eastern countryside to the nightclub buzz of the capital.

In the 1960s, the American folk musician Pete Seeger gave the song a new lease of life when he converted 'Guantanamera' to an anti-Vietnam war anthem using verses by Cuba's revolutionary poet José Martí. All over the world, it has been adopted by singers associated with left-wing struggles. But Fernández never received a cent in royalties. He confessed in later life, 'I never suspected that it would be world famous. On the radio, I sang this tune with every number.' Twenty years after his death, the song still echoes round the narrow cobbled streets of Old Havana, where crowds of tourists join in choruses with the wandering guitar trios.

Trova, bolero, feeling – music for protest, music for love

In a tribute to his mentor, Sindo Garay (below), the songwriter Carlos Puebla laughingly revealed that Garay had celebrated his hundredth birthday at least three times – 'Whenever he needed money!' From 1868, when he wrote his anthem for the Independence War, 'La Bayamesa', Garay composed lyrical songs to suit every political development, and stirring love songs in between.

While guajiras are songs in praise of Cuba's natural beauty, another guitar-based tradition, which was harnessed for political purposes, also emerged in the East of the island – the trova. In mediaeval Spain, troubadours moved between towns and villages with a guitar or lute, dispersing news and gossip through their catchy, often satirical songs. In the French-speaking Caribbean, during the revolutionary 1790s, troubadours stoked the anti-French fires, and during Cuba's War of Independence, they unified the islanders against the Spanish. Their trovas were the island's earliest patriotic songs, though they were, ironically, delivered in the strict ten-line verses of the Spanish décima and accompanied by Spanish guitars.

One of the most moving trovas from the War of Independence was 'La Bayamesa', written in 1868 by the godfather of trova: the composer, singer and guitarist Sindo Garay. This heroic song tells of a woman in the town of Bayamón, heartland of the independence movement, who burned her house down rather than hand it over to the Spanish. At the start of the twentieth century, as the country recovered from the war, composers like Garay mingled love songs and romances with political messages.

One of the most unconventional stars of trova was María Teresa Vera, a small, slight woman who became known as 'Mother Trova', and whose career began in the clubs of Havana in the 1920s, at a time when women musicians were a rare sight. Many of Vera's songs are still performed today: her 'Veinte años' (Twenty Years), a poignant duet between two voices and guitars, is the most exquisite embodiment of Cuban romance.

Today most Cuban towns have a 'Casa de Trova' – a Trova House, usually located in one of the colonial mansions put aside for 'cultural use'. Trova houses operate like musical community centres and are often associated with the memory of one particular singer or composer. In the evening local residents and groups of tourists looking for a sing-song sit on hard benches and join in the familiar repertoires, including the inevitable 'Guantanamera.'

In many towns, including Havana, barber shops and cafés have also traditionally been the meeting places for trova singers and their friends. The island's most famous shop-turned-commercial trova house was founded in 1931 in a narrow street in Old Havana. A grocer called Angel Martínez extended his premises to accommodate a café-bar, which he called La Bodeguita del Medio. He attracted poets and trova singers and their bohemian and politically active friends, drawn to hear the likes of the leading guitar group, Trío Matamoros, the rebellious trova composer and performer Sindo Garay and his protégé Nico Saquito, and visiting musicians such as Nat 'King' Cole, Edith Piaf and Josephine Baker, who dropped in after performing elsewhere in town. It was there in the fifties that the young poet and guitarist Carlos Puebla perfected songs which became rallying cries for the followers of the guerrillas in their confrontations with General Batista's forces.

In the years following the revolution, the trova was transformed by a new generation of musicians who took it in a different direction. The figureheads included Silvio Rodríguez, Pablo Milanés and Sara González, who drew on influences as diverse as The Beatles and Latin-American-Indian folk music. They renamed the style 'Nueva Canción – New Song', but it remained the same mix of politics and pleasure that Sindo Garay had created nearly a century earlier.

BOLERO AND FEELING

The Cuban bolero, which derives from the trova, is the epitome of the romantic love song. The first documented bolero, written at the end of the nineteenth century, was called, typically enough, 'Tristezas' (Sorrows). From the beginning, boleros were poetry set to (guitar) music, songs whose rhythms were governed by the rhythms of the lyrics, inside a 2/4 beat. Trova and bolero

Maria Teresa Vera, 'Mother Trova', drank cognac, smoked cigars and lived a modest life. She was Cuba's first feminist heroine, the first Cuban woman on record. Her debut recording was in New York with Sexteto Habanero in 1918, when she was also touring as a guitar duo with Lorenzo Hierrezuelo.

travelled, together with son, from their birthplace in Santiago to Havana's cafés and streets at the turn of the century, carried by guitar duos and twin harmony voices (tenor and baritone) or solitary singers.

Visiting opera companies from France and Italy are thought to have inspired the first boleros, and even today the lead singer will have the same high, passionate tones as an operatic tenor. Sindo Garay, though primarily associated with trova, also wrote some hauntingly lyrical boleros. One of his greatest fans was the guitarist Compay Segundo, who began his singing career in Santiago as half of the popular Los Compadres. He possesses a gritty baritone second voice – hence the name Segundo.

By the twenties, the bolero was one of many styles in the repertoire of son trios who performed in Havana's cafés and dancehalls. By the thirties it was essential for all play-lists. The world-travelling Lecuona Cuban Boys included bolero sheet music with rhumbas and congas on their ceaseless tours of the

US and Europe, under the baton of Armando Orefiche. His bolero 'Havana mi amor' was a hit tearjerker for any Latin living abroad.

The forties and fifties were the peak period for bolero internationally. The centre of the bolero industry shifted to Mexico, where it remains today. The original 'Peanut Vendor' singer, Antonio Machín, moved to Spain in the forties and introduced the bolero there. This tradition has also lasted and has given rise to such late-twentieth-century phenomena as Juan Gabriel and Julio Iglesias. One of the most moving songs in the tradition, 'Dos gardenias' by Isolina Carillo, is a roller-coaster of emotional intensity which is still a favourite duet among Cuba's older musicians, including singers Omara Portuondo and Ibrahim Ferrer, whose cheeks glisten with tears at many performances.

In the late forties, under the influence of American jazz singers – particularly Frank Sinatra, Sarah Vaughan, Ella Fitzgerald and Nat 'King' Cole, whose

CUBA: THE ROOTS OF SALSA

songs poured from Cuban radio – bolero evolved into the peculiarly Cuban style known as 'feeling' or 'filin''. The usual accompaniment switched from guitar to an upbeat cocktail-jazz piano. The pioneers of feeling are two guitarist–songwriters, César Portillo de la Luz and Rosendo Ruiz Jnr, who provided a group of interpreters with their material. The piano accompanists Bola de Nieve, Peruchín and Frank Emilio Flynn, and guitarist José Antonio Méndez, backed the expressive voices of two former members of the sixties hit girl group, Las D'Aida – Elena Burke and Omara Portuondo.

In the wake of Cuba's revolution, the nueva-trova generation also transformed feeling. Pablo Milanés pays tribute to the style's godfathers in two 1980s albums *Filin 2* and *Filin 3*, which include his silky voiced modern covers of José Antonio Méndez's 'Novia mía' (My Girl) and the gorgeous love song forever associated with César Portillo de la Luz, 'Delirio'.

While trova houses dotted around the island attract tourists seeking low-key entertainment, feeling nights are now hard to find. Apart from self-conscious preservationists like Pablo Milanés, and the dying generation of old-timers, including Omara Portuondo, feeling is a fading art, though the Roof Bar of the St John Hotel in Havana still hosts an appropriately dark and smoky Salón de Feelin', where tourists drop in for a late-night drink, oblivious to the eminent credentials of the husky singer performing with the piano in the corner.

Anacaona, the legendary Cuban Indian, wife of the chief and wild sybarite, was immortalized by Cuba's most famous all-woman orchestra. Founded in 1928 by eight sisters from the wealthy Castro family, it still performs today. Graduate singers include Machito's sister Graciela, and Chucho Valdés's sister – today's unrivalled jazz great – Mayra Valdés.

Chapter 2

SPANISH HARLEM:
The immigrants' tale

JESUS COLON

In 1918, 16-year-old Jesús Colón (right) stowed away on the *S.S.Carolina* from San Juan to New York. Discovered in a linen cupboard, he spent the trip washing dishes. In Spanish Harlem he roomed with his brother Ramón (left) and took a string of menial jobs. This bright, articulate teenager soon met writers, poets and musicians, and wrote stinging vignettes about the wretchedness of immigrant life. He wrote in English – the language of NuYorican culture, and his work influenced the sixties generation US-born poets and writers who performed to jazz backing on the Lower East Side.

PRECEDING PAGES: **Cruising down Fifth Avenue: a Puerto Rican Day Parade in the late fifties – a positive statement of Puerto Rican presence in the city.**

You should see the hundreds of Puerto Rican grandmas like you on a
    wintry, snowy day,
Standing by the window and watching the snow fall,
As Ramito, our folk singer, said when he came here,
'Like coconut flakes falling from the sky'.

'Grandma, Please Don't Come!' by Jesús Colón, from *A Puerto Rican in New York and Other Sketches*, 1961.

IN THE FIRST decades of the twentieth century, hundreds of thousands of Puerto Ricans streamed off the boats and onto the streets at Battery Point, south Manhattan, exempt from the Ellis Island immigration processing which Europeans and other Latin Americans had to endure. The 1917 Jones Act had converted the former Spanish colony into a United States Commonwealth state, which granted Puerto Ricans American citizenship and entitled them to live and work in the US. The foundations were laid for America's largest immigrant community, which would provide New York with a Latin music scene in which Puerto Ricans were the main players.

The islanders had seen colour pictures of the skyscrapers and had heard the exhilarating dance crazes of the Jazz Age: the lindy-hop and the jitterbug. But the first-hand excitement still awaited them. They carried guitars with their suitcases, and songs in their heads. Some arrived as stowaways, including Jesús Colón, who wrote the poem above. The first winter was often the biggest shock.

By the 1920s, the neighbourhood north of Central Park and south of Harlem, around 116th Street, was transformed into 'El Barrio' – Spanish Harlem. Jewish delis and Italian grocery stores were replaced by Spanish corner shops (bodegas), barbers, boarding houses and cafés. Entertainment grew alongside the community; scores of guitar trios sang plenas in the high, raw Spanish style along with Cuban son songs and boleros. At Christmas, Puerto Rican carols (aguinaldos) were pulled out – songs that everyone knew – and their airs filled the snowy streets as the singers walked from one apartment block to another.

Erratic employment was available for the newcomers in docks, tobacco factories and laundries, and there was work for carpenters, barbers and tailors. Women worked in sweatshops. Thousands of men were cigar-makers (tabaqueros), the most politicized workers, who left Puerto Rico as the tobacco industry was mechanized and the world turned to cigarettes. From this first generation emerged poets and writers, songwriters, singers and musicians, whose politically sharp works provided a reassuring bond in the hostile new country.

In the thirties, the community was united through Spanish-language radio stations: live broadcasts from local nightclubs were a major source of home entertainment. The American record industry sent talent scouts into the Caribbean in the first decade of the century: both The Victor Talking Machine Company and Columbia Phonograph Company were capitalizing on the new market with recordings of Cuban son and Puerto Rican danzas, plenas and aguinaldos. A 1980s UK record compilation, *The Music of Puerto Rico: 1929–40,* recreated the variety of subjects covered by a selection of lyrical singers. Musicians were ferried in from both islands to record 78s, usually staying extra days in the city to play in the cafés, social clubs and dancehalls; some stayed permanently.

Throughout the 1930s, more musicians moved to New York, driven from Puerto Rico both by the Depression and by the destruction of small-scale farming through the development of intensive single-crop agriculture (sugar, coffee and tobacco). Many musicians were lured by the American music which filled the radio airwaves. The Cubans, including Miguelito Valdés and Desi Arnaz, left to escape the civil war against the dictator General Machado. Though the Cubans set the trends, most musicians were Puerto Rican, with a handful of Dominicans.

After World War I, a surge of Puerto Rican islanders, including a number who had fought in the US Army, moved to New York. The majority had started out playing in the highly trained municipal brass bands which operated in every town on the island, and had later been introduced to jazz by black American soldiers during their army service. Their skills at reading music were prized by New York's jazz bandleaders and also by the producers of several Broadway shows, including *The Blackbirds of 21* and *22* and *Shuffle Along*, starring Josephine Baker.

One of the first popular dance bands was run by Vicente Sigler, who arrived in the city from Cuba in the early 1920s. Since few Cubans lived in New York at that time, he hired mainly Puerto Rican and Dominican musicians who even provided backing for Cuban son Trío Matamoros at one recording session. A young Cuban flute player, Alberto Socarras, played with Sigler briefly before setting up his own rival band featuring the recently arrived Puerto Rican trumpeter Augusto Coen. The match was short-lived, however: Coen soon founded his own band, which leant closer to the American Swing formula.

An unlikely mecca for visiting Latin musicians was a grocery store called 'Almacenes Hernández' on Madison Avenue near 115th Street. Its owner was a young Puerto Rican pianist, Victoria Hernández, who arrived in New York in 1919. When she boosted her stock to include the first 78s, the shop became a magnet for local music fans. In the mid-twenties her brother, Rafael, turned up, on discharge from the US army, where he had played in James Reece Europe's celebrated regimental band, The Hellfighters, composed chiefly of Harlem's African-American musicians. Victoria turned over the back room to music – she gave piano lessons and Rafael composed songs which would become anthems for Puerto Ricans on both sides of the water. In 1930 Victoria founded the label Hispano and acted as advisor to the major recording companies on their productions. She also promoted Cuban and Puerto Rican bands and managed her brother's groups. Rafael became the most sought-after composer of his era; his repertoire includes the unofficial Puerto Rican anthem 'Lamento Borincano' which united the community throughout the Depression.

Alberto Socarras arrived in New York in 1927. His prototype Latin-Jazz band briefly featured Dizzy Gillespie.

VICTORIA & RAFAEL HERNANDEZ

Victoria Hernández was running a grocery-cum-record store in Spanish Harlem when her brother Rafael arrived from San Juan. The modest, meticulous young man set the standard for the city's many guitar trios with his first group, Trío Borinquén (Puerto Rican Trio). Victoria managed his band and he named his second line-up, Cuarteto Victoria, after her. Hernández composed more than 2000 songs, odes to his homeland (like the famous 'Lamento Borincano'), stark tales from the barrio and limpid love songs. Many are still covered, and they are guaranteed to stir national pride, in salsa, Latin Jazz or ballad style.

The 1930s were marked by the arrival of three Puerto Rican tenors, known affectionately by the nicknames 'Davilita', 'Canario' and 'Ramito'. These three men, wearing the appropriate hillbilly farmer costumes with straw hats, and sporting machetes, brought the flavour of the Caribbean countryside to New York's clubs. Their patriotic songs still evoke an emotional response from audiences of third- and fourth-generation Puerto-Rican New Yorkers and have inspired cover versions by scores of musicians, including the salsa composer and bandleader Willie Colón, whose parents were part of the 1930s migration.

Late in the decade, a couple of teenage Puerto Rican singers newly arrived in New York had success with repertoires of mostly Cuban songs. Daniel Santos, reputedly hired after he was overheard singing in the bath, became an idol of Latin New York. His Valentino looks and lazy, emotional voice had women at his concerts sighing out loud. Fifteen-year-old Myrta Silva was spotted singing during the interval at a local theatre. She recorded a protest song called 'La llave' (The Key), which criticized the US Government's plan to open a military base on Puerto Rico (the protest failed). In 1939, when she was sixteen, Rafael Hernández hired her to sing in his Cuarteto Victoria. Both Santos and Silva would eventually sing in Cuba with the feted Cuban orchestra La Sonora Matancera, which boasted over one hundred vocalists since its formation in 1924. Myrta Silva was a hard act to follow even for her successor, the arch-diva, Celia Cruz.

DANIEL SANTOS

For over half a century, the dark Valentino looks and smooth, languid voice of Daniel Santos (1911–92) created near-hysteria all over Latin America. Santos had an unusual and original sense of pitch which intensified his appeal. A Puerto Rican by birth, he is most associated with Cuban music, particularly boleros, but his career began in New York in several key thirties guitar groups: with Cuarteto Flores he succeeded in replacing the 'linnet-throated' Davilita. He found his niche in Cuba in 1948 when, with La Sonora Matancera, he recorded one of the most seductive boleros of all time, 'Dos gardenias'. Even when he was in his seventies, Santos's casual delivery of his hits could still fill concert halls.

The popular thirties guitar group Cuarteto Victoria, led by Rafael Hernández (third from left), with teenage singer Myrta Silva. Bobby Rodríguez (right), who later changed his name to Capo, became a much requested Puerto Rican songwriter. Myrta Silva found her niche singing on Puerto Rican television, presenting live music shows, and dubbing voices on Hollywood cartoons.

Throughout the thirties, Cuban son songs and Puerto Rican plenas rang out around the barrio, played by trios and quartets. The Cuban Trío Matamoros was top of the bill. Their vivid songs, precise harmonies and distinctive Spanish guitar accompaniment were said to be responsible for the gradual replacement of the small 8-stringed Puerto Rican cuatro guitar with the larger, more powerful, 6-stringed Cuban tres. In Cuba the café groups expanded to sextets and septets, and were copied in New York under the influence of records by Septetos Habanero and Nacional's evocative songs. Rivalling the Cuban sextets in the Puerto Rican clubs were plena groups formed in the wake of the inflammatory success of Canario's group.

On a grander scale, the most significant musical event in the thirties was the arrival in Manhattan in 1931 of Don Azpiazu's full-scale Cuban Orchestra which unleashed 'El Manicero' (The Peanut Vendor) from the stage of the prestigious Palace Theatre on Broadway and launched a world craze for Latin music – for rhumbas, congas and boleros – which has waxed and waned in different guises ever since. Several Broadway composers became infatuated with Cuban music around that time – most famously George Gershwin, who wrote the 'Cuban Overture' after a research trip to Havana in 1930. A spate of Cuban and Mexican themes found their way on to the Broadway stage and into Hollywood films, introducing the Spanish-Cuban bandleader Xavier Cugat to American audiences.

In Havana in 1929, the prolific composer and pianist Ernesto Lecuona had recorded a tribute to the Caribbean Indians called 'Siboney'. It became all the rage in Cuba's dancehalls before spreading to New York. Lecuona would become a regular performer – in white tie and tails – in classical settings at Carnegie Hall, but he also composed scores of swinging dance tunes, brassy rhumbas and swoony romantic boleros for his dance band, the Lecuona Cuban Boys. This ruffle-sleeved outfit became the leading evangelists for Latin music in Europe through the 1930s and 1940s.

For the first few decades of the century, most of the burgeoning Latin Caribbean community enjoyed their entertainments locally, often at home. Piano rolls were superseded by wind-up gramophones (known in Spanish as 'Vitrolas', after the Victor company). Rent parties – an idea borrowed from the black community during the Depression and Prohibition – paid the rent and made illicit drinking easier. For musicians, they were a meal ticket. The Cuban bandleader Fernando Storch Caney ran a Puerto Rican-style guitar group in 1930. He explained to musicologist Max Salazar how these parties worked: 'Guests were pinned with a small strip of coloured cloth, indicating they had paid the 25-cent entrance fee. We played boleros, guarachas and son hit tunes like "Son de la loma", in a slow swing...two guitarists would set the tempo and sing in unison...the muted trumpet, rattling maracas and claves rounded out the sound...we were paid with money collected from the sales of food and beer. On good nights, we earned as much as $5.' Wealthier families hired more ambitious line-ups and charged more.

At the same time, cafés and bars with evocative island names like Flor de Borinquén and El San Juan still employed the more folksy guitar trios and quartets, while the growing number of dancehalls and social clubs presented mixed programmes and more elaborate line-ups. In summer, the Puerto Rican workers' associations and trades unions held camps outside New York, ending the days with campfire sing-songs of nostalgic hit songs and ad-libbed commentaries on the new life. The social clubs and cigar-workers' societies

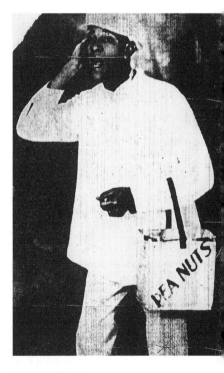

The original 'Peanut Vendor' – Antonio Machín. Composer Moises Simón wrote the famous song in a café in Old Havana.

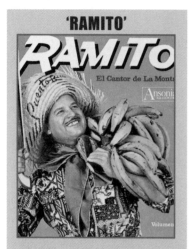

'RAMITO'

Puerto Rico's 'Ramito' – Florencio Morales Ramos – was nicknamed 'El Cantor de La Montaña' (The Mountain Troubadour). He landed in New York in 1926, bringing with him the rough, Spanish-descended décimas – songs of the jíbaros, the mountain farmers. On stage he wore the traditional jíbaro costume – machete tucked in his waistband and upturned straw hat – and carried a repertoire of evocative songs, like 'La tierra mía' (My Land). The response to his clear tenor tones, the stretched vowels and exaggeratedly rolled R's spanning lazily across the rhythms, was near-hysteria. Improvisation is essential in this style of song, and both Ramito and his brother Juan ('Moralito') inherited the skill from their mother, a rare exception in a male tradition. Ramito's performances were exhilarating, spontaneous affairs, built on topical, long verses – he once included a song about President John F. Kennedy's assassination – but he was also an eminent songwriter and folklorist who revived many near-extinct Puerto Rican song styles. Ramito represented the Spanish song tradition, but the most lasting song about the jíbaro's condition is the Afro-Rican plena version of the national anthem, Rafael Hernandez's 'Lamento Borincano'.

held political and educational evenings, with poetry and story-telling, comedy routines, dances and talent contests. The pianist Charlie Palmieri remembered winning piles of pencils when his mother paraded him through the social clubs.

Beyond family entertainment, the city buzzed with jazz and blues. Tour buses took visitors to Black Harlem's Savoy Ballroom, Cotton Club and Small's Paradise, where some of the century's most innovative musicians played Swing and orchestrated blues, just a few blocks from Spanish Harlem. The black, white and Latin lindy-hopping crowds tended to dance in their own territories, but the musicians, as always, crossed the boundaries. The effect of these cross-fertilizations began to be heard in Latin clubs, where jazz was still dance music.

Cuban and Puerto Rican horn players found work in jazz bands and in the orchestra pits of Broadway musicals. The Cuban flautist Alberto Socarras played with his small group in the warm-up slot at the Cotton Club and the Savoy Ballroom, but also broadcast his rhumbas and boleros on WMCA radio live from the Latin Campoamor Club. He hired a young trumpeter, Dizzy Gillespie, 'to add that American flavour' to his mix of Cuba and jazz. In his autobiography, *To Be Or Not to Bop*, Gillespie called Socarras 'the Cuban maestro with the magic flute'.

When the Swing Era was officially launched in 1935, the hit song was Benny Goodman's 'It Don't Mean a Thing, If It Ain't Got That Swing'; the lindy-hop was its dance and the Savoy Ballroom, filling an entire block on 140th Street and Lenox Avenue in Harlem, was its 'mecca'. The resident Chick Webb Orchestra fronted by Ella Fitzgerald drew queues round the block for every show. Webb's exuberant young trumpeter and musical director was Mario Bauzá, a twenty-two-year-old Cuban who befriended his opposite number, Dizzy Gillespie, in Socarras's band.

After Chick Webb's death in 1932, Bauzá and Gillespie moved together into the eccentric Cab Calloway's orchestra where they sowed the early seeds of Latin Jazz – or Afro-Cuban jazz, as Bauzá referred to it. The two men separated in 1940 and in 1941 Bauzá invited his brother-in-law, the singer Machito (Frank Grillo), over from Havana; Machito's sister, the singer Graciela, soon followed. The scene was set for a revolutionary new sound. Machito named the band the Afro-Cubans. Their 1943 recording of 'Tanga' (an African word for marijuana) was the first crystallization of his ideas, irresistibly danceable big-band Afro-Cuban jazz. The band were hired at the most fashionable clubs, and played to audiences from both black American and Latin camps – genuinely Afro-Cuban-American music, the sound of the New Latin New York.

BARRIO LIFE

By the start of World War II, barrio life was settled but schizophrenic, especially for the first generation who spoke Spanish at home and English at school, and listened to America's dance music and singers on the radio and

Efraín Suarez, owner of the
Spanish Harlem store Made
in Puerto Rico, holding a
San Juan phone book with
mambo stars on the cover.

JOE CUBA

Joe Cuba (Gilberto Miguel Calderon, born
1931) walks through Spanish Harlem,
greeting old friends and passersby like a
favourite politician. He dips into Casa
Latina Records to check on sales of his
sixties boogaloo CDs, which are enjoying
a comeback since Tito Nieves's 1997 chart
success with house remixes of Cuba's
1966 hit *Bang! Bang!*. That rollicking
English-language song was Latin music's
first million-seller. It took Cuba's Sextet on
tours with James Brown and Motown's
top acts. Cuba recalls playing Madison
Square Gardens ahead of Brown: 'I threw
the audience about ten million whistles
(pitos) that play a tune as we played our
theme, 'El Pito' (I'll Never Go Back to
Georgia). They were still playing them as
James Brown was trying to get on stage.'

island music at family get-togethers. Los Reyes de la Plena's 'En la ciento diez y seis' (On 116th Street) reveals the adjustments and tensions experienced by the two generations in those early decades of Spanish Harlem:

> On 116th Street, there's a certain girl...
> I took her to the movies and I took her little hand,
> I took her to the theatre and there I told her I loved her...
> She called me 'Papi'* and said it in English,
> and 'Darling, if you love me, I'll marry you.'
> Because I'm from Ponce and she's from Mayaguez,
> Her mother won't talk to me, because I married her daughter.
>
> [*an Hispanic term of endearment from wives to husbands]

The conga player Joe Cuba (Gilberto Calderon), who grew up on 116th Street – where he still lives – was one of the first generation of genuine Puerto Rican New Yorkers who lived the life romanticized in Leonard Bernstein's *West Side Story*. Violent gang fights, cinematic rooftop chases and battles with home-made zip guns were daily occurrences. The enemy was everyone else, particularly the Italians, but even included the newly arrived Puerto Ricans: 'We called them "Hillbillies" and "Ringy Jingy Boys", ' says Cuba, 'because of the jangly sound of their guitars.' Their heroes were Ramito and Canario, who sang about life in the mountain villages, and were too hick for these tough young Manhattanites, who listened to Swing and jazz and Cuban rhumbas, wore zoot suits and spoke English. Cuba remembers hogging the listening booths at Victoria Hernández's music store with his friends and colonizing Abbey's Luncheonette for late-night sessions round the jukebox. This clique, all percussionists, went on to occupy significant niches in salsa and Latin Jazz: Willie Bobo worked with the West Coast jazz bands; Changuito went home to Cuba and cofounded Los Van Van; Carlos 'Patato' Valdez built a career in Afro-Cuban jazz and roots rumbas. Only Joe Cuba achieved mainstream success with a string of 1960s boogaloo crossovers.

Cuba's break came when the hip Puerto Rican band Alfarona X visited New York without their regular conga player, Sabu Martínez, who had been called to Hollywood to play on a film soundtrack. Cuba stepped in. 'The gig was at the Park Plaza Hotel,' he recalled. 'I earned $28 – a fortune then.' His first band played in an American-Latin show at the Stardust Ballroom downtown. After the shows, the Latinos playing in various downtown clubs would race up to Spanish Harlem to an after-hours club called Baldies. 'We played there till seven in the morning,' Cuba remembers. 'Everybody would go there for breakfast in their tuxedos, half drunk, and we'd get down to the nitty-gritty music.'

Non-Latin American interest in Latin music swelled in the thirties and forties through a spate of Hollywood kitsch musicals featuring exotic song-and-dance intervals. The musicians played live on the radio and at swanky New York nightclubs. Hollywood's favourite Latin bandleader was the Spanish-Cuban violinist Xavier Cugat, who had hits with songs by both Sinatra ('The Shawl') and Bing Crosby. Cugat also had a residency at New York's prestigious Waldorf Astoria, where his orchestra performed on

Miguelito Valdés (1916–78) was a boy-boxer in one of Havana's famous rumba barrios. In 1929 he forsook boxing to sing with his former guitar teacher Maria Teresa Vera's Sexteto Occidental. In 1937, he and six friends signed to the Marianao Beach Casino as Orquesta Casino de la Playa, entertaining swimsuited American tourists with rhumbas and congas. Their hit number was 'Babalú', sung by Valdés, who accompanied himself on a conga drum. In 1939, Desi Arnaz took 'Babalú' into the US charts; the following year Xavier Cugat hired Valdés to succeed Arnaz in his band, billing him 'Mister Babalú' and paying $150 a week. Valdés was a natural showman with a refined vibrato to his warm tenor voice. His fast, deft scatting and rolling rhyming-slang would shame many modern rappers.

luxuriously draped stage sets. His leggy singers in glitzy costumes included three wives: Carmen Castillo, Abbe Lane and 'Charo' Baeza. Cugat's secret was his immaculate musicianship and the simplified Cuban rhumbas and congas he tailored for the American dancers. His band was a nursery for young musicians who went on to form their own influential dance orchestras, with greater attention to authenticity.

In 1939 Cugat signed up the Cuban singer Miguelito Valdés, who had played in Havana with the popular tourist band, Orquesta Casino de la Playa. Valdés's risqué act – conga drum strapped to his waist, hip-shaking rhumba, and ad-libbed chanting in African tongues – delighted the society crowds. He had a hit in 1941 with the Americanized rhumba 'Babalú' but his version was overshadowed by one by fellow Cuban exile Dezi Arnaz, who also sang with Cugat for a few months before shooting off to Hollywood where he met and married the all-American Lucille Ball. The couple's staggeringly successful networked television series, *I Love Lucy*, pushed America's Cubans into the national spotlight. Arnaz took with him a new dance craze – the conga – which he kicked off in Miami, in imitation of the snakey carnival dances of his childhood. The rhumba and the conga became the dances of the decade.

In the wake of World War II, New York was a club-goers' paradise, starkly divided on racial and social terms. Downtown supported white America's taste for Cugat's exotica, and the easy-going Puerto Rican cocktail-Latin piano style of Noro Morales, while the Harlem dancehalls catered primarily for the black crowd. The Latin scene had its own places, named after venues in Havana and San Juan – La Conga, Havana-Madrid, the Latin Quarter. As always, many musicians swung effortlessly between both camps. The least adulterated versions of Latin music were played by some of the greatest bands in Latin New York's history, both Cuban and Puerto Rican. They followed Machito's Afro-Cuban jazz, and the impressive big band was led by the Cuban pianist José Curbelo, a master talent spotter who hired the seventeen-year-old Tito Puente in 1939 to play timbales. Curbelo told how he had been so depressed by the lack of good percussionists in New York that he was contemplating returning to Cuba. He went along to one of the weekly hiring sessions at Roseland Ballroom – 'In the afternoons, two or three thousand musicians turned up and the bandleaders went to hire. I was handed a leaflet about a gig, and that's where I saw this young drummer. I thought I was back in Cuba – I hired him on the spot, and took him straight to Miami on a job.' Puente was seventeen, and still at school. Curbelo's orchestra became a staple on the Latin-Jazz circuit in both Harlem and Spanish town. In 1946 Curbelo also picked up Machito's band boy, a young Puerto Rican romantic singer called Tito Rodríguez.

In the early 1940s, a new style of orchestrated Puerto Rican folk music ruffled the surface of Latin New York when trumpeter César Concepción brought the rural plena to the metropolis and converted it to a big-band format, led by the raging tones of singer Joe Valle. 'Ponce', their tribute to the birthplace of plena, is still being revived today.

Multi-talented Xavier Cugat (1900–1990) was a violinist, cartoonist (for the *Los Angeles Times*), painter, 'Tango King' and 'Rhumba King', composer of film-scores for Valentino and Chaplin, and Hollywood bandleader.

All through the forties and fifties, the Audubon Hall in Spanish Harlem and Hunts Point Palace in the Bronx were great neighbourhood Latin crowd-pullers. Hunts Point was run by an Italian musician-turned-promoter Federico Pagani, who persuaded Tito Puente to launch his own band, The Piccadilly Boys, when he was demobbed from the US Navy. A year later, in 1949, Puente formed a dance orchestra, hiring the dapper Cuban singer Vicentico Valdés and the Cuban conga player Mongo Santamaría. Their first recording, a song called 'Abaniquito', is the first American mambo on record. It appeared on the historic album *Mamborama*, which effectively launched the dazzling new era of mambo.

Nineteen-forty-nine was a significant year. Apart from the fearsome *Mamborama*, the Cuban pianist Pérez Prado issued the first of a series of numerical mambos from his base in Mexico City. Mambo No. 5 crash-landed in New York just as the mambo was sneaking up on the city's dancers. The same year, Federico Pagani discovered a rundown hostess club on Broadway at 52nd Street and offered it to Machito's Afro-Cubans for Sunday afternoon sessions. Mario Bauzá suggested an all-Latin night and called it the 'Blen Blen Club' as a tribute to his friend and Dizzy Gillespie's conga player, Chano Pozo, who had recently been killed in Harlem. Queues formed around the block, prompting Pagani to open four nights a week and promote only Latin bands. He renamed the club the Palladium and it became world famous as the 'home of the mambo and cha-cha-cha'. Machito's dazzling band was a star attraction, but the competition was impressively fierce, with each band having its own loyal and vociferous following. Slap bang in the centre of Manhattan, at its most exclusive Broadway address, this all-Latin mecca would become the most talked-about venue in America, drawing in not only Havana's greatest musicians, but also Hollywood's most glamorous stars. Marlon Brando turned up to play congas; Kim Novak and Eartha Kitt danced mambos. From 1949 until 1966, when it was demolished to make way for a car park, the Palladium had a reputation which reached all round the world. Within its heavily draped walls, the musical identity of homegrown Latin New York was consolidated.

ABOVE: **The Mambo Aces Andy (Vásquez) and Joe (Centeno) pioneered two-man synchronized routines including the 'Round-the-back-Lindy' and the 'Through-the-legs-Charleston'.**
BELOW: **Millie (Distafano) and Pete ('Cuban Pete' Aguilar) wove rumba, tap and modern dance into their act.**

Tito Rodríguez

The dapper Puerto Rican singer Tito Rodríguez was one of the three 'Mambo Kings'. Born in 1923 in San Juan, he arrived in New York in 1940 as a 17-year-old hopeful and moved in with his elder brother, Johnny, who hooked him up with singing jobs around Spanish Harlem. Within two years Tito's light-skinned good looks and soft, smooth voice had won him a job with Xavier Cugat, the Don of the Downtown black-tie-and-cocktail-dress (white American) supper-club circuit. He then moved on to another Downtown band, run by Puerto Rican pianist Noro Morales, before joining José Curbelo's Cuban orchestra in 1946. Curbelo's drummer was the teenaged Tito Puente; a previous singer had been Machito. Thus the paths of the three future mambo kings crossed even before they formed their own rival bands.

Tito Rodríguez's first band was a combo called the Mambo Devils, expanded from 1948 to a full orchestra. His repertoire of mambos and cha-cha-chas was tailored to the sophisticated Palladium dancers rather than to the diluted Downtown tastes catered for by Cugat. The three Kings' versions of mambo and cha-cha-cha were quite different but jazz was important to all three. Tito Rodríguez's blazing uptempo reworkings of some American classics can be heard on *Live at Birdland* (1963), with Zoot Zims, Clark Terry and Al Cohn, recorded at the famous jazz club along 52nd Street from the Palladium. But while Machito and Mario Bauzá emphasized the *Afro-Cuban* line in their songs, both Puente and Rodríguez courted the dancers with the latest crazes. Rodríguez's voice revealed the influence of American singers such as Nat 'King' Cole, and his 1963 record, *From Tito with Love*, spelled out his passion for boleros.

In 1962 his brother Johnny moved back to Puerto Rico and Tito began a series of extended visits to the island. Although the official reception was always warm, he was cold-shouldered for a while by many musicians because he was seen as a grand NuYorican who had deserted 'home'. But he returned to stay in 1971, keeping secret the fact that he had untreatable leukaemia. A sell-out concert at Madison Square Gardens in 1973 was in fact a farewell; he died a month later. The live recording of the concert, *25th Anniversary Performance*, backed by the orchestra of his former Palladium rival, Machito, was a final tribute in front of his ecstatic home-crowd.

Tito (Pablo) Rodríguez, dancing piano-top pachanga with a sixties line-up, was established as a singer in the leading Palladium bands. He launched his first big band in 1963; their eminent guest-players guaranteed success, but the main draw was always Rodríguez. Audiences clamoured for his clear and velvety voice, brilliant improvisations and soul-sustaining boleros.

Wednesday night at the Palladium was 'Mamboscope', compered by Cuban dancer Frank 'Killer Joe' Piro, who ran mambo classes before the show. Mamboscope drew the Hollywood set; here Marlon Brando exhibits his conga skills with the band. Friday nights included Pie-eating and Girls' Legs Contests, during which M.C. Federico Pagani pushed the skirts up with a stick to measure the legs.

Through the second half of the 1950s, rock'n'roll influenced the Latin community just as it did every other style of popular music. Bands shifted their material to keep up with the new trend: Celia Cruz recorded 'Rock an' Roll' with La Sonora Matancera – a cheeky number that revealed the close connection between the two styles. At the same time, black American doowop also inspired many young American-born Latino singers. America's most successful doowoppers, Frankie Lymon and the Teenagers, comprising two black Americans, two Puerto Ricans and a Dominican, had a top ten hit in 1955 with 'Why Do Fools Fall in Love?'. Lymon's manager, George Goldner, set up the Tico label to straddle both the doowop and the new young Latin bands. In 1954 Joe Cuba founded his first sextet with a honey-voiced singer called Cheo Feliciano, just in from San Juan and working as a bandboy for Tito Rodríguez. They became the toast of the Palladium. Cuba's appeal lay in his punchy, modern, jazzy arrangements, and in his innovative inclusion of a vibraphone in the simple line-up.

In the late fifties, a young pianist and musical jack-of-all-trades called Al Santiago consolidated his skills in the CasAlegre record shop and the Alegre label (the latter modelled on Cuba's Panart). His 1958 set of five Alegre All Stars albums, featuring the peak of local soloists in copy-cat jam session imitations of Cachao's Cuban Descargas, were compulsory listening for new York's young musicians. The creative centre for Latin music was still the Palladium and visits from Cuba's star bands (Beny Moré and José Fajardo, and Orquesta Aragón) continued to inspire the locals, but in 1957 a buzz percolated from Puerto Rico about a bombshell new band called Rafael Cortijo's Combo, fronted by the raunchy, charismatic black singer Ismael Rivera. In 1959 the Combo brought a new ingredient to the rhythm mix – a modernized, big-band version of the folksy Puerto Rican bomba perfected in their hit 'La bombon de Elena', which freshly inspired homegrown modernists in their creation of the next phase of Latin music in the US. Teenagers like Willie Colón studied their moves and musical techniques along with American bands and singing groups, and moulded the cacophony of music which surrounded them into what would become ¡SALSA! And that is another story.

PEREZ PRADO

'Uh-Huhhhh': the deep, visceral grunts which punctuate Pérez Prado's songs and his manic piano solos were a trademark. The wild man of mambo began his career playing freestyle organ accompaniment to silent movies. He played alongside Arsenio Rodríguez and Miguelito Valdés in Orquesta Casino de la Playa but was sacked for his jazzy arrangements – his style was influenced by Swing jazz. In 1944 he founded his own band and moved to Mexico City, where a brief, intense partnership with the singer Beny Moré led to the four-million seller record, *Que rico el mambo*. In 1955 Prado's trumpet-led 'Cherry Pink, Apple Blossom White' was number one in the US charts.

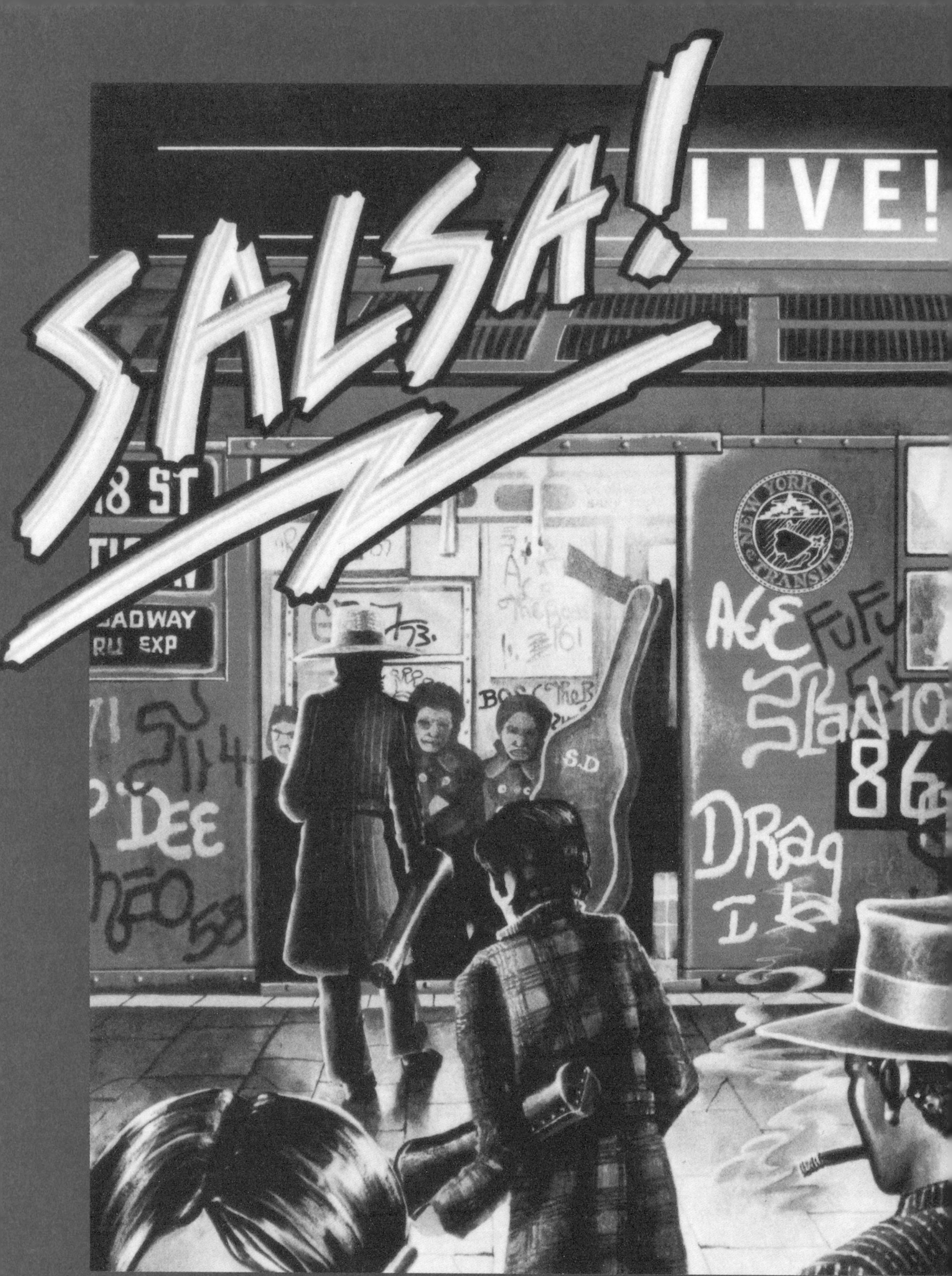
SALSA!
LIVE!

Chapter 3 Salsa in the USA

AT THE END of the fifties, scores of Cuban musicians bought one-way tickets from Havana to New York City and settled in Spanish Harlem and the Hispanic communities of Brooklyn and the Bronx. They stepped off Havana's danzón and mambo carousel into the brassy ether of the Palladium and New York's network of neighbourhood nightclubs, dancehalls, hotel ballrooms, after-hours bars and social clubs.

The music on offer ranged from folksy guitar trios to sophisticated dance bands still playing fast and brassy mambos and smoochy boleros. But the supremacy of the mambo had already been undermined earlier in the decade when Cuban bandleader and flautist Gilberto Valdés brought the charanga band to town. Valdés's wildly rhythmic arrangements were powered by the Afro-Cuban conga player Mongo Santamaría, and subsequently by a talented young freelance Dominican musician called Johnny Pacheco, who played drums with Valdés as well as accordion with a handful of merengue bands in town. Valdés's enthusiasm for charanga fed Pacheco's interest in Cuban music: the bandleader presented him with an antique wooden Cuban flute and initiated him in the high, trilling Cuban technique.

A run of Cuban charanga orchestras visited New York's clubs in 1958, and the following year the group Fajardo y sus Estrellas, with their slick showband dance routines, performed during the young Senator John F. Kennedy's presidential campaign. The dashing flute player José Fajardo subsequently wooed

his Latin fans at the Palladium. The most revered Cuban flute band, Orquesta Aragón, also left their mark. By 1962, when Fajardo eventually moved to New York, taking the inventive bass player Israel 'Cachao' López with him, many New York musicians were already infatuated with the charanga sound. Johnny Pacheco and pianist Charlie Palmieri were the first to go – in 1959 they abandoned their quintet and formed a full-size band, Charanga Duboney,

LEFT: **New York, birthplace of salsa, has played hide-and-seek with Latin music for decades. In recent years, salsa has burst beyond the barrio.**
ABOVE RIGHT: **A mural depicting 'La Gran Manzana' (The Big Apple), on the wall of Gaby Oller's Music Store, which provided for Latin musicians for decades.**

The Palmieri brothers, pianists Eddie (left, born 1936) and Charlie (right, born 1927), were first-generation Spanish Harlem–New Yorkers, precocious musical talents who followed each other through the history of New York's Latin music for nearly five decades. At 14, Charlie joined Machito's orchestra; Eddie started out with Tito Rodríguez. Their solo careers began with charangas – Eddie's Perfecta, featuring Barry Rogers's pivotal trombone; and Charlie's melodic Modorna, with Johnny Pacheco. Generous, modest Charlie became a brilliant teacher and director, and a romantic soloist, composer of such wry tunes as 'Stop the World, I Want to Get On', written after he had suffered a disabling stroke. Eddie is salsa's eccentric, manic genius, who prefaces his songs with long, mathematically calculated, impressionist solos.

with Pacheco playing the antique wooden flute. Their one album together, *Palmieri*, is a showcase for Pacheco's recklessly light-fingered style and Palmieri's effortless, rhythmic technique. Most of all, its four fiddles inject irresistible swing. 'Musical differences' split the band after eight months: Palmieri kept the name and stayed with the melodic style, while Pacheco's new group, Charanga, was an uptempo, more showy affair, with two singers (Fajardo-style) and for the first time in New York the whole band dancing. A young pianist called Al Santiago, who had just launched Alegre Records, signed Pacheco, and *Johnny Pacheco y su charanga* sold more than 100,000 copies in six months. Santiago then brought out Charlie Palmieri's bestseller, *Charanga at the Caravana Club*, and the charanga boom was on.

The dancers' enthusiasm encouraged other bands to switch formats: the visiting Puerto Rican singer Mon Rivera joined one of Pacheco's school-friends, trombonist Barry Rogers, and hired Charlie Palmieri and his kid brother Eddie to play piano for his Alegre album *Mon y sus trombones*. This record's rough, edgy quality inspired Eddie Palmieri to hook up with Rogers – they recorded an exceptional debut album, *La perfecta*, in 1962. Brother Charlie Palmieri named their style 'trombanga'.

Charanga proved to be a highly versatile style. Throughout the seventies, whole sections of musicians moved between bands and created new line-ups. A mass break-out from Ray Barretto's band led to the formation in 1973 of the influential Típica 73, which launched many important soloists. This group's young violinist, Alfredo de la Fé, had served his apprenticeship with José

Cover of Eddie Palmieri's debut album, *La perfecta*, 1962. Eddie is 4th from left; Barry Rogers can be seen at the back, brandishing his trombone.

LEFT: **Celia Cruz recording in Miami in 1997.**
ABOVE: **Costumes like this fabulous flamenco-inspired affair took her Cuban dress-makers weeks to make.**
BELOW LEFT: **Soulmates Celia Cruz and Tito Puente, enjoying an off-stage joke.**

Celia Cruz

No one in Latin music has ever approached the status of Celia Cruz in her more than fifty-year reign. She is quite simply the Queen of Salsa. She can walk virtually anonymously through Manhattan, but an honorary degree from Yale, the freedom of most major US cities and her handprints in the Hollywood Walk of Fame officially acknowledge her as an American-Latin. In any Latino neighbourhood her presence attracts riots of well-wishers and autograph hunters.

Celia Cruz's vast repertoire of songs contains the history of salsa – from the earliest, fresh-voiced records with the brassy Afro-Cuban son band, La Sonora Matancera (who led her out of Cuba in 1959), through her sixties recordings with Tito Puente, when she sang soul-stirring tributes to the Afro-Cuban saints and joined the New York set, to her unchallenged dance through salsa's history, guided by Johnny Pacheco and picking up gold discs and Grammies for albums with Fania's other top bandleaders: Larry Harlow, Willie Colón, Ray Barretto, 'Papo' Lucca. Her performances with the Fania All Stars

will never be forgotten. Every subsequent new generation has fallen for her charms; more recent bandleaders – José Alberto, Oscar D'León, Willie Chirino and Isidro Infante – have lured her into salsa raps and Latin ballads alongside the brighter, faster modern American salsa. But her most enduring musical relationship is with Tito Puente – 'El Maestro' as she calls him – who simply says: 'There will never be another Celia Cruz; she has everything.'

In person, Celia Cruz emits a contagious glow; on stage it bursts into full flame. Her performances are a whirl of movement and joyfulness, feet and hips twisting and shimmying, reflecting light-beams off her outrageous costumes and Tiffany jewels. Her penetrating voice, with its operatic range and sure, sophisticated sense of timing, her computer-fast improvisations and fast, playful onomatopoeic scats are exceptional by any standards. Even her trademark catchline – a barking call 'Azúcaaaaar!' (Sugar!) – brings on goose-bumps. All her skills are exercised in the finale to her shows, 'Bemba colorá' (Thick Red Lips), in which she sings, with feigned humility:

'Don't forget the name of this poor singer,
I've worn my best dress,
I've given all I can...
My name is *Celia Cruz*.'

With La Sonora Matancera, during the 1940s.

Fajardo in Havana; its lead singer José Alberto, 'El Canario', would become one of salsa's top stars. Percussionist Orestes Vilato would go on to join West Coast guitarist Carlos Santana in the wake of his worldwide success with the first Latin rock album, *Abraxas*. In 1976 Típica 73 split: singer Adalberto Santiago and Vilato reformed as Los Kimbos, built around two trumpets and an electric guitar. The rest of the band kept the name and the style and in 1979, on a visit to Cuba, recorded an historic album, *En Cuba: Intercambio* (Cultural Interchange), with their idols, Orquesta Aragón.

In 1966 the Palladium lost its drink licence and closed down. According to the celebrated pianist Charlie Palmieri, 'The end of the mambo, the closing of the Palladium, the Cuban crisis, changed everything. After that, musicians stopped coming in, there was no more sheet music from Cuba, so the young musicians had to learn to write their own, and the musical arrangements changed.' By then the first generation of bilingual American-Latinos, the Nu-Yoricans, were living between two cultures: their parents still expected to return 'home' to Puerto Rico or Cuba, still talked in Spanish, still ate Caribbean food, and continued to dance danzas and plenas, mambos and danzóns. Their children went to American schools, dressed like their neighbours and wanted to be Americans.

David Maldonado, an influential manager in nineties salsa, grew up in Spanish Harlem in the era of sharkskin suits and beaver fur hats, dancing 'The Mashed Potato' and jiving to Motown records. 'We'd go to christenings and weddings with our relatives and interrupt their music with "Twist and Shout"', he recalled. 'And then suddenly there was this music that was LATIN, but they were singing in English, and they dressed like us and they talked like us...It was so hip! That was the boogaloo. And through that we discovered Eddie Palmieri, Tito Puente, Ray Barretto. Holy smoke!'

Along with the boogaloo (in Spanish, bugalú) came the dengue, the jala-jala and the shing-a-ling, all mambo and cha-cha-cha offspring. While soul and r'n'b bands were inventing dance crazes in Harlem, the Latinos were concocting their own, every bit as irresistible as the Hully Gully and the Twist. A modernist charanga band called Orquesta Broadway was founded by the three Zervigón brothers and singer Roberto Torres, who arrived from Havana in 1962. These quiffed rock'n'roll hipsters, reared on the slick brilliance of Orquesta Aragón, sparked a mayfly dance craze with their 1964 album *Dengue*, which converted Pérez Prado's invention (the dengue) into an uptempo, on-the-beat, Latin-soul feast. The main claim to fame for the jala-jala was that it launched a pair of wildly uninhibited and exceptionally talented musicians: the florid pianist Ricardo 'Richie' Ray and the shrieking falsetto singer Bobby Cruz.

The boogaloo craze was started by multi-instrumentalist and singer Johnny Colón, who had previously sung with Swedish West Coast jazz vibes player Cal Tjader. Colón's two trombone–two saxophone line-up (he played trombone) recorded the first and one of the most sophisticated boogaloos, 'Boogaloo Blues'. Shortly afterwards, an ex-Charlie Palmieri vocalist, Pete Rodríguez, released a souped-up Latin soul song, 'Michaela'. But the greatest success was the Joe Cuba Sextet's 1967 hit 'Bang! Bang!', the first million-seller. Its riotous party atmosphere epitomizes the boogaloo style; a raucous collision of hand-claps, musicians calling each other's nicknames, children's choruses, all backed by a superb vibes-led jazz dance sextet and fronted by the cool young voice of Cheo Feliciano. Cuba also invented the memorable

'Wabble Cha', in which, as he describes it, 'Everybody dips their body from one side to the other at the same time, like a big Mexican wave.'

The best boogaloos were more sophisticated than their cod-English lyrics and simplified rhythms imply. But some musicians resented their youthful style. Promoter Ralph Mercado recalls that 'Eddie Palmieri wouldn't play boogaloo, but Charlie released "Boogaloo Mania".' Celia Cruz relished the tongue-twisting rhythms of her boogaloos with La Sonora Matancera. Ray Barretto, who had a serious reputation beyond the Latin scene, playing congas with many leading jazz legends all through the fifties, released a slow-burning boogaloo-charanga, 'El Watusi', on his 1962 album *Charanga moderna*. This crept into the US and UK charts in 1963 and lodged there, a sharp dance track with a searing flute solo and a battery of Barretto's Afro-Cuban drumming. In 1964 Cal Tjader, a member of Dave Brubeck's original 'Take 5' trio, reworked Dizzy Gillespie's Latin-soul feast, 'Guachi Guara' (Soul Sauce) and shot into both the US and UK charts. The boogaloo era ended abruptly in 1969, leaving many young musicians ready for reinvention in the coming 'salsa' scene.

Inevitably, the charanga boom also waned. Perhaps Johnny Pacheco anticipated this when he switched to the brassy, trumpet-led Afro-Cuban format known as conjuntos. His role models were La Sonora Matancera and Arsenio Rodríguez, who had both recently arrived in New York from Havana. Pacheco's new band, Pacheco y su Tumbao, included a tres guitarist and a bongo player – a telling formula associated with the son. Their crisp new sound was immortalized on *Canonazo*, recorded by Al Santiago.

THE FANIA STORY

In 1964 Pacheco met an Italian-American divorce lawyer called Jerry Masucci at a party in a New York hotel. Masucci had worked in Havana right up to the closure of Cuba's visa department and retained a passion for the place. Pacheco's career was built around Cuban music. The two men struck a deal and launched Fania Records, a label that would become the most influential in Latin music's history and that would remould Cuban music into a sound more appropriate to Latin New York, the sound they called 'Salsa'.

Fania became known as 'The Latin Motown' – supercharged hit records poured from the studio and into the charts all over Latin America. Producers and arrangers took the diverse rhythms from Cuba's song-books and gave them lyrics which matched their own Latin-in-America lifestyle and arrangements which were influenced by the buzz of jazz, soul, r'n'b and rock that surrounded their lives.

Pacheco's first acquisition was the classically trained oboist and pianist Larry Harlow, a rule-breaking ex-music teacher who had studied music in Cuba while Masucci was there. Their first record in 1966 was *Heavy Smoking* (a reference to marijuana). Next, Pacheco bought from Al Santiago a half-finished album by a group of Brooklyn teenagers, led by seventeen-year-old trombonist Willie Colón. Pacheco introduced Colón to another teenager, the singer Héctor Lavoe, who had sung a few gigs for him already. Their first record together, *El malo* (The Bad Guy), in 1967, was a raw, minimalist collection of songs about teenage barrio life with an inner-city edge. The record sleeve, created by Santiago's ex-designer Izzy Sanabria, now working for

JOHNNY PACHECO

The debonair Johnny Pacheco, with his silver pompadour hair, gold jewelry, well-smoked cigar and black wooden flute, is a symbol of aristocratic New York salsa. Not only did he co-own the legendary Fania label and direct (and perform in) the phenomenal Fania All Stars super-group, but his award-winning productions spread their fame beyond the barrios of New York. A Dominican New Yorker with Cuban music in his soul, Pacheco's greatest joy, he says, was producing Celia Cruz's first album, *Celia and Johnny*, for Fania, in 1974. The multi-instrumentalist played accordion, percussion, clarinet and flute, for merengues and every Cuban style, but he is most associated with sixties pachanga.

The 'Bad Boys' of salsa, Willie Colón (left), aged 17, and Héctor Lavoe, aged 21, photographed in 1967 for their first record, *El malo*.

Pacheco's Fania, established the 'Bad Boy' image of their early records.

The same year, Fania landed a prize catch – conga player Ray Barretto, whose 1967 album *Acid* was a hard-edged fusion of r'n'b and jazz featuring Barretto's expansive new singing partner, Adalberto Santiago. Barretto was on a roll: the following year, 'Hard Hands' gave him a lifelong nickname and presented a topical experiment in jazzy poems backed by two trumpets and dense percussion breaks.

In 1997 Fania Records' first pianist and bandleader, Larry Harlow, founded 'The Fania Legends' – veterans of the Fania All Stars, who toured like a sixties rockers' super-group. The group's diverse members included Alfredo de la Fé and seminal Cuban-American flautist José Fajardo; percussionists Cachete, Nicky Marrero and Roberto Roena; singers Adalberto Santiago, Pete 'El Conde' Rodríguez and Ismael Miranda; Yomo Toro; and the maniacal director, Larry Harlow.

Fania expanded rapidly, moving into a prestigious office-studio complex on Seventh Avenue. In the beginning, Pacheco and Masucci worked around the clock, delivering records in Pacheco's Mercedes. Masucci recalled their sleepless routines: 'I used to listen to Symphony Sid on the radio and if by 2 a.m. he hadn't played our latest records, I would get out of bed, go and buy him a pastrami sandwich, take it to the studio and wait there until he played them!'

Early in the seventies, Jerry Masucci reconnected with his occasional partner Ralph Mercado, who by that time controlled most of New York's top Latin dance venues. Their first joint venture, in 1971, was a historic show with a super-group of Fania artists at the Cheetah club in Manhattan. Masucci remembered the chaos involved: 'There were two days of rehearsal; the musicians had never seen the music, never played with each other, all the material was written on little pieces of paper and sheet music which Johnny [Pacheco] and Bobby Valentín [the bass player] took to a hotel room and transformed. Somehow on the night it was magic. We filmed it as *Nuestra Cosa Latina – Our Latin Thing*. That's really where the salsa explosion started. After that we did the Yankee Stadium show in 1973 to 20,000 people. Crazy!'

The Yankee Stadium concert was released on film in 1974 as *Salsa* and the two-album set *Fania All Stars Live at Yankee Stadium* captures its breathless programme of songs and instrumentals, conducted by Johnny Pacheco in a splendid patchwork coat, with Celia Cruz regal in bejewelled caftan and Afro wig. El Gran Combo, the leading band in Puerto Rico, played alongside duelling congueros Ray Barretto and Mongo Santamaría; Celia Cruz delivered a stunning twenty-minute improvisation on her hit 'Bemba colorá', and the big band joined in with guests from jazz (Billy Cobham and Jan Hammer), rock (Jorge Santana) and Africa (Manu Dibango – whose saxophone-led Afro-Disco hit 'Soul Makossa' was then high in the charts).

In the early seventies era of sharp new salsa, Celia Cruz was rescued from the limitations of the pre-revolutionary Cuban style and introduced to New York's younger generation through her role in Larry Harlow's salsa musical, *Hommy – A Latin Opera* (a Latin version of The Who's rock opera, *Tommy*), which premiered at Carnegie Hall in 1973. Cruz played the Tina Turner role, renamed Gracia Divina, with Cheo Feliciano as El Padrino (The Godfather). In the same year she became the only woman to penetrate the elite magic circle of Fania when Pacheco and Masucci tailored a new label, Vaya, specially for her. Her first album for the new label, *Celia and Johnny*, in 1974, was an immortal, upbeat set which went gold and launched several hits, including the unimaginable feat of rhythmic virtuosity, 'Químbara'. It was the first of scores of award-winning albums produced by the cream of Fania's bandleaders.

RAY BARRETTO

Conga master Ray Barretto (born in New York in 1929) is equally at home in Latin Jazz's improvising spaces and in the more structured dictates of salsa's dancefloors. His long career has brought him honours in both – including the 1990 salsa Grammy with Celia Cruz for *Ritmo en el corazón* (Rhythm in the Heart). Barretto's international reputation grew from his rhythm work behind the great jazz soloists since the fifties, but in salsa he has also groomed many young Puerto musicians in his bands since. The nickname 'Hard Hands' came from his tough, attacking technique, which seems at odds with the tall, slow-moving man who has the air of an academic – until the music ignites a spark and his face contorts as the rhythms shoot through his palms and fingers. Barretto's course through Latin music has been based on conviction; unlike most bandleaders who swing under pressure from the latest trends, he refused to join the disco, merengue or rap crazes.

Fania's bands toured all over Latin America, stimulating waves of imitators in Colombia and Venezuela. Because the bandleaders could hand-pick their ideal singer, some extraordinary partnerships emerged. Pacheco's dream alliance with the smokey-voiced Puerto Rican Pete 'El Conde' (The Count) Rodríguez began in 1973 and has continued, on and off, until today; Larry Harlow launched the seventeen-year-old Puerto Rican high tenor Ismael Miranda, whom Pacheco called 'El Bonito' (The Pretty Boy), both now members of the touring 'Fania Legends' group.

Willie Colón and Héctor Lavoe remained a magical team for five years, until 1974, when Colón handed the band over to Lavoe and entered into what would become one of Fania's most potent partnerships: with the young Panamanian singer–songwriter Rubén Blades. Blades already had one album to his name – *De Panama a Nueva York* – when he started work in Fania's postroom in 1973. In 1974 Ray Barretto signed him as a back-up singer and a year later he sang chorus on a Colón–Lavoe album, *The Good, the Bad and the Ugly*. The following year he and Colón hunkered down on a set of historically significant recordings. Their efforts included the largest selling Latin album, *Siembra*, released in 1979. Songs like Blades's 'Pedro Navaja' (about the demise of a petty gangster) and 'Plástico' (about the perils of the consumerist society) shifted salsa from the limitations of love to social realist story-poems which became anthems for generations of Latin American youth.

The 'Fania Sound' was created by a clique of inventive bandleaders, composers, arrangers and engineers who brought their passions to the studios. Johnny Pacheco and Larry Harlow were diehard Cuban music aficionados who tweaked and reworked the brassy mambo model; Harlow was also a technology fiend: his 1973 album *Electric Harlow* introduced electric piano to salsa. Pacheco included a few merengues for the Dominicans. Louie Ramírez, the virtuoso percussionist and prolific producer and Louis 'Perico' Ortiz, the Puerto Rican trumpeter, both had strong jazz leanings – Ortiz had performed with Mongo Santamaría's band before arranging for Fania; jazz-influenced prodigy 'Papo' Lucca moonlighted from the Puerto Rican band La Sonora Ponceña. Each band also depended for its individual sound on the magical configurations and emphases of the different instruments, particularly within the brass and horn sections. Several left-field instruments – baritone saxophone, clarinet, electric guitar, tres guitar – were dropped in to give fresh textures.

Fania's leading renegades, Colón and Blades, broke every rule in salsa's in-house guide – including reversing the sacred clave. Colón made constant references to Puerto Rican music in covers of revered songs by the island's hero, Rafael Hernández. He also introduced the Puerto Rican cuatro guitar player Yomo Toro to the Fania stable at the historic

FANIA

**EL MALO
WILLIE COLON**

SIDE A
SLP 337
STEREO

1. **JAZZY**
(Brewster · Colon · Taylor)
2. **WILLIE BABY**
(W. Colon)
3. **BORINQUEN**
(D.R.)
4. **WILLIE WHOPPER**
(W. Colon)

Recording Director: JOHNNY PACHECO
Produced by: JERRY MASUCCI

Yankee Stadium show, to uncontrollable flag-waving and cheering from the NuYorican majority in the audience. Colón went beyond Cuba and Puerto Rico: he incorporated Brazilian and other Latin American folk traditions into his songs, even persuading the fanatical Cuban patriot Celia Cruz to sing samba in an early collaboration.

Severed from the Cuban mothership, Fania still maintained an umbilical connection with Puerto Rico. New songs arrived in the office through the post and through the door, and Pacheco and Masucci went on shopping sprees to San Juan. Masucci recalled the scene in the Tin Pan Alley street Calle Serra, where the songwriters sold their latest works. Masucci said, 'I would spend a week there and come back with ten hits. I got all Ray Barretto's first hits from a Cuban called Hugo González.'

ABOVE: **The Fania family at its late-seventies peak, with the Queen, Celia Cruz, at the centre, Cheo Feliciano to her left, and Rubén Blades behind.**
BELOW: **Puerto Rican singers Héctor Lavoe (in Nashville mode) and Cheo Feliciano, Madison Square Gardens, 1987.**

The island's leading songwriter, 'Tite' Curet Alonso, worked as a postman and journalist in San Juan while his songs were in the charts all over Latin America. He provided Fania's artists, particularly the Puerto Rican institutions – Ismael Rivera, Cheo Feliciano and El Gran Combo – with a stream of poetic, award-winning songs which were covered and reissued for decades. Like all Fania artists, he received no royalties, only fees.

Although Fania had an effective monopoly on salsa throughout the seventies, there were plenty of challengers. Many Puerto Rican singers and musicians who were guests on Fania's shows and records still ran their own independent labels back home, and some New York bands were too uncommercial for Fania's tastes and were signed to a handful of more eclectic labels. SalSoul, for instance, recorded the uncompromising Conjunto Libre and a pair of influential descarga albums by Cachao.

An enterprising rival, SAR Records, was housed in a cramped record warehouse on Manhattan's Tenth Avenue. Behind the label were Sergio Bofil, Adriano García and singer Roberto Torres, who dusted off the old Cuban songbooks and reunited musicians with reputations in Havana's pre-Castro heydays: former Beny Moré trumpeter Alfredo 'Chocolate' Armenteros and pianist Alfredo Valdés, who had played solo on Ray Barretto's 'El Watusi' hit. Roberto Torres eventually moved to Miami in 1983, relaunched as Guajiro Records, and re-established his career as a singer. SAR became Caiman and continued their recordings in the Cuban vein.

Throughout the seventies, Jerry Masucci hoovered up the opposition and built up Fania's monopoly. He bought out the main rival, Tico Records, and inherited back catalogues of music by two Mambo Kings, Tito Puente and Rodríguez, as well as Celia Cruz, Charlie Palmieri, Joe Cuba and the wild Cuban diva La Lupe, who was briefly Puente's leading lady. Around 1980, amid rumours of serious tax problems at Fania, Masucci moved house to Argentina ('to play tennis'), leaving Pacheco in charge of a fading empire. This was a cue for a new Venezuelan-Dutch conglomerate, TH (Top Hits)–Rodven to move in. Founded at the height of Venezuela's oil boom and masterminded by the knowledgeable Tony Moreno, TH–Rodven was able to dent Fania's monopoly.

Moreno went for Puerto Rico's fresh new solo singers, not necessarily New Yorkers: Andy Montañez (who left the supergroup El Gran Combo) and Tommy Olivencia, who had both been largely ignored by Fania, and two very

Willie Colón & Rubén Blades

The musical partnership of Willie Colón and Rubén Blades (1977–1982) was colossally important to salsa, providing rebellious audiences with songs to match their lives.

William Anthony Colón was born in 1950 and grew up in Brooklyn, steeped in American and Puerto Rican music. His first hit album, at 17, *El malo* (The Bad Guy), introduced twenty-one-year-old Puerto Rican singer Héctor Lavoe, whose emotionally charged voice delivered provocative songs to a clarion call of Colón's rough-and-ready, trombone-led salsa.

Rubén Blades was born to Cuban–St Lucian parents in Panama City and trained as a lawyer. Cuban music and Beatles' songs were his inspiration, and anti-US student demonstrations sparked a political awareness. In New York from 1974, he graduated from a job in Fania Records' postroom to the Fania All Stars – singing alongside Lavoe with Colón on trombone. The pair had met at a Colón–Lavoe concert in Panama City in 1969.

Blades's first solo Fania record, *Metiendo mano!* (Feeling up) – produced by Colón – established their alliance. Blades brought a smooth, precise singing style and a continental Latin-American perspective to his magical-social-realist lyrics. He found the perfect partner in self-taught, streetwise NuYorican Colón, who laced his songs with music from the Americas and the Caribbean. Their sensational 1978 album, *Siembra* (Seed), was salsa's bestseller for nearly two decades, typically trashing salsa's traditional themes of lost love and dancing.

The often stormy partnership ended in 1982. Both left Fania: Blades signed to Elektra (and later Sony), emerging in 1984 with a synthesizer sextet, Seis del Solar (Six from the Tenements), and a remarkable crossover album, *Buscando*

América (Looking for America), filled with doowop, reggae, Cuban and rap influences. Colón signed to RCA but continued to produce Fania's top names, including Celia Cruz and Héctor Lavoe. His own albums featured uncompromisingly satirical lyrics.

Colón performed at President Clinton's Inauguration Ball in 1992 and in 1994 stood for the Democratic Congressional elections. Blades ran for President in Panama. After a tumultuous reunion in San Juan in 1995, backed by Blades's band Son del Solar, the pair released *Tras la tormenta* (After the Storm). Blades took a Grammy for *La rosa de los vientos* (Rose of the Winds) in 1996 and a year later sang in Paul Simon's Broadway musical *The Capeman* alongside rising salsa superstar Marc Anthony. Blades now lives in Panama City, Colón in Mexico City. They are both politically as well as musically active, though their political time has yet to come.

Rubén Blades, not much of a dancer, plays maracas during the chorus of a song.

young, raw singers, Frankie Ruiz and Eddie Santiago. The company's fierce marketing turned them into major, top-selling artists and put Puerto Rican salsa firmly onto the map. In Venezuela, they lifted an awesomely talented singer called Oscar D'León from his band Dimensión Latina and set him on the path to major international success. In the nineties, Moreno broke away and formed MPI (Moreno Productions Inc.) in Miami, where he continued to lead the field in young, uncultivated talent from all around Latin America.

By the eighties, Fania's monopoly was also being eroded from within. First Rubén Blades defected to Elektra records in 1984 and released a mould-breaking album, *Buscando América*, with his new rock-influenced sextet, Seis de Solar. Blades mixed in doowop and salsa with Latin American folk rhythms behind his typically stinging realist lyrics. He won a Grammy and earned a place in the wider American music arena. The same year, Willie Colón transferred to RCA and recorded an underrated, Caribbean-flavoured album called *Criollo*, carrying steely satirical lyrics.

LA LUPE

In 1962 Cuba's most controversial, sexually explicit singer, Lupe Victoria Yoli Raymond, known always as La Lupe, left for the US in tears. Her electrifying act at La Red Club was intolerable to the new, austere regime; Fidel Castro personally intervened to curb her. In New York, Mongo Santamaría and Tito Puente encouraged her wild singing and performances, which ignited several records. Her greatest legacy is her graphic version of Peggy Lee's 'Fever' – part Eartha Kitt, part Edith Piaf – with a cackling, witchy kick which even Miss Kitt could never match. Latin music does not tolerate wild women – La Lupe died unknown in 1992.

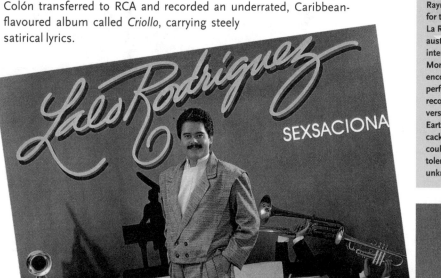

ABOVE: **Former Eddie Palmieri teenage singer Ubaldo 'Lalo' Rodríguez, whose embodiment of romantica/erotica, *Sexsacional!*, hit the charts in 1989.**

THE ROMANTIC AND THE EROTIC

In 1984, a casual, after-hours studio doodle sparked a new direction in salsa. Fania's leading producer, Louie Ramírez, was working late with his singing partner Ray de la Paz, the pianist Isidro Infante and guest vocalist José Alberto. Ramírez unwittingly unleashed a style of salsa which would become known as 'salsa romántica'. The four knocked off a collection of smoochy songs with romantic Spanish lyrics, languid bolero vocals wrapped around an upbeat salsa tune, a formula used to perfection when Frank Sinatra crooned across big-band Swing arrangements. From the night's work emerged an album called *Noches calientes* (Hot Nights), which sold around half-a-million copies and launched a new obsession with romance.

Ramírez's prototype was imitated by the Puerto Rican band Conjunto Chaney, fronted by a most unlikely romantic hero, the skinny, boyish Eddie Santiago, whose scratchy voice suited the increasingly passionate urgency of his lyrics. His first solo album, *Atrevido y diferente* (Daring and Different), in 1986, confirmed that salsa was in the hands of the romantics. But macho romance is but a pelvic thrust away from the erotic, and the new young Puerto Rican singers took the romantic formula to new realms of explicitness with a style dubbed 'salsa erotica', in which romance was either overrun by blatant lust or, in many cases, tinged with crass misogyny. A relatively mild song, 'Ven, devórame otra vez' (Come and Devour Me Again), was a huge hit for Eddie Palmieri's former vocalist Lalo Rodríguez – many hits were successful, partly because of their X-rated lyrics. The backing music for these songs was overwhelmingly formulaic, and hypnotically soft. Many musicians referred to it disparagingly as 'salsa gorda' – limp salsa.

JOSE ALBERTO

In the *Mambo Kings* movie, José Alberto (Justiniano)('El Canario': The Canary) played the fifties mambo idol Johnny Casanova, and sang Beny Moré's gorgeous bolero 'Como fué (How Was It?)?' For his next video, *Bailemos otra vez* (Let's Dance One More), in 1987, he rehired the look and broke the salsa erotica conventions. He is a Cuban music fanatic, a Dominican New Yorker, who visited Havana in 1978 with his band Típica 73. His 'invisible flute' solos are legendary: trilling, agile melodies which become 'real' flutes with his favourite sparring partner, Dave Valentín.

LEFT: Celebrating the launch of late eighties 'salsa romántica': producer Louie Ramírez, 'The Quincy Jones of Salsa' (left), and singer Ray de la Paz (right). Percussionist Ramírez brought hits to salsa's key names and also to his own vibes-led Latin Jazz.

OSCAR D'LEON

Oscar Emilio León Samoza (Oscar D'León) is salsa's most compelling performer. The six-foot-tall former Caracas taxi driver learned double bass off records by Pérez Prado and Machito and modelled his glorious singing style on Beny Moré. With his first band, Dimensión Latina, founded in 1972 with trombonist César 'Albanodiga' (Meatball) Monge, he developed a passion for plush, rhythmic trombone choruses which have infused his immaculately polished orchestras ever since.

CROSSOVERS AND FUSIONS

The eighties were a decade of seething change in salsa. Latin musicians became visible to their neighbours and began to have an impact on mainstream US music. This marked the beginning of non-Latin musicians' infatuation with salsa. Bill Cosby bought Tito Puente's evergreen hit 'Oye como va' to use as the theme tune for his networked television series; David Byrne sang a duet with Celia Cruz for the soundtrack of Jonathan Demme's film *Wild Style* before co-producing with Johnny Pacheco and a cast of New York salseros his own quirky take on salsa under the title *Rey momo* (King Funny Face); August Darnell conjured an alter-ego and took off around the world with his exotic Latin musical show as Kid Creole and the Coconuts.

Latin music was becoming trendy. The most significant intervention from the Latin camp – Rubén Blades's *Buscando América* – catapulted Blades onto the cover of *Life* magazine. In addition to his Grammy, it also won him a role in the Robert Redford film *The Milagro Beanfield War*. In 1987 the Cuban-American writer Oscar Hijuelos was awarded the prestigious Pulitzer prize for his novel *The Mambo Kings Play Songs of Love*, an erotic-realist tale of barrio life in the mamboing fifties. Hollywood recreated the book's lusty story with Antonio Banderas as the love-sick, trumpet-playing Mambo King, and the film's cast included Celia Cruz, José 'El Canario' Alberto and the original Mambo King, Tito Puente.

Cuba's music, previously hidden behind the US embargo, started in the late eighties to percolate through to the US salsa scene. New influences also began to appear in New York. In 1987 the political folk singer Pablo Milanés played to a surprised and excited audience in Central Park, and Orquesta Aragón and Irakere both travelled to the US on education passes. Prized cassettes and grainy videos of Cuba's new salsa bands Los Van Van and Son 14 circulated among New York's Cuban intellectuals and curious salsaphiles.

As the eighties drew to a close, salsa charts and nightclubs were still awash with romantic and shamelessly erotic salsa. But the calm was shattered by a tidal wave of new merengue bands which arrived in New York following a dramatic plunge in the island's economy. Over half a million Dominicans moved to New York around 1988, bringing with them an insatiable appetite for merengue. Washington Heights became virtually Dominican overnight. Its clubs switched to exclusively merengue programmes and cocaine-fuelled audiences danced at crazed speeds, driven by the sizzling güira percussion and throbbing tambora drums. Salsa bands were forced to merengue. Ever pragmatic, Ralph Mercado installed a 'Merengue Unit' in the Broadway offices of his RMM label and signed the most successful local bands: Millie, Jocelyn y Los Vecinos – classy salsa-influenced merengue veterans – and various newcomers, including the slick, rap-inspired, two-girl, two-boy New York Band; Víctor Roque's La Gran Manzana (The Big Apple) and Jossie Esteban y La Patrulla 15 (15th Street Patrol). Roque's use of tasteless rap-style lyrics and electronic beats behind the conventional merengue arrangements were hugely popular after his 1989 hit 'La soga' (The Rope: 'Tie her up if she won't do what you tell her'). Just as the boogaloo had shaken the mambo generation in the sixties, so merengue forced salsa's bandleaders to go with the flow or sit in the commercial cold.

MILLIE, JOCELYN Y LOS VECINOS

The vivacious Millie Queseda (right) is the First Lady of Merengue. When she formed Millie, Jocelyn (left) y Los Vecinos (The Neighbours) in 1975, she and sister Jocelyn were merengue's first merengueras. Ironically, Millie was never a purist – she had lived in New York too long and from the beginning cut merengues with salsa and ballads. Her recent comeback after the death of her husband, *Millie ...Vive* (1998), included a stirring duet with Puerto Rico's top salsero, Gilberto Santa Rosa: 'Siempre amigos' (Friends Forever); the follow-up featured duets with new stars Elvis Crespo and Víctor Víctor. Lively and down-to-earth Millie now has more than twenty dynamic albums under her belt.

HIPHOPPING THE LATIN WAY

For young American Latinos – reared on disco, rock, rap and a diet of MTV and Coca-Cola – something was needed to fit both their reality and their tastes. The first generation of Latin hiphop was nurtured by a clique of club and radio DJs and record producers in New York and Miami. Thousands of teenagers danced to young one-hit wonders miming their songs in Manhattan's alcohol-free Hearthrob and 10:18 clubs. Club DJs and producers and radio DJs from New York's Hot 103FM station were supplied by a record pool run by the soft-spoken Puerto Rican Eddie Rivera. In 1987 Rivera drove his teenage protégés in the Hot 103FM float down Fifth Avenue during the summer Puerto Rican and Cuban parades. Madonna's 'La Isla Bonita' was ricocheting around the streets of San Juan, Puerto Rico and Spanish New York. The Latin hiphoppers sang at beach parties and in parks in New York and Miami to thousands of kids in bikinis and newly fashionable Lycra. The girls included Sa-Fire, Lisa Lisa, Nancy Torres, Nayobe, The Cover Girls, Double Destiny (two Bronx twins), Sweet Sensation, Giggles, and the Miami rivals, Expose and Company B (Miami's 'Latin Supremes' in platinum wigs); the boys comprised Latin Empire (two bilingual Puerto Rican rappers MC Puerto Rock and MC K.T.), Information Society, Spanish Prince, and the rap trio: Two Puerto Ricans, A Blackman and A Dominican.

Behind the young singers was a clique of DJ-producers known as the 'Brat Pack', led by Tony Morán and Albert Cabrera, aka The Latin Rascals. They operated from a small single room in Manhattan where they created new hits – sound collages handmade from cut-up tapes of chart hits by the likes of Mick Jagger, Aretha Franklin and Duran Duran. Their friendly rivals included L'il Louie Vega, Kenny 'Dope' González, Andy 'Panda' Tripoli, Aldo Marín, David Cole and Robert Clavilles, and the best known, John 'Jellybean' Benítez, a graduate with Madonna of Manhattan's disco scene. A decade later, this pack were running America's Latin dance music: Benítez with H.O.L.A. (Home of Latin Artists) Records, launched in 1996 with the pioneering merengue-hiphop group Proyecto Uno; Marín with Cutting Records, skirting closer to conventional salsa and merengue in its futuristic dance mixes for the late nineties phenomenon Fulanito. Louie Vega (by now without the 'Li'l' prefix) was reshaping hits by 'King' Tito Puente.

Rae Serrano (centre) with Amoretto, whose 'Clave Rocks' (1988) looped Tito Puente timbales explosions into an electro-song, laying the foundations of nineties Latin house.

While Latin hiphop at this time mostly meant hiphop with Spanish lyrics, it did pave the way for more interesting experiments in the following decade. 'Clave Rocks' by Rae Serrano – a Puerto Rican producer who provided electronics for rap icon Afrika Baambaata – was a crackling dance track, featuring Tito Puente playing cat-and-mouse timbales with a Roland drum machine. The same year, 1988, Willie Colón penetrated the crossover shield with a 12" Latin dance single called *Set Fire to Me*.

This was the era of Gypsy Kings mania, when Spanish guitars and flamenco hand-claps were de rigueur in pop and dance music. In 1988 the celebrated merengue balladeer Sergio Vargas released a stunningly effective flamenco-merengue-hiphop version of Gypsy Kings' 'Bamboleo'. In Spain, two sisters known as Azúcar Moreno (Brown Sugar) created a repertoire of catchy electro-flamenco songs backed by thunderous hand-claps and rippling guitars. Such mutant Latin singles transformed the charts and inspired major record companies to notice Latin music. Rap had exploded onto the Latin scene but the traffic also occasionally worked in the opposite direction, as when the timbalero Jimmy Delgado played on Kurtis Blow's rap classic 'These Are the Breaks' in 1986.

Jamaica's new dancehall artists and the new experiments in drum-and-bass rhythms also appealed to young Latinos. The Panamanian Brooklynite known as 'El General' (Edgar Franco) shaved his head and released a set of Spanish raps, including 'Pu Tun Tun', which was covered and re-covered by Puerto Rico's first ragga-muffinos, Vico C and Negro DJ. Reggae's influence was particularly strong in Colombia where Grupo Kerube converted a merengue hit into a salsa-reggae chant called 'Las chicas de los ojos cafés'. Cuban-American DJ Mellow Man Ace had a hit with a Ja-Rican reggae tune, 'Mentirosa, Welcome to My Groove'.

The crossover success of Amoretto's 'Clave Rocks' in 1988 was in part due to promotion by David Maldonado, who ran a dynamic English-speaking office on Broadway. One of his office boys was Marc Anthony Muñiz, who sang occasional back-ups in the Latin hiphop clubs and dreamed of becoming a rock star. Maldonado's clients then included one-hit wonder singer Sa-Fire,

ABOVE: **Eddie Rivera in his SoHo loft in 1987. Rivera was at the hub of the nascent Latin hiphop scene. From his office-apartment he distributed the latest records and remixes to radio and club DJs and groomed the new wave of teenage Latino wannabes.**
RIGHT: **In 1988 the London label Rhythm King issued this compilation, drawn from the playlist of New York's Hot 103FM station and described on the sleeve as 'where salsa meets the silicon chip'.**

producer Louie Vega, Puerto Rican teenyboppers Menudo, and Latin-Jazz trumpeter and former Fania arranger, Louis 'Perico' Ortiz. His most famous client was Rubén Blades, the original crossover kid. Maldonado's aim was to bring salsa into the electronic age, and 'Clave Rocks' fitted his plan. It took the disco-fusion of Miami Sound Machine's pioneering 1985 smash hit 'Conga' further into the electro-age while retaining a 'live' trumpet solo from 'Perico' Ortiz and a cascading timbales solo from Tito Puente.

In 1986 Maldonado and Ralph Mercado added a Latino dance music label, SoHo Latino, to the RMM roster. Mercado was by then the 'Dean' of Latin Music in New York, the leading US promoter of Latin music. They inserted their acts ahead of the salsa acts at 'Thursday Nights at the Palladium', in an attempt to close the gap between the generations. While most mimed their hits, one sassy eighteen-year-old called La India poured her high, girlish voice into a microphone and got people talking. Through her then-husband, Louie Vega, India sang back-ups on several hiphop productions and in 1992 she was introduced to Latin music's most respected Latin pianist, Eddie Palmieri. The success of their resulting album, *Llegó*

La India, via Eddie Palmieri (Here Comes India), convinced Ralph Mercado to stay with her despite widespread criticism of her weak, erratic voice. It proved to be a good hunch: her 1998 album *Sobre el fuego* was a Grammy nominee.

As much late eighties, early nineties mainstream salsa sank into a romantic rut, a few valiant, determined producers struggled to create original music. The formidably inventive pianist Sergio George had joined as in-house producer for Ralph Mercado's new RMM (Ralph Mercado Management) label in 1988, and launched a new era. His emerging style mixed his opposing passions for brass-heavy (particularly trombone-heavy) mambo and laid-back melodic arrangements and influences from the year he spent with Colombia's top producer, Fruko. He was especially successful with the singers Tito Nieves and José Alberto, who had apprenticed with the leading Cuban-styled seventies Fania bands Conjunto Clásico and Típica 73 respectively, and with the trombone duo Los Hermanos Moreno (brothers Willie and Nelson), who worked a set of Cuban classics in their gutsy, brassy style. By then, Mercado had most of the Fania legends and many of the new generation.

Sergio George's intention was to bring back salsa's punchy identity. His first – and highly unlikely – major success was with an all-Japanese combo Orquesta de la Luz, led by a singer called Nora who spoke no Spanish. He proved to the sceptics that this group produced skilful salsa, sometimes more impressive and imaginative than that of many local bands.

Within a decade RMM held the monopoly in American Latin music, which Fania used to control, with subdivisions for jazz (Tropijazz), dance (SoHo Latino), rock (RMM Rocks), salsa (RMM) and merengue (Merengazo), and a new generation of arrangers and producers to work on the 'RMM Sound'. George directed the RMM orchestra at spectacular stadium shows of the label's artists in New York, Miami and San Juan. As in the Fania days, many

In 1949, the Tokyo Cuban Boys covered rumbas by the Havana Cuban Boys; in 1988 Orquesta de la Luz performed word-and-note perfect salsa, learnt phonetically from records; singer Nora Shiji imitated Celia Cruz. New York producer Sergio George recorded their hit album *Salsa de Japón* in 1990, and they performed with their idols, unable to speak to them, but singing in perfect Spanish.

San Francisco

Although the main focus of salsa in the US has been New York and Miami, the West Coast has a thriving Latin music tradition dating back to the thirties and forties when several Cuban musicians moved West to escape all the competition in New York. Most were percussionists who found work in the pioneering Latin Jazz bands of Cal Tjader and George Shearing. The West Coast Latin Jazz scene is still strong today (see Chapter 10). Bandleader Xavier 'Cugie' Cugat became Hollywood's favourite and his one-time front man Desi Arnaz came West and married the comedienne and dancer Lucille Ball. Their networked sit-com *I Love Lucy* delivered Cuban music straight into America's living rooms. A couple of decades later, Carlos Santana's dreamy version of Tito Puente's 'Oye como va?' (Listen, How's It Going?) took West Coast Latin music to rock audiences worldwide via the Woodstock Festival.

Santana's band was the tip of a local Latin rock band iceberg, which included Azteca and Malo. It embraced the

John Santos's most exciting performances are his animated and minutely detailed musical lectures on Afro-Caribbean percussion, but his drumming is also a focal point in local bands.

Nicaraguan percussionist Chepito Areas and, from the 1972 album *Caravanserai*, versatile percussionist Coke Escovedo (also Mexican), who ran Azteca with his brother Pete. Today Pete is an elder statesman of the Bay Area's Latin scene, host at the trendy Mr E's club and father of timbales player Sheila E, who was a member of Prince's sensational stage shows in the 1980s. Her whimsical Latinized dance albums feature both her father and her godfather, Tito Puente.

In the early eighties Pete Escovedo incorporated into his clan a local Puerto Rican percussionist and musicologist called John Santos, who was director of Orquesta Batachanga. Santos's bias was imaginative, eclectic, Cuban-influenced salsa jazz. With partner and pianist Rebeca Mauleón, Batachanga metamorphosed into the Machete Ensemble, which took its folkloric brief wider and brought in survivors from the local Latin Jazz scene, Armando Peraza and Orestes Vilato, and guests from the East Coast, like Tito Puente and Cachao. Today Santos is a local guru, consultant, guest producer and percussionist for a number of bands, including Conjunto Céspedes, which combines a serious, educational bent with downright funky salsa.

For slick, rootsy salsa, Johnny Polanco's is the West Coast's best loved band. His reputation was clinched after he performed at Tom Cruise and Nicole Kidman's Hollywood wedding party, following in footsteps made by Xavier Cugat and Desi Arnaz fifty years earlier.

At the hub of San Franciscan salsa is Conjunto Céspedes, led by dynamic singer 'Bobi' Céspedes (seated, left) and nephew Guillermo.

musicians playing salsa did not land the golden (RMM) opportunity, but unlike in the Fania days, there were now other options as the major US labels cottoned on to the potential of the market and ran their own Latin music labels.

By the mid-1990s, Ralph Mercado's Broadway offices resembled the energetic beehive that Fania had once been. Familiar faces from the top salsa album covers passed through: Celia Cruz collecting fan mail, Tito Puente dropping off sheet music; José Alberto photocopying new arrangements for his band. But now they were joined by the new kids on the block, the salsa-and-merengue rappers 3-2 Get Heavy and Limi-T XXX, standing around awkwardly in their baggies and back-to-front baseball hats, waiting to meet the Dean, Mercado (as often as not wearing his own hat twisted round).

Sergio George's greatest successes at RMM were with David Maldonado's ambitious office boy, the slender youth known as Marc Anthony, and a young Puerto Rican backup singer, Víctor Manuelle. Marc Anthony's 1993 album, *Otra nota* (Another Note), launched a new era of twenty-first century salsa, heavily influenced by the new Cuban sound and by rock and rap. George left RMM in 1996 to establish his own stable, Sir George Records, and was replaced by another classically trained pianist, Isidro Infante. His reputation is less buccaneering, perhaps, but he brought a solid record for classic productions and tackled a wide spectrum of styles – from a salsa Beatles tribute (in English) to Grammy-level albums by Marc Anthony and other youth icons, La India and Michael Stuart, as well as the retro-production *Back to the Mambo, a Tribute to Machito* by José Alberto and Celia Cruz's *Mi vida es cantar* (My Life Is to Sing), her best in years. Meanwhile, as Marc Anthony simultaneously wooed salsa and Latin hiphop audiences, Sergio George rode in with his next protégés, his most radical experiment to date, the trio Dark Latin Groove (DLG). Their mosaic of salsa, reggae, rap and house music resembles a slowly scanned FM radio dial in uptown Manhattan, the sound of the future of Latin music being produced from its spiritual home in the heart of New York.

CONJUNTO CLASICO

Conjunto Clásico was one of the delights of live salsa in eighties New York. Founded in 1979 by bass player Ramon Rodríguez and percussionist–singer Raymond Castro, Clásico remodelled Arsenio Rodríguez's trumpet-led template. Their sharp city sound built from three trumpets has appeared on nearly thirty hit albums. In the early days, their young singer, 'Tito' Nieves (right), was a tall, thin baseball ace with a dramatic–operatic tenor; since going solo in 1986, his rotund body and beefy voice have earned him the nickname 'The Pavarotti of Salsa'. Straight Clásico-style salsa remains his forte, but the 1989 salsa version of 'I'll Always Love You' paved the way for snappy salsa-house remakes of sixties Latin-soul hits, including 'I Like It Like That', in 1997.

Chapter 4 CUBA:
Salsa in revolution

GEORGE RAFT'S marble-lined Hotel Capri in downtown Havana was a symbol of the city's contradictions in the late fifties during the closing years of General Fulgencio Batista's corrupt regime. Below the hotel's rooftop pool and casino, the city was out of control; the music, the gambling and the prostitution which supported Raft's bank balance and those of the island's other controllers (Batista, the American Mafia and legitimate US investors) were on a spinning decline and the throngs of American tourists who cruised the streets at night were thinning out. American investors began to withdraw and several nightclubs shut down.

In the midst of all the chaos and corruption, however, fifties Havana concentrated into one city some of the most brilliant and inventive musicians of the time and the city still hummed and danced to what was perhaps the world's most exciting music. On a nocturnal trawl you could have caught Beny Moré and Celia Cruz singing under the stars at the Tropicana, heard Olga Guillot's commanding voice penetrating the night air at the Sans Souci, seen Rita Montaner at the Montmartre, Nat 'King' Cole in the grand cabaret of the Hotel Nacional, and the consummate Orquesta Aragón at venues all over town. You could have spotted Ernest Hemingway downing daiquiris in the Floridita bar, and, if you passed the stringent rules, joined the (white) society elite for cocktails and cha-cha-chas at their racially segregated haunts: the Country Club, the Vedado Tennis Club, the Yacht Club and the Jazz Club. You would find young black Cubans at the Tropical, an outdoor beer garden away from the city centre, where they danced mambo and rock'n'roll and invented new crazes. You could have slipped into early morning descargas, the after-hours recording sessions run by mambo bass player Cachao for the prestigious Cuban label Panart, or caught up with pianist Bebo Valdés as he drove from work as House Orchestra Director at the Tropicana to rival musical free-for-alls which also lasted till dawn.

Resistance to Batista's brutality and corruption came from all quarters, but one singer–songwriter was particularly important in fitting songs to the moment. In the trova tradition, Carlos Puebla used his songs to rally and support the opposition. Puebla told the journalist Rafael Lam, 'In 1952 I planted myself in the Bodeguita del Medio restaurant to sing with Los Tradicionales group. Before singing, I would check to see that there were no Batista supporters around me because things could get rough if they heard me. The atmosphere was fabulous. We didn't earn a salary, we depended on what people gave us.'

A carnival float drifts past the mural of Ernesto 'Ché' Guevara, on the side of his former office block. The lights in his offices are permanently switched on.

Tony Evora, then a young graphic designer and occasional percussionist in Beny Moré's band, remembers the sharp contrasts: 'Woolworths was a treasure trove of records for local music aficionados, a bazaar right in the heart of Havana. It was known as "El Ten Cen" (The Ten Cent Shop) because everything was sold at very low prices. What was amazing was all the music on the radio and in the clubs while at the same time young people were being persecuted by Batista's police and tortured in damp obscure jails.' Eddie Zervigón, a meteorologist by day and flute-player by night, also remembers the violent unrest: 'In 1957 and 1958, a big bomb in the Tropicana blew up the woman who was laying it.'

The decade moved inevitably towards the final showdown between Batista's army and the guerrillas. The city became a war zone, with curfews, bomb scares, explosions and street fighting. But, as in most wars, music remained a vital commodity. The diminutive singer Pío Leyva recalls the day in 1957 when he bunked off from working as a cigar roller to join his friend the guitarist Compay Segundo in a recording studio: 'We had finished recording the first song, "La mujer del peso" (The Woman with One Peso) and were about to start a second when we had to stop because of shots outside from an attack on the President's palace. We just stopped recording, lit our cigars and waited until things calmed down.'

The same year, Batista organized a morale-boosting music festival, 'Fifty Years of Cuban Music', for the many musicians who had become successful abroad. It was the last time many would set foot on Cuban soil. Miguelito Valdés returned as the crossover star 'Mr Babalú' who had sung at the Waldorf Astoria with Xavier Cugat. Machito and Mario Bauzá were carving a niche with itchy, danceable mambo-jazz, and mambo king Tito Puente – honorary Cuban – scuttled off to Havana's barrios for Afro-Cuban drumming sessions between appearances. After the emotional reunion of the festival, the city returned to its countdown to revolution.

'AND THEN FIDEL ARRIVED'

New Year's Day, 1959: Eva Kirkhope, a Cuban who now lives in London, was a young girl in Havana. 'We first heard the news on the radio that Batista had fled the night before, and that Fidel Castro would speak on the radio,' she recalls. Castro's guerrilla army had moved across the island from the East, building up support as it went. They took Batista's army by surprise on the outskirts of the capital, but the president had already flown to Santo Domingo the night before. 'Fidel said that Batista had gone, and there was to be a military junta. He asked people to oppose it with a general strike. We kids had to stay indoors. On 8 January, Castro entered Havana. The junta was dissolved and Fidel made his first public speech. Everybody went onto the streets; there were riots between Batista's supporters and Fidel's supporters. Mobs raided the casinos and destroyed the hated slot machines which had provided Batista with a personal income. Later, the soldiers went round the clubs looking for women (and men). They were very attractive, different, with long hair and beards – and guns.'

The stark neon letters on the roof of the Havana Hilton spelled out 'HABANA LIBRE', announcing to the city below that Cuba was now Cuban and Havana was free – of the United States, at least. Almost immediately after the overthrow of Batista, the hotel's cabaret and bars returned to some semblance of business as usual; before long, cocktail dresses and light suits came to be replaced by berets and uniforms and, later, by cheap Russian suits.

In April 1962 Castro visited President Kennedy in New York to negotiate his new reformist policies. In a marvellously modern piece of media manipulation, Castro, Ché Guevara and entourage checked out of their official midtown hotel and into Harlem's St Theresa hotel, where Castro delivered speeches from the balcony. Photographs of Ché lolling on his hotel bed, puffing on a cigar, fix the moment. The trip failed. Back in Havana, Castro took up Nikita Khrushchev's persistent offer of support for his revolution and announced that Cuba was to be a Socialist Republic. At that point, the trova singer Carlos Puebla came into his own: settled into his official residency at the Bodeguita del Medio bar in Old Havana, he wrote songs for every new occasion and new law passed. He performed 'Y en eso llegó Fidel' ("And Then Fidel Arrived") and 'Alfabetización' (Song to the Literacy Campaign) on platforms alongside the new leaders, his catchy tunes calculated to sweeten the messages of the new austerity.

As Castro continued to cosy up to the Russians, a group of anti-Communist Cubans landed from Miami at Cuba's Bay of Pigs, mistakenly assuming US backing and intent on quashing Castro. During the fiasco several were killed and the rest imprisoned (they were later traded back to the US), among them Gloria Estefán's father. In 1962 the US government imposed a trade embargo. Castro nationalized all American-owned companies, and the sea between Miami and Havana was effectively sealed off.

In 1960 Celia Cruz and her husband, Pedro Knight, left Cuba for a tour of Mexico with her orchestra, La Sonora Matancera. They were on the plane to Mexico City, when the bandleader Rogelio Martínez stood up and announced: 'We won't be going back.' At first they thought it would only be for a few years, but none of them has ever returned. Gradually several artists who left were written out of Cuban history: even Celia Cruz and the formidable bass player Cachao were omitted from the first, 1981 edition of Elio Orovio's respected *Dictionary of Cuban Music* (in 1997 they were reinstated). Until recently, many young Cubans did not even know of Cruz's existence and her contemporaries had no clue as to her subsequent massive success around the world. 'I think she moved to Mexico and gave up singing,' an old man living in her childhood street told me. But in the more liberal nineties, Cruz's unmistakeably potent voice could once again be heard as her songs echoed around the streets of Havana.

In the immediate wake of the revolution and the Bay of Pigs invasion, curfews increased, tourism dwindled and many favourite haunts were closed down. The remaining clubs, bars and hotels often had to rely on the jukebox to entertain the dancers. Musicians continued to flock to the airport, causing a shocking drain of talent which was never officially announced. In 1964 the government started blocking exit visas, particularly for musicians. Those who left could see that the lifestyle they had enjoyed under Batista would not continue.

In 1963 the country went into mourning at the deaths of Rita Montaner and Beny Moré, two singers who were almost deified in Cuba – before and after the revolution. Whether Moré would have tolerated the new austerity is impossible to imagine, but his 1959 song, 'Se te cayó el tabaco' (Give up the Tobacco – a symbol of Batista), reveals where his politics were at the time. Rita Montaner died a few months ahead of Moré; both were given state funerals which drew the country to a halt. Old Cuba died with them (reborn in Miami); the process of building a new music to suit the new society began.

RCA Victor and Columbia had controlled Cuban music's output to the world until the fifties when the crisis worsened and they backed out. Several Cuban-owned labels cashed in on the situation and flourished. From 1957, Panart Records released Cachao's avant-garde jam sessions as *Cuban Descargas* and *Cuban Jam Sessions in Miniature*. The sessions had a major impact on musicians in both Havana and New York.

From 1962 all Cuban industries were gradually nationalized – including record companies. Several company directors and record producers had already left by then, taking precious tapes to New York in the countdown to shutdown. Panart and the key independent labels Gema and Puchito were absorbed into one nationalized company, EGREM, which traded exclusively for the next thirty years. Because of lack of vinyl to reissue them, priceless archives lay silently on EGREM's shelves until the eighties, when a series of curious label bosses from London (Joe Boyd, Nick Gold and Mo Fini) persuaded the authorities to license them to their UK companies. A trickle of albums on the Globestyle, Hannibal, World Circuit and TUMI labels triggered an avalanche in the late nineties of releases of labels from Europe and the US.

In the wake of the revolution, the lifestyles of musicians inevitably changed.

They became salaried employees of the government, members of the Musicians' Union, paid according to experience and qualification until they retired, and then paid a pension. Because of the exodus, there were gaps not only in the clubs and recording studios, but also in radio and television, newspapers and magazines. For many musicians, opportunities dwindled, but for one section of the population – the black musicians whose opportunities had been severely limited under the old system – things looked up. Not all musicians wanted such a formal contract but those who rejected the new system found it difficult to perform at all.

Tours and gigs were organized through the unions; new venues and foreign territories emerged: musicians found themselves playing to mystified audiences in Moscow or Budapest, to grateful Cuban soldiers serving in Angola, and to factory workers' co-operatives and students at home. Bands like Irakere and Los Van Van spent most of the eighties abroad, bringing in hard currency to the ailing economy – and living on $25 a day. Not surprisingly, many musicians 'disappeared' during those trips, especially after Castro decreed that they could keep a percentage of their earnings and they began to taste dollar prosperity.

Under the new regime, qualifying as a full-time professional musician involved a formal education which excluded the self-taught. Many grand names in Cuban history would not have made it through such a system. Neither the adored Beny Moré, nor rumba drummer Chano Pozo, who transformed Dizzy Gillespie's band in the 1940s, would have qualified: both were intuitive musicians who learned to play in the exhilarating pressure-cooker confines of the Afro-Cuban religious ceremonies and secular rumbas of their home neighbourhoods.

The four-piece vocal harmony group Los Zafiros (The Sapphires), founded in 1962, were Cuba's answer to American doowoppers: The Coasters and The Platters.

Chucho Valdés, a classically trained pianist, had to conduct his own intensive research into the Afro-Cuban folk music which infuses all of his compositions. He was fortunate enough to have learnt to improvise and to play jazz at home with his father, the eminent pianist Bebo Valdés (who left the country in the sixties). 'When I studied at the conservatory, there were no classes in jazz or improvisation,' he says, 'Now I'm a professor of popular music, the course includes both.'

The first generation to reach their teens in the late 1960s were involved with a more frivolous revolution – against the authorities. Eva Kirkhope recalls that she was captivated by Swinging London, 'The Beatles were symbols of capitalism and decadence, and the clothes and music that went with them were considered counter-revolutionary, but my mother made me whatever Twiggy

was wearing in the magazines we passed round. False eyelashes were essential – I got some from a girl at the Tropicana, and we stuck them on with chewing gum. We had to have the latest Beatles' and rock records which were

JESUS ALEMANY

Finding rehearsal space in Havana is not easy; Jesús Alémany works out in a local park between rehearsals with his 15-piece band Cubanismo. Alémany is a startling new trumpet 'voice' who developed his style and musical identity during fifteen years spent with the son revivalist group, Sierra Maestra, and as solo trumpeter in the Tropicana cabaret's rigorous 25-piece orchestra. He directs Cubanismo in a repertoire of dance rhythms, including the pilon, pa'ca and mozambique, virtually unplayed today. His pure, high-register trumpet solos follow the tradition of the great high-flying son musicians Félix Chappotín and 'Chocolate' Armenteros; his breathtaking horn arrangements swing like Beny Moré's.

banned from the radio – we used to listen to them on the American stations coming from Miami, and a boyfriend got hold of bootlegs through someone who worked in a studio.'

The American influences gradually diminished as Cuba became more isolated, but, early on, *rocanoleros* (rock'n'rollers) like Los Kent copied the new music they surreptitiously listened to – particularly The Beatles. Vocal groups were the most popular – the Del Rey, Los Bucaneros, Las d'Aida (Aida's Girls). Los Zafiros (The Sapphires) – a preppy close-harmony quartet, backed by a rumbling, echoey electric guitar – imitated The Platters, and were the top idols. They played in Europe and even met The Beatles. But their American style created trouble with the authorities and they were subjected to censorship. A rose-tinted, docu-fiction version of the era was recreated in the 1997 Cuban film, *Zafiros locura azul* (Sapphires Blue Madness).

All through the sixties, unprecedented changes took place in the music scene as American culture lost its hold. New Cuban dance crazes and bands were encouraged to fill the void. Songwriters and composers delved into the neglected trove of Afro-Cuban music which had been completely suppressed by the previous regime. Until the nineties, when Cuba began to open up, only touring musicians were aware of the variety of music being made in other countries. Bob Marley – who lived so near – was virtually unknown in Cuba until the Brazilian singer Gilberto Gil performed 'No Woman, No Cry' at the Latin American Song Festival in the resort of Varadero in 1988. Jazz players maintained connections with their American counterparts through the European festival circuit and brought prized records back from their trips. Cuba's new alliances in Latin America influenced the composers of the new political folk song – nueva trova – movement. Festivals became a source of entertainment for the Cuban people and provided work for the musicians. They were also attractive to tourists and the guest musicians opened a window onto the outside world.

SOCIALISMO CON PACHANGA: A decade of dance crazes

So what guarantees a successful revolution? New dance crazes, obviously. In 1959 the American-Cuban songwriter Eduardo Davidson created a looser, funkier variation of the cha-cha-cha, called pachanga, which so captivated young Cubans that Ché Guevara coined the catchphrase, 'Socialismo con pachanga!' Davidson left for America in 1961, taking his pachanga with him. In Havana, the singer Pacho Alonso and his band Los Bocucos had a hit called 'La pachanga' which was successful as far away as Moscow and Dakar.

The pachanga triggered a series of new dance crazes, including the pilon, the mozambique, the simale, the changui, the pa'ca, and many forgotten local variations. The pilon was launched in 1965 by Enrique Bonne Castillo in his hometown, Santiago de Cuba. Bonne Castillo organized a troupe of about fifty carnival percussionists and drummers called Los Tambores de Oriente (The Drummers from the East), who jived through the streets like a Brazilian samba school. The pilon was named after a brand of coffee and was also the name for the mortar used to crush the beans. Couples dance separately, marking time with hip shakes and jumping up and down. The detail is the hand jive, with the fists mashing on top of each other in time with the beat (grinding the coffee beans). The mozambique (pronounced mo-zam-bee-kay) was a hit which was picked up in New York and also carried through to the 1990s. Its prime exponent was a percussionist known as 'Pello el Afrokán'

(Pedro Izquierdo Padrón), who put together a huge band of drummers using Afro-Cuban rhythms on a son framework. The short-lived pa'ca, adapted from a Venezuelan folk dance, was revived in 1998 by the salsa-jazz big band Cubanismo, led by trumpeter Jesús Alémany. Their repertoire included not only modernized versions of the pa'ca but also of the mozambique and the pilón, and in their live shows, during the number 'Salsa pilón', the band's formidable brass section sway in unison and mash fists between riffs.

NUEVA TROVA: New Politics, New Song

Meanwhile, foundations were being laid for a new era of trova songs. At the helm was Carlos Puebla, whose position in Cuban history was guaranteed in 1965 when he performed at an historic rally in Havana to commemorate the life and death of Ché Guevara. 'On the unforgettable night when Fidel read out Ché's farewell letter – that same night I wrote the song, "Hasta siempre, Comandante" (Forever, Comandante). It is a song of farewell, not death.'

> We learned to love you from historical heights,
> Where your shining bravery put shadows on death,
> Your strong and glorious hand fires history,
> When the whole of Santa Clara awakens to see you,
> You come burning the winds with rays of spring sun
> To raise the flag with the light of your smile.
> Your revolutionary love takes you on to new fights
> Where they await the firmness of your liberating arm.
> We will continue forward as if by your side,
> And with Fidel, we say to you, 'Forever, Comandante.'

In a quiet garden in Havana, Puebla paraphrased Castro's own maxim: 'It was proposed that we should rescue our culture. All musicians have been integrated into the Revolution; each one does it their way – as long as it is within the Revolution.' The 1998 TUMI album *Hasta siempre, comandante* began with Castro's speech and included a selection of contemporary song-tributes to Ché, one of which was Puebla's moving composition.

The first generation of Castro-ite trova songwriters were a collective of students at ICAIC, the Cuban film institute, led by Sara González. Influences included Puebla and the old soneros, but most of all The Beatles and the emerging young singers in Chile, Argentina, Uruguay and Brazil. They called their guitar-backed songs 'nueva trova' (new song). Silvio Rodríguez and Pablo Milanés flew too close to the flame and were sent on special military service on account of their long hair (Rodríguez), wild Afro (Milanés), their jeans, and because they were cool, in an unambiguously American way. Gradually, nueva trova songs became hits. In 1967 the Casa de la Américas organized a festival, Encuentro de la Canción Protesta (Meeting of Protest Song), with guest performers from Latin America and the Caribbean, including old legends from feeling and trova. The shows drew hundreds of thousands of chanting fans. Several of the hosts and their guests flew on to Santo Domingo for a 'Siete Días' (seven-day) festival of trova music; their status in a pan-Latin network had begun to gell.

By the 1990s, Pablo Milanés and Silvio Rodríguez were pillars of the establishment, relatively wealthy fifty-somethings, who travelled widely, and ran their own recording studios in Havana. Rodríguez's small Ojalá Studios and

CARLOS PUEBLA

Carlos Puebla's strong, Spanish features (perfectly captured here by the Cuban caricaturist 'David'), upright posture, guitar played high on his chest, and theatrically deep, baritone voice, give him the air of a flamenco singer. 'Una noche de Puebla y de mojitos' (A night with Puebla and rum cocktails) was how the Cuban poet Nicholas Guillen described an evening at the Bodeguita del Medio in Central Havana in the years before the Revolution. The bar was then the underground meeting place of political poets, artists, musicians and songwriters, and the ideal place for Puebla, an old-style troubadour, poet and songwriter, to test his rallying trovas on friends. Under Castro, he continued to try out his officially commissioned songs there before performing them in the Plaza de la Revolución – alongside the Government leaders. Today, the Bodeguita is a watering-hole for tourists.

the sophisticated independent Abdala Studios were eventually superseded by EGREM's high-tech state-of-the-art complex which opened in 1988 in the leafy Havana suburb of Miramar.

FITTING IN

Before the revolution, a form of apartheid operated among musicians, with some bizarre consequences. The flute player Eddie Zervigón, who moved to New York in 1962, remembers the racial dynamic before the revolution: 'Black and white musicians had separate unions and played to separate audiences. Black people couldn't dance in the mulatto or white society and the only people who could move freely were the musicians. Most charanga bands played to black society, until Tito Gómez and Orquesta Riverside started to be invited by the white society crowd. Then they wanted Orquesta Aragón, and then Fajardo – who had three orchestras and would sing one set and move on to another band at the next dance.' The conjuntos, which played the brassy, more Afro-Cuban music, had the darkest-skinned players, but Conjunto Casino, and Chapottín's and Chocolate's all began to play for white audiences too. 'The Tropicana's colour bar was extreme, but one of the few black artists allowed to perform there during its Batista heyday was Celia Cruz.'

The pressure to conform to the new rules left several artists isolated. One singer, Lupe Victoria Yoli Raymond – or La Lupe, as she was known everywhere – was a particular problem for the authorities. Her revolutionary spirit was entirely at odds with official definitions and she was cautioned for 'bad behaviour', though bohemians and intellectuals adored her. Picasso called her 'a genius' and Sartre, 'a musical animal'. On stage, La Lupe would run around, singing, shrieking and pulling at her clothes. In 1962 she left Cuba, but the New York salsa system, which at first welcomed her with open arms, also found her antics hard to take after a few years of starry success. There was no place for sexually abandoned women in New York's macho culture either.

After 1959 the restricted press and news services were the official bulletin-boards for the Cuban people, but news travelled through rumour and gossip; Chinese whispers shot through the population and official propaganda was spread via the radio and television wars fought between the US and Cuban

ABOVE: **Havana's Tropicana nightclub is an incongruous relic of pre-Revolutionary hedonism. Fantasy chorines have paraded through its lush grounds since the fifties, when Beny Moré and Celia Cruz sang alongside Frank Sinatra and Nat 'King' Cole.**
RIGHT: **The irrepressible master percussionist Elio Reve (1930–98) burst on to the Havana salsa scene in 1956 with a sharp, timbales-heavy revamp of eastern dance rhythms.**

governments. By the eighties, each had a powerful station firing propaganda between Miami and Havana. The songwriters were the true chroniclers of the decades. Composers of the leading salsa songs, particularly Elio Reve, Juan Formell, Adalberto Alvarez and the nueva canción pack, hitched coded, double-edged lyrics to dance rhythms so that the whole country could sing along with Los Van Van's 'La Habana no aguanta más' (Havana Can't Take Any More), about the problems of mass migration into the capital from the impoverished countryside, and Silvio Rodríguez's 'La era', about the need to export revolution.

THE REGENERATION

Through the sixties and seventies, Cuban musicians composed, recorded and played all over the island, unhampered by conventional European and American pressures of touring schedules and quick album deadlines. Isolated from the mainstream of Latin music, they began in the eighties to re-engage with the non-Communist world through Europe and particularly the UK. By the mid-nineties, Cuban music was back on the Latin music map and in demand everywhere – even in the US. By then, New York's Latin musicians had transformed the fifties Cuban model and their 'salsa' was influencing bands worldwide. But salsa was anathema to Cuban musicians, who dismissed it as 'an imperialist theft of Cuban music', ignoring the fact that many musicians playing salsa in New York and particularly in Miami were also Cubans.

Back in Havana, percussionist Elio Reve arrived from Santiago in the East with a fast, raunchy old rhythm called the changui, which he had adapted and first performed in 1956. A year later he left his band, which then reorganized as Ritmo Oriental and focused in its shows as much on dancing as on music. The violinists were all trained dancers as well as musicians – on stage they still roll and bend like a line of chorines and many of their hits are double-entendre songs about dancing, including 'Nena, así no se vale' (Girl, It's No Good Like That). Meanwhile Reve hired another set of musicians including, in 1968, a prolific young songwriter and bass player called Juan Formell, a graduate of the university's music school who brought a passion for The Beatles and a head full of original ideas. Some time after Formell had left Reve in 1969 to found his own band, Los Van Van (The Go-Gos), the songwriting duties fell to

83

keyboards player and songwriter Juan Carlos Alfonso. Alfonso, who stayed the course longer, remaining until 1988, when he founded his own band, Dan Den. From these offshoots of the original Reve line-up emerged some of the most significant Cuban music since the revolution, certainly the most exhilarating and danceable.

The seventies were launched with Van Van's explosive first album, *Los Van Van*, which toughened the elegant flute-and-violin-flavoured charanga style with Juan Formell's mobile electric bass and the quick, inventive percussion of Changuito (José Luis Quintana, who was simultaneously a member of the soundtrack department at the National Film Institute). Between them they invented a new hybrid which they called songo, described by Formell as not a rhythm but a style, with influences from rock, jazz and Brazilian music, and powered by Formell's heavy, angular bass. By the nineties, the songo was being incorporated by many progressive American salsa bands working in the RMM stable under Sergio George, while Cuba's own bandleaders, particularly Juan Carlos Alfonso, were adding New York salsa ideas to their music.

Los Van Van is a constantly evolving organism, with regular changes of personnel, regular new inventions – and a torrent of hit songs. In 1981 Formell pitched three trombones into the mix, to work against the three violins. The effect was electrifying, and almost clinched the Van Van sound. It was perfected by the arrival of one of the sexiest singers on earth, Pedro Calvi, whose onstage dancing is a distinctly counter-revolutionary activity. Changuito became a roving conga trouble-shooter who drops in occasionally; Formell's son Samuel plays timbales. Calvi was later joined by a young, dreadlocked sprite of a singer called Mayito, whose youthful energy and sexiness keeps the older macho on his toes. And Formell drives around town in his expensive sports car, planning what to do next to shake up the salsa world.

For much of the eighties, Pedro Calvi was the most desired man in Cuba. As lead singer with Los Van Van he made an art form out of dirty dancing. Age shows no sign of withering his charms – young women still queue to undergo the Calvi treatment (above).

EXPERIMENTING WITH SOUND

As Los Van Van was getting into its stride, the Havana Film Institute, ICAIC, set up a department to produce soundtracks for Cuban films. On the team with Changuito in 1963 was the piano prodigy Chucho Valdés, who worked in an experimental orchestra, El Teatro Musical de la Habana, with like-minded musicians, including Paquito D'Rivera. They began to explore new combinations of jazz, rock music and Afro-Cuban music. In 1970 they established themselves as a formal band which they called Irakere – a Yoruba name for the sacred part of the forest where holy drummers play. Afro-Cuban music was to be at the core of their compositions. Valdés's cousin Oscar, the singer and percussionist, incorporated the batá drum into the band and led them through some deeply religious passages. One of Irakere's first hits was 'Bacalao con pan' (Codfish with Bread) – the schoolchildren near Valdés's house used to chant the title as he passed by. During his time at ICAIC, between 1963 and 1974, Valdés wrote a sophisticated Afro-Cuban jazz symphony called 'Misa negra', which, he said in retrospect, 'had opened the door to a new world within [Afro-Cuban] folkloric music. It's a very exotic work, with a little bit of everything – jazz, Caribbean and even Brazilian music.' Irakere was – at its eighties peak – the most sophisticated modern jazz band in the world: every instrument played by a virtuosic soloist, every number as suited to dancing as to studying.

As Irakere pursued the jazz and Afro-Cuban folk line, son was being modernized, 'New Cubanized', by a dedicated songwriter and singer, Adalberto Alvarez, a big bear of a man with a rich tenor voice. His band, Son 14, formed in 1978, recorded scores of hits, which have been covered in hundreds of versions all over Latin America and by US-based salseros. Son 14 was noted for the singers behind Alvarez and was a training-ground for the late nineties pop-salsa icon Paulito F. G. (Fernández Gallo). Since the opening up of Cuba, Alvarez has taken Cuban salsa deeper into the Caribbean for inspiration on the hit albums *Toca-Toca* and *Magistral!!!*.

OPENING UP

All through the eighties, Cuban music began to intrigue the outside world. Europe's burgeoning Latin music scene, incorporating salsa and Latin Jazz, played a major part in raising its profile. Ronnie Scott's Jazz Club in London plugged into the networks that were being laced together between the many festivals and clubs that kept the Cubans on tour in Europe for months. A number of independent record labels in the UK also boosted interest, and the 1984 BBC television documentary, *What's Cuba Playing At?* was a revelation.

Back in Havana the singers who had slipped into Celia Cruz's high heels when she moved to New York now entertained foreign tourists at festivals and hotel cabarets and in the Tropicana extravaganzas. Caridad Cuervo, Omara Portuondo and Elena Burke sang the classics and favourite boleros. They even broke into pop. Burke made an album of Juan Formell's early pre-Los Van Van songs and saw her daughter Malena move to the US and became a nineties crossover singer. Celina González, the 'Queen of Country Music' presented a prime-time radio show with her band Campo Alegre after her singing partner (and husband) Reutilio died in 1971. It also featured her protégée, the young singer–songwriter Albita Rodríguez, who was then a leading light in the nueva trova movement. González's career was transformed by interest from the UK when World Circuit records released *Fiesta guajira* in 1983 and took her to

Juan Formell (Los Van Van) & José Luis Cortés (N.G. La Banda)

In the wake of the Cuban revolution, Juan Formell's Los Van Van revolutionized dance music with a new dance called the 'songo', and N.G. La Banda, led by José Luis Cortés, rode out the nineties with salsa timba-brava.

Formell emerged in Elio Reve's radical sixties Orquesta, where he introduced electric bass, electric guitar and kit drums, electrified the violins and wreaked havoc with the son. In 1969 he left, taking percussionist José Luis Quintana ('Changuito') and pianist–songwriter César Pedroso with him to make up the core of Los Van Van (The Go-Go's) and to build a new electric charanga. In 1981 his astonishing idea of adding three trombones to lay great swathes of swinging rhythms opposite the violins clinched the sound. His thick, electric bass-lines cavorted with Changuito's mesh of conga rhythms in the newly created songo.

ABOVE: **N.G. La Banda (with leader José Luis Cortés in the suit) take their music to the streets.**
LEFT: **Juan Formell (far left) and Los Van Van.**

Juan Formell's songo influenced the fresh wave of musicians who emerged in the 1990s, particularly José Luis Cortés, 'El Tosco' (The Tough Guy). Cortés left Irakere in 1988 with four fellow horn players and joined other familiar Havana musicians as the Nueva Generación (New Generation: N.G.) band. Their aim was 'to search for the Cuban music of the future'. Cortés created the most musically advanced dance music in Latin America, exhilarating, complicated 'concept salsa' called 'timba', which rubs rumba and son against jazz and rap. La Banda's first success, 'Necesito una amiga' (I Need a Girlfriend) is typical of their lyrics, which bristle with street talk, obscene slang and made-up phrases which become slogans for Cuban youth. Singer Tony Cala is an extraordinary improviser, heir, says Cortés, to Beny Moré. The band's popularity is all-pervasive in Cuba. La Banda is leading Cuban salsa into the next century.

Los Van Van evolved with Formell's enthusiasms, from synthesizers and electronic drums in the late eighties to topical santería, New York-style salsa and American rap in the nineties. Audiences adore the antics of singer Pedro Calvi, who pulls eager female fans on stage to dance with him. In the late nineties Formell introduced a young singer, Mario 'Mayito' Rivera, to attract the young generation – his long, sinuous songo-raps guarantee that. Indeed, part of Los Van Van's spectacular success has always lain with their lyrics – stories drawn from street-talk, scandals, gossip, even criticisms of official policies. Titles became catchphrases for the whole island.

London. Omara Portuondo left the cult fifties girl group Las D'Aida in 1967 and made a career with bittersweet boleros and the uptempo Cuban variation known as feeling (in Spanish, 'feelin''). She too was reborn through London's new interest in Cuban music after a chance encounter with her old friend Compay Segundo at the EGREM studios a decade later landed her a role in his historic recording of *The Buena Vista Social Club* album.

THE NEW GENERATION

In 1988 Havana's music scene was shocked by the departure from Irakere of the band's celebrated flute player, José Luis Cortés – 'El Tosco' (The Tough Guy) – who ganged up with fellow rebels who had apprenticed in the city's leading bands. They called themselves Nuevá Generación – or N.G. (pronounced En-ay-hay) La Banda. Cortés's songs taunted his mentors with his aggressively cocky punk-political philosophy. 'Let them dance, make them listen,' he threatened. The group justifiably swept the board and were particularly popular with Cuban youth – especially young black audiences. Cortés's first song, 'Abriendo el siglo' (Opening the Century), reveals his confidence.

Cortés considered every detail of his band's performance. He ran a radio contest to gauge the popularity of its name and its slogan 'La banda que manda' (The Band in Command). The music is complex and calculated, neither jazz nor salsa, but a brilliant take on each. Hand-picked singers were chosen for their contrasts – the sophisticated sonero crooner Issac Delgado was pitched against the rough Afro-Cuban rap and rumba calls of Tony Cala.

At the dawn of the nineties, the speed of change of Cuban music escalated in the face of increasing outside exposure and foreign record deals. Beginners and veterans found themselves with unimagined opportunities: the keyboards player Juan Carlos Alfonso, who had provided Elio Reve's orquestra with a string of catchy hits, was running the band Dan Den (a typical Cuban double meaning – not only the sound of the tick-tocking cowbell but also a word-play criticism of the despised ration books). Alfonso followed Juan Formell's trombone-heavy model but steered his salsa close to the suave Puerto Rican sound.

A new crop of soloists emerged from the great eighties outfits – Issac Delgado from N.G. La Banda, and Paulito F. G. (Fernández Gallo) from Adalberto y Su Son. Adalberto y Su Son led the new pack in the nineties – Paulito F. G. was to be Cuba's greatest heartthrob since Beny Moré (though no rival in vocal talent). A third youthful soloist Manolín – 'El

ISSAC DELGADO

Singer Issac Delgado has paved the way for Cuba's new breed of solo timberos (Cuba's salseros) to enter the US salsa fray. He was chosen for grooming by impresario Ralph Mercado in 1996, and led smiling onto a superstar bill with José Alberto, Celia Cruz (who avoided him) and local pin-up Marc Anthony. His warm, infectious style won the night; his diverse background in improvised jazz and progressive salsa with N. G. La Banda and with his own tight band pays off in his intelligent, versatile performances. His 1997 album *Otra idea*, recorded in New York by Isidro Infante, was another first: it united Cuban musicians from both sides of the political divide, the first such collaboration since the Revolution.

The greatest influence on Juan Carlos Alfonso (born 1963) – the keyboards player nicknamed the 'Skinhead of Cuba' – was Led Zeppelin. He even arranges trombones in percussion blocks to imitate their rhythm section. His band Dan Den is closer to American salsa than to jumpy Cuban timba; Alfonso's taste for trombones grew during his four years on keyboards with Elio Reve's eighties band. He founded Dan Den in 1987.

Juan Carlos Alfonso

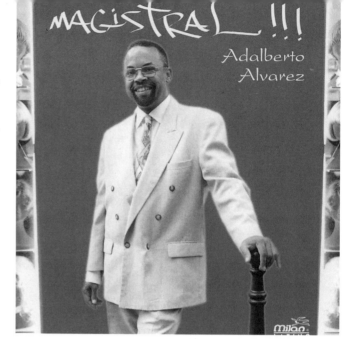

'I believe in tradition,' says Adalberto Alvarez, one of Cuba's most dedicated musicians and most covered songwriters (18 salsa versions of 'La soledad es mala consejora' [Loneliness is a Bad Advisor], for instance). Alvarez has created a modern son tradition with his bands Son 14 and Adalberto y Su Son.

PAULITO F. G.

The singer Paulito F. G. (Fernando Gallo) presented late-nineties Cuban salsa with a problem: should an instinctive musician with such stylish good looks and magnetic stage presence but no formal education qualify for superstar status? Though Paulito is a self-taught, natural performer and songwriter, he passed through the rigorous bands of Adalberto Alvarez and Dan Den and in 1992 formed Paulito y su Elite and was announced by several hit songs. Paulito is something of a Cuban salsa 'new man': the 37-year-old's stage act is sensual and intimate rather than hard and raunchy; he sings about breaking hearts and broken love, and is a romantic rather than a street-talking, hard-living rebel.

Médico de la Salsa' (The Salsa Doctor) was at medical school while the others were cutting their teeth on Havana's salsa platforms. In 1994 he swapped the stethoscope for a microphone and released his first album, *Una aventura loca* (A Mad Adventure), followed by a string of hit singles which landed him a residency at Havana's prestigious club, El Palacio de la Salsa (the Salsa Palace) in the Hotel Riviera.

With open cheque books appearing once again in the capital and European journalists flying in to check out the scene, an extraordinary range of new music started to surface. At a public party at the Salsa Palace, held in honour of Harry Belafonte's wedding anniversary in 1997, a group of singers called Vocal Sampling kicked off their tribute with an a cappella version of Belafonte's fifties hit, 'Banana Boat Song'. Without an instrument between them they captured perfectly the calypso lilt and even the Trinidadian accent. Sampling were signed up by Madonna's former label, Sire. They were joined on stage by salsa-rock singer, Rojitas (a roquero with a seventies footballer's haircut), who performed a Beatles medley with the dreadlocked Mayito from Los Van Van. Their versions of Los Van Van's hits included a pumping 'voice bass' imitation of Juan Formell's surging bass lines, and the room erupted into dancing couples. El Médico, who had delivered his wife's baby that afternoon, was in the audience, sitting among the new hip crowd of young, privileged Cubans destined to shake up global salsa in the following century.

The most talked-about bands to emerge from Cuba in the late nineties were Bamboleo and David Calzado's Charanga Habanera. Although quite different musically, both have been fronted by beautiful bold, bald-headed singers who mix rap lyrics with Cuba's new salsa dance rhythms. Calzado's singers leap acrobatically around the stage in a new Cuban slant on break-dancing. In 1997 the cheeky Calzado pushed his luck too far at a Festival of Youth, when he boasted about smoking marijuana and made obvious double-entendre jokes about Fidel Castro. He also encouraged his young, adoring audience in their erotic dance, the pelota (like sex standing up). Calzado was 'grounded' for six months and missed a prestigious European tour. Dance crazes have returned to the story and young revolutionary Cubans are as adept as their parents were at creating catchy steps. Manolito (Simonet) y su Trabuco's hit single 'El águila' (The Eagle) drove crowds of fans to wave their arms like eagles in flight, while Manolito crowed lewd bird-calls and instructions from the stage. The new generation even gave their music its own identity, calling their songo-driven salsa 'timba', to distinguish it from the New York variety.

In 1997 a huge open-air dancehall called the Tropical, famous for the dance steps created on its rough stone floors, hosted a week-long salsa-and-son marathon for the *Guinness Book of Records* during which more than 40,000 people danced to the 100-hour soundtrack provided by the revolution's most important bands – from the ninety-year-old Compay Segundo's sweet guitar-based songs of the countryside to Charanga Habanera's raw, electric blend of every music style since.

CARVING UP THE CAKE

By the late 1990s, Cuba was once again a sellers' market: the Ministry of Culture held its first post-revolution music trade fair, CUBADISCO, in 1997 and a year later Cuban records were being traded under licence at the first MIDEM Latin fair in Miami. This time round the American multinationals were not part of the deal, but several US-based Latin independents found

David Calzado (right) is one of Cuba's new capitalists, leader of the revolutionary young band, Charanga Habanera. He owns one of Cuba's few sports cars, but still rehearses in this shanty town where he grew up.

LEFT: Gathered round the piano in this Havana bar (from left to right) are the pianist Rubén González and singers Pío Leyva, Ibrahim Ferrer and Manuel 'Puntillita' Licea. All were winding down their careers when the *Buena Vista Social Club* and *Afro-Cuban All Stars* projects transformed their lives. In 1998 they not only toured Europe and the USA but also appeared on stage at Carnegie Hall.

Buena Vista Social Club & Afro-Cuban All Stars

The Buena Vista Social Club album is the fairy-tale ending to the story of a group of musicians from the footnotes of Cuban history. Most of them were in their seventies, their careers were waning or seemed to be over, their days were measured in cigar butts, shots of rum and coffee and occasional musical gatherings. Then, in 1996, a tall American blues guitarist and a short English record company boss arrived in Havana.

Ry Cooder and Nick Gold (of World Circuit Records) invited the guitarist and dedicated traditionalist Juan de Marcos González to scout for Cooder's dreamteam to record an album of classic Cuban songs. The project exploded: three records emerged where only one was planned, and more have followed, sparking a worldwide craze for classic Cuban music and turning the veterans into globe-trotting superstars.

The first record, *The Buena Vista Social Club*, is a magical guitar-based feast featuring Cooder's bluesy rumbles and Hawaiian sighs, the crisply picked guitar lines of Compay Segundo and Eliades Ochoa's delicate lute playing. The album won a Grammy and Wim Wenders made a documentary of its incredible story. The second, *The Afro-Cuban All Stars,* is bright and brassy, trumpet-led, big-band Cuban salsa, fronted by a mesh of mature, effortless voices. Most striking are Ibrahim Ferrer and Pío Leyva and the sole woman on the project, Omara Portuondo. And the last, and unplanned child of the sessions, *Introducing ...Rubén González,* is a seemingly casual illustration of a reborn pianist in full flight.

When Cooder arrived, the 84-year-old González had retired because of arthritis and did not even own a piano; 89-year-old Compay Segundo was running a local guitar band called 'Los Muchachos' (The Boys); 60-something Omara Portuondo was singing in a piano-bar, and 74-year-old Ibrahim Ferrer, a former backing singer for Beny Moré, had also retired. Within a year, all four were performing in Europe's leading concert halls. Says Ferrer: 'Juan de Marcos gave me my life back.'

ABOVE: **Compay Segundo** (left), who has played through a century of Cuban music, with the American blues guitarist Ry Cooder.

ABOVE: In between organizing the Buena Vista Social Club members, Juan de Marcos González plays traditional tres guitar in Sierra Maestra.
LEFT: Ibrahim Ferrer, singing a duet with Omara Portuondo.

loopholes in the government's embargo and went talent hunting. Former Fania records boss Jerry Masucci rose from retirement and visited Cuba in 1996. He signed both Paulito F. G. and Dan Den to his Nueva Fania label and was set to scoop up more when he died suddenly in 1997. Ralph Mercado, who had picked up where Masucci left off with American salsa, recorded Issac Delgado for his RMM label, and – ignoring threats from Miami's Cubans – put him on a bill, with Celia Cruz, at Madison Square Gardens.

What finally guaranteed Cuba's return to the Latin music family was the marvellous trio of 1996 recordings for the small independent UK label World Circuit, including Ry Cooder's production, *The Buena Vista Social Club*. Compay Segundo, eighty-four-year-old pianist Rubén González and seventy-year-old bolero singer Ibrahim Ferrer were suddenly superstars, touring more intensively than they had ever done in their heydays.

Today, Havana's hotels race to keep up with tourists' demands and Cuba is once again the Caribbean's hippest destination. The scent of illicit Cuban cigar smoke hangs heavy in New York's most fashionable clubs; Havana Club rum sells in London's most respectable dance bars, and Cuban musicians are scattered in tour coaches all over Europe. The same venues that featured as backdrops for stories about Havana's heady night-life and visitors like Sinatra, Nat 'King' Cole and Hemingway in the glossy American magazines of the fifties are back in business with today's glamorous icons. And European (and American) talent scouts are checking the credentials of every busking guitar band singing 'Guantanamera' in the tourist bars of newly renovated Old Havana where European package tourists practice their salsa moves. As Juan de Marcos González, musical director of the Buena Vista Social Club, driving through Havana in his bright green VW beetle, a Ché beret covering springing grey dreadlocks, declares, 'It's like the Wild West out here – and who knows what will happen next?'

ABOVE: **Dancing on the roof of Havana's Hotel Inglaterra, in the shadow of the Cathedral tower.**
LEFT: The 1990s has seen women in Cuba emerge in most musical guises. The trumpet-led all-women group Son Damas follows the tradition established by Anacaona in the thirties.

Plena is one of Puerto Rico's traditional styles, first performed in the rural areas around Ponce, on the south coast of the island and in Loiza Aldea in the north. Lush forest is the backdrop for this nostalgic re-creation of a traditional plena, whose key instrument is the time-keeping tambourine drum called a pandereta.

92

PUERTO RICO, SALSA COLONY

Chapter 5 PUERTO RICO:
Salsa colony

ON LANDING IN Puerto Rico in 1493, Christopher Columbus described the island as 'The Jewel of the Caribbean'. To the indigenous Taino Indians – who were ultimately all-but wiped out by the conquestadores – it was 'Borinquén' (Island of the Brave Lord). Columbus renamed it San Juan Bautista (St John the Baptist) and later 'Puerto Rico' – 'Rich Port', and called the first city San Juan.

For the tourists who arrive there today, the first stop is invariably the beautifully renovated Old Town with its maze of blue-cobbled streets and Spanish Colonial architecture. But, despite such details, San Juan frequently feels like an American city, more like Miami than Havana or Santo Domingo. Its locals flit between Spanish and a lilting American English. Modern Puerto Rico occupies a similar place to Havana before Castro's Revolution – an offshore tourist resort for free-spending visitors to American-owned hotels, nightclubs and casinos.

The significant difference between Puerto Rico and Cuba is the extent of American involvement. In 1898 the US government assisted Puerto Rico's war of independence from the Spanish and then occupied the island. The 1917 Jones Act decreed that Puerto Ricans were US citizens, free to come and go from the mainland, obliged to serve in the US forces and speak English, but unable to vote. That moment marked the conception of 'El Barrio' and Spanish Harlem in New York, the start of the mass exodus from the island. On 25 July 1952, Puerto Rico was made a Commonwealth State. The Governor, Luis Muñoz Marín, raised two flags in Old San Juan as a military band played both the 'Stars and Stripes' and 'La Borinqueña' – the new official national anthem. In December 1998, Puerto Rico rejected a second attempt to make it the 51st State of the Union. While America's investment has kept the island's standard of living higher than that of any other Caribbean island, Puerto Rico has sacrificed some of its cultural independence, a smouldering issue which is constantly being raised in songs.

San Juan is a typically piebald city, with shanty districts and impoverished barrios alongside affluent residential neighbourhoods and tourist sections. A short walk from the resort district of Condado is Santurce, traditionally a musicians' neighbourhood, which contains Puerto Rico's own Tin Pan Alley – a narrow street called Calle Serra, where many local independent labels are housed. Most Puerto Rican salsa stars began their careers with a label based in this street – an open-air snack bar serves as a meeting-place for passing record producers and behind-the-scenes creators of the island's music.

Casual tourists might easily miss the richness of Puerto Rican music as they consume rum cocktails, and listen to flamenco, watered-down salsa and international music shows. The islanders themselves flock to the Roberto

Clemente Stadium to dance to the salsa which fills the charts of Latin America. Every July the touring bands return home and the island rocks to a week-long frenzy of Fiesta Patronales (Patron Saints' Festivals) – outdoor concerts held in every sizeable town. For the grand finales, the legends turn out in full strength. By driving around, it is possible to see every significant and upcoming band – for free.

The Puerto Rican poet Lola Rodríguez de Tio described Cuba and Puerto Rico as 'two wings of the same bird', but Puerto Rico's native music has often been overshadowed by big brother Cuba and its NuYorican cousins, even though the island possesses many celebrated musicians and composers who have fed into the mainstream of Latin American dance music and jazz and have been key players in salsa throughout most of the twentieth century. The connections are most obvious in the traditional styles, though these also give the islands their distinctive heritage.

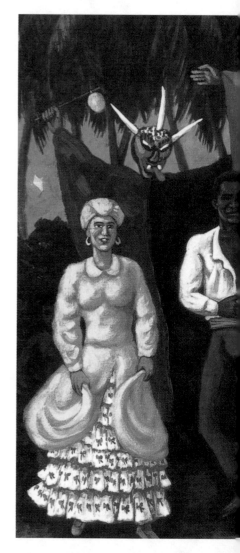

DANZA

The most European of Puerto Rico's dance music is the elegant, formal danza, created in mid-nineteenth-century San Juan from an infusion of the French contredanse with the flavours of the Caribbean. Like the Cuban danzón, it has a brisk, military-band quality, though its original appeal is alleged to have been its slow tempo which allowed dancers to perform without sweating.

The first danzas – instrumentals played by brass bands and small orchestras consisting of piano and strings – were recorded in 1910. A precocious young pianist and prolific composer called Juan Morel Campos souped up his romantic and humorous pieces with novel, local percussion, and aimed their syncopated rhythms at the city's racially mixed working-class audiences. Campos took his reputation to the genteel, southern port of Ponce where he founded a fireman's band to launch the opening (in 1883) of the gaudy red and black fireman's headquarters, today a tourist attraction. The island's national anthem, 'La Borinqueña' (The Puerto Rican Girl), was one of the first danzas with lyrics, a metaphor for the island's beauty, written in 1868 during an attempted uprising against the Spanish.

THE BOMBA AND THE PLENA

Two related styles, the bomba and the plena, are tied to the history of the island's black population. Their ancestral homes are in the two areas most densely populated by slaves: the northern coastal town of Loiza Aldea, built around a sugarcane mill, and the southern port of Ponce. During the years of slavery, Loiza attracted workers from the countryside on Christian holidays (saints' days) for riotous bomba sessions. A local family would host a session, crowds would collect, and the appearance of the wooden, barrel-like bomba drums signalled the start of night-long singing, dancing and drumming.

Traditionally, the bomba drummers sit in a line, each playing a different sized instrument, criss-crossing with patterns from smaller drums (subidors), maracas and wooden sticks (palillos). The rhythm is strong and propulsive, with a syncopated African lurch. The singers chant onomatopoeic fragments of African words and improvise in imitation of the drum. The

LEFT: This painting by Cajiga of Old San Juan shows a traditional plena group at the Fiesta of Loiza Aldea. The women flashed their skirts in time with the small hand-drums (panderetas); the 'vejigantes' (bladder carriers) wore spikey masks derived from an ancient Spanish festival and terrorized each other in 'trick or treat' type scares.
BELOW LEFT: Loiza Aldea is the traditional centre for bomba music and dances, still performed at the homes of families who carry the tradition from the days of slavery. The key connection — seen here — is between the solo dancer and the driving bomba drummers.

dancers move in a circle in front of the drummers and as the music builds one emerges and glides towards the musicians for a solo. At that point, the dancer's movements dictate the drummer's patterns. Bombas have traditionally been resisted outside black or working-class circles but mass tourism has seen them repackaged as 'folkloric', and included in tourist programmes.

Plenas first appeared in Ponce at the end of the nineteenth century when a pair of English-speaking singers called John Clarke and Catherine George – 'Los Ingleses' – arrived from Barbados or St Kitts and settled in Ponce's black ghetto – known, ironically, as 'La Joya del Castillo' (Jewel of the Castle). The couple busked in the streets with their daughter Carolina, who played the pandereta (the tambourine with no bells). They played guitar and tambourine, and composed songs to local music, poignant and humorous commentaries on the daily life of the black working-class people. The songs were known as plenas, possibly a Spanish version of 'Play now!'.

A tourist-perfect photograph taken in a village near Ponce, on the south coast. This is the classic plena trio line-up: two guitars, two harmonizing voices and the timekeeper, the pandereta, which travelled to New York's Spanish Harlem in the early twentieth century and brought an instant reminder of home. Today plenas are enjoying a comeback through a number of neo-traditional bands, such as Plena Libre.

The plena was popularized beyond Ponce by a ploughman called Joselino Oppenheimer, known as 'Bumbún'. Like 'Los Ingleses', he lived in La Joya, but worked in the sugarcane fields, where he composed his songs and taught his ploughboys to sing the choruses. At night he performed in local bars to an accompanying accordion or harmonica and güiro and the double-beat rhythm (bum-bun) on a pandereta. Bumbún was a showman drummer, rolling his instrument across his shoulders, over his head or along the floor, without losing the beat. Pandereta and accordion were the essential instruments for plenas.

Bumbún's compositions remain part of the plena repertoire. Songs like 'Cuando las mujeres quieren a los hombres' (When the Women Love the Men) and 'Tanta vanidad' (Such Vanity) are still reworked today by neo-traditionalists. With time, a cuatro guitar and double bass were added to the mix, and the plena proved as versatile as its Cuban cousin, the son. A successful plenero must shine at improvisation, providing a satirical or saucy take on the news and gossip. Like calypso and son, plena serves as a musical newspaper and scandal sheet.

MUSICA JIBARA

The jíbaros (literally 'those who escape civilization') occupy a romantic and mythic place in Puerto Rican culture. With their wildly upturned straw hats and 5-stringed cuatro guitars, they represent an idealized rustic lifestyle which has not existed for centuries. The original jíbaros were communities of Spanish peasant farmers and escaped African slaves, who lived in farming villages in the mountains. The jíbaro songs (the equivalent of Cuba's guajira music) are accompanied by the locally invented cuatro guitar (played with a plectrum), a güiro and sometimes a bongo drum.

Jíbaro lyrics romanticize the country idyll and rustic images in ten-line verses in décima patterns. The two main jíbaro styles are seis and aguinaldo. The seis are complex songs, improvised or written in verses, some in décimas, others in free form. The aguinaldo is a Christmas carol, cranked into life by the record industry every year around November. Traditionally, aguinaldos have been performed by parties of singers (parrandas) who go like carrollers from house to house, collecting food and tots of rum on the way. The most famous and best-loved jíbaro musician today is cuatro player Yomo Toro – known as 'The Funky Jíbaro' because of his rock-style solos. Although he has lived and worked in New York since the early 1950s, Toro, with his electrified cuatro, has carried the atmosphere of the Caribbean countryside into many New York salsa hits, particularly those by Willie Colón, who took him off the folk circuit into the salsa arena. Toro's annual aguinaldo records provided the soundtrack to Christmas for New York's barrio for many years.

MILESTONE MOMENTS IN PUERTO RICAN SALSA

Puerto Rican music has maintained a distinct identity throughout the twentieth century despite the potent influences of American jazz and Cuban music. It has a more Caribbean, laid-back quality, less frenzied than American salsa, less African-syncopated than Cuban salsa. The songwriter 'Tite' Curet Alonso hears 'a definite calypso feel in the salsa here'. The island has been a breeding-ground for singers and has contributed many great voices to Latin music: the warbling, soaring country falsettos of Ramito and Canario, the honeyed croonings of Ismael Rivera and Cheo Feliciano and today's new kids in the barrio, Víctor Manuelle and Jerry Rivera, as well as the rough, nasal tones associated with the country style of Héctor Lavoe and Frankie Ruiz.

A modern Puerto Rican sound began to develop within the first decades of the century, when contact with American musicians began. In 1917, as the Jones Act qualified islanders for the US forces, a Sergeant James Reece Europe went to San Juan to enlist musicians for his all-black regimental band, The Hellfighters. Reece Europe signed up Rafael Hernández, a San Juan trombonist, Hernández's brother Jesús, and a few other likely candidates, and trained them in Harlem. They spent the final year of the war in France, entertaining troops with American jazz, popular show tunes and brass-band pieces. After demobilization, many musicians stayed in New York and joined the orchestras of a new wave of musicals. Rafael Hernández went to Havana and directed a cinema orchestra until 1925, then returned to New York and back to the basic guitar-voice and percussion with his Trío Borinquén and Cuarteto Victoria. One of Hernández's favourite singers was an ambitious young girl called Myrta Silva who became a leading light in Puerto Rican music. His songs provided the Puerto Rican canon with classics which have been reworked throughout the century.

From the 1920s and 1930s San Juan's beach hotels, cabaret theatres, casinos and dancehalls were designed to the same deco template as those in Havana and Miami. The spectacularly fashionable Escambrón Beach Club held court through the thirties to a band led by trumpeter Rafael Muñoz, whose speciality was a slow and very sensual style of bolero which the band dropped in among the tangos, pasadobles and rumbas. The highly paid Muñoz trained many young musicians for stardom, including cabaret pianist Noro Morales and the trumpeter César Concepción, both of whom made their names in New York. Muñoz's son Ramón went on to play timbal with Tito Rodríguez's leading mambo band at the Palladium.

Between the World Wars, the US government introduced a plantation system in Puerto Rico which forced thousands of peasant farmers off their

A painting by the San Juan artist Cajiga tells the story behind Rafael Hernández's 1929 composition 'Lamento Borincano' (Puerto Rican Lament) – the island's unofficial national anthem. A small-time jíbaro farmer goes to market to sell his produce and buy his wife a new dress, but because America has taken over the land for sugar, the market has collapsed and a centuries-old rural lifestyle has been destroyed.

land and into the towns. Thousands moved into New York's swelling barrios, taking the emotive jíbaro songs and bright cuatro guitar tunes with them. Rafael Hernandez's 'Serenata jíbara' and 'Lamento del copla' (Lament of the Poet)) reveal his continued support for the jíbaros' situation and were panaceas to homesick Nueva Yorkers as well as to city-locked jíbaros on the island.

During the Second World War, contact with American musicians again broadened musical bases. The Swing bands of Glenn Miller, Jimmy Dorsey and Count Basie flooded the radio and transformed the island's music – modern salsa still possesses a distinctive 'Swing' in the horn sections. A young singer called Ruth Fernández joined a Ponce band with the revealingly Americanized name of Mingo and the Whoopee Kids. Fernández – later Senator Ruth Fernández – was the first female Puerto Rican singer to record with a big band in New York.

Cuban music was also highly influential at the time. Around 1940 the ten o'clock *Arsenio Rodríguez Show* on short-wave radio launched a trend for trumpet-led line-ups. Plenas also enjoyed a new popularity in the early 1940s, when the trumpeter César Concepción and his singer, Joe Valle, re-dressed them in the bold and brassy format of the Cuban conjuntos.

In contrast to the luxurious American hotel venues, many local musicians worked in neighbourhood bars and dancehalls. Rafael Ithier, a young guitarist, played that circuit before going to fight in Korea. On his return he took up the piano and moved upscale to the swanky hotel band Orquesta Panamericana. At the same time, Orquesta Internacional featured another young pianist, Enrique 'Quique' Lucca, who, like Ithier, would eventually create a dance orchestra which defines Puerto Rican music. Racial discrimination kept many bands off the hotel circuit but in 1945 a fearless young black percussionist called Rafael Cortijo got his band, Los Dandies, into a hotel casino because they performed a revue show rather than a dance routine .

The most significant early postwar band was Moncho Lena's Los Ases del Ritmo (The Aces of Rhythm) led by percussionist Lena and singer Mon Rivera. The two met in a danceband playing the pop tunes of the day: 'We had to play "In the Mood" and samba and pasadoble and tango,' Lena told David Carp for *Descarga Online* in 1998. In 1952 Lena and Rivera broke away and landed a contract as Los Ases del Ritmo at the Coconut Hut club. When Mambo Master Tito Rodríguez brought the celebrated big band to his homeland a few month's later, Lena's band were the support. The following year the Aces of Rhythm were invited to the Palladium, where their presence inspired the song 'Que rica es', by Lito Peña.

> They have bands by the thousand
> Over there (Machito, Tito Puente, Rodríguez).
> I will have to listen to all of them.
> I'm going to a dance played by Moncho Lena
> But I won't stay if he doesn't play
> the Puerto Rican bomba.

In 1951 a band emerged which represented a milestone in Puerto Rican music. Rafael Ithier switched from playing piano in a tuxedo with Orquesta

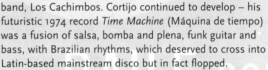

Ismael Rivera & Rafael Cortijo

A cocaine habit and three years in an American gaol for possession were just two of the many tragedies in the life of the singer Ismael Rivera. But for Puerto Ricans everywhere, his glorious melancholy voice was and is an expression of their soul.

One of salsa's most potent partnerships was launched in San Juan in the early 1950s, when Rivera hooked up

The percussionist and bandleader Rafael Cortijo, who put Puerto Rican bombas on the salsa map.

with the rule-breaking percussionist Rafael Cortijo. The Cortijo Combo's first hit record, *El bombón de Elena* (Elena's Candy), in 1954, rocked San Juan's clubs and dives, while successive hits landed the band a slot on daytime television.

Rivera's clear, emotive, husky voice was a dream for songwriters. In New York, the Puerto Rican nationalist Boby Capo provided him

Ismael Rivera, called by Beny Moré 'El Sonero Mayor' – the greatest improvising singer.

with universally haunting boleros like 'Sale el sol' (The Sun Goes In); at home, 'Tite' Curet Alonso tailored songs for him, such as 'Las caras lindas' (The Beautiful Faces), where his voice moves with a solo cuatro guitar.

The bubble burst in 1962, when Rivera was gaoled. Though Cortijo welcomed him back in 1966, in a recording *Bienvenido!/Welcome!*, the two men soon went their separate ways, Rivera with his new band, Los Cachimbos. Cortijo continued to develop – his futuristic 1974 record *Time Machine* (Máquina de tiempo) was a fusion of salsa, bomba and plena, funk guitar and bass, with Brazilian rhythms, which deserved to cross into Latin-based mainstream disco but in fact flopped.

Cortijo's death in 1983 shocked the island, but when Rivera died, after a long silence induced by vocal polyps, Puerto Rico virtually shut down; his songs were played on every radio station and flags flew at half mast.

Panamericana to jamming with a small group led by the black conga player Rafael Cortijo and a husky crooner called Ismael Rivera at a dockside brothel known as La Riviera. La Riviera's dancers were hooked on mambos and rock-'n'roll which came in through the port from Cuba and New York. Cortijo's combo used the energy and tension of rock but stayed close to the roots music of bombas and plenas. He transposed the bubbling rhythms of bomba for saxophone, trumpet and piano-led unit. Their 1954 release *El bombón de Elena* (Elena's Candy) was a compelling debut which launched a string of hits.

In the mid-fifties, Cortijo's band had the status of The Beatles at home and were regulars on the live daytime television show hosted by singer Ruth Fernández. An album of the show, *El alma del pueblo* (The Soul of the People), reveals the extraordinary range of styles they had to play in those days– from the Spanish kitsch of 'Volare' to merengues, boleros, mambos and unexpectedly free jazz solos. In 1959 the Combo made their debut at the Palladium and other hip Latin clubs in New York. Their 1961 hit 'Quítate de la vía, perico' (a double-entendre song about drugs), tore through the clubs. As musicians with no training, Cortijo and Rivera were inspirations to poor black Latinos – Rivera's drugs problem and vulnerability made him even more adored. Their songs are still among the most quoted in the Puerto Rican book; their birthdays are fiestas in San Juan. At the peak of their popularity, schools eventually closed down when they played free concerts because students never returned from their lunch breaks.

'TITE' CURET ALONSO

With his trademark straw hat and quiet, retiring manner, Catalino 'Tite' Curet Alonso is an unlikely source of some of salsa's greatest hits. If royalties had ever been paid, he would be a millionaire; instead, he worked as a mailman and a journalist on *El vocero* in San Juan. 'My lyrics are like news,' he says, 'They have a narrative style.' He tailors the narrative to the singer – particularly in his favourite partnership with Cheo Feliciano. Alonso has written hits for non-Puerto Ricans (Celia Cruz, Johnny Pacheco), but remains fiercely competitive about Cuban music: 'Salsa is Cuban in its origins,' he admits, 'But, remember, the English invented football and boxing but they don't have all the champions.'

The fifties saw a steady drain of musicians to New York, heading for Broadway and the Palladium. In 1952 Cheo Feliciano, a young singer from Ponce, was hired as Tito Rodríguez's valet and in 1957 Joe Cuba took him on as lead singer for his Sextet. Within weeks, Feliciano was on the Palladium's stage, and five years later his songs 'Bang! Bang!' and 'El pito' (I'll Never Go to Georgia) were in the US charts.

In 1954 the bass player of Orquesta Internacional, Enrique 'Quique' Lucca, took over the band, changing its name to La Sonora Ponceña. He added a third trumpet, under the influence of Cuban conjuntos like Sonora Matancera, and introduced his young prodigy pianist son, 'Papo'. Papo's unrivalled versatility – as composer, multi-instrumentalist and producer – have kept the band at the forefront of the salsa league.

With the mambo and the Palladium waning, most musicians returned home. Singer Myrta Silva handed over the microphone with the illustrious Cuban band La Sonora Matancera to Celia Cruz and became a leading radio and television personality in San Juan. The sixties were disastrous for Cortijo's Combo – Ismael Rivera's gaol sentence in the US for possessing cocaine caused the band to spin into chaos. Pianist Rafael Ithier led a breakaway with percussionist Roberto Roena, trumpeter Rogelio 'Kito' Vélez and saxophonist Eddie Pérez. They called themselves El Gran Combo – a compact two trumpets/two saxophone sound led by Ithier's velvety piano and two singers. Ithier's slick, almost mathematical approach to arranging seduced audiences everywhere. As an acknowledgment of rock'n'roll, his front-line singers harmonized in voice and danced in synchronized formation.

In 1966 percussionist Roberto Roena went solo and produced a rough-diamond album entitled *Se pone bueno* (It Gets Better), with a nuclear age band called Los Megatones. His singer was Camilo Azuguita, a Panamanian with a liquidly soulful voice. Their mambo jazz workout of Dave Brubeck's 'Take Five' is a high point on the album. Roena founded his permanent band, The Apollo Sound, in 1969, and used a series of local producers to harness his wild, untutored energy.

With Roena gone, Ithier's Gran Combo settled into a groove of smooth hit songs polished by rigorous rehearsals which set the tone for the Puerto Rican sound – more conservative than experimental, but no less exciting.

During the sixties and seventies, New York was the focus for salsa, but its record producers and tour organizers began to include Puerto Rico in their plans. Al Santiago – whose Alegre records launched Johnny Pacheco and the Palmieri brothers onto vinyl – had set up an office in San Juan and hired postman–songwriter 'Tite' Curet Alonso to run it. Following the success of his Alegre All Stars superstar jam sessions, he turned up in San Juan in 1963 to organize the first Puerto Rican All Stars album which featured the El Gran Combo rhythm section, former Cortijo percussionist 'Kako' and trumpeter César Concepción.

Jerry Masucci and Johnny Pacheco kept a close eye on San Juan and scooped up hits for their Fania artists. Many Puerto Rican musicians joined the Fania clan – 'Papo' Lucca introduced a jazz element to Celia Cruz productions and played piano on the historic Fania All Stars shows in the 1970s; bass player Bobby Valentín worked closely with Johnny Pacheco on the arrangements; former El Gran Combo percussionist Roberto Roena joined as a bongo player and dancer, and Ismael Rivera and Rafael Cortijo both took their places on the stage. Cheo Feliciano emerged from drug rehab with a magical

El Gran Combo, on tour in Japan, living up to the title of their 1998 celebratory album *35 Years around the World*. Rafael Ithier is centre, wearing a jacket.

La Sonora Ponceña & El Gran Combo

The slick, swinging dance music and catchy hit songs of La Sonora Ponceña (from the Southern town of Ponce) and El Gran Combo (from the capital) have occupied Puerto Rico's salsa charts for nearly half a century. The two bands are national institutions.

Ponceña was founded in 1954 by Enrique 'Quique' Lucca and has been directed since the sixties by Quique's son, the pianist 'Papo'. EGC rose from the ashes of Rafael Cortijo's Combo in 1963, and is still run by Rafael Ithier, the pianist who led the breakaway. Such stability has brought both bands a smooth, polished sound, matured and burnished through the years.

'Papo' Arsenio Lucca's eclectic tastes and love of Cuban music dominates Ponceña's material – an early hit was a cover of Arsenio Rodríguez's song 'Fuego en el 23!'. 'Papo's' rhythmic jazz-piano style lends the songs an unmistakable swing carried by the smooth textures of four trumpets and three singers' voices dovetailed with the precision of a doowop act. Ponceña have included that rare thing in salsa, a female vocalist,

Pianist 'Papo' Lucca (above) and with his band La Sonora Ponceña (right, arms folded).

Yolande Rivera – one of several former singers (Luigi Texidor, Pichi Pérez and Tito Gómez) who return for periodic anniversary celebrations, such as the 40th anniversary party at Madison Square Gardens in 1993 and the superlative album *Birthday Party*.

The 13-piece EGC are more akin to the sophisticated brassy forties Swing bands of Count Basie or Stan Kenton, injected with syncopated Cuban rhythms. The mathematically precise, split-second timing of two trumpets, two saxophones and a trombone, and the tightly choreographed voices and dance steps of the three singers – Charlie Aponte, Jerry Rivas and Papo Rosario – have been as inseparable from EGC's identity as Ithier himself. Like Ponceña, EGC has cultivated a stable cast but has also been a springboard for many artists. The percussionist and legendary dancer Roberto Roena left in 1969 to start his looser, more eclectic, Cuba-oriented Apollo Sound band, leaving a legacy of dancing singers with the band.

The nineties saw a round of celebratory EGC albums and concerts marking over 50 releases and culminating in the 1998 album *35 years around the World*, whose 34 songs more than justify the band's nickname, 'The University of Salsa'.

comeback album, *La voz sensual de Cheo*, written in 1972 by 'Tite' Curet Alonso. In 1974 Cortijo released a shockingly avant-garde album called *Time Machine* – a futuristic clash of sounds from Brazil, funk and guitar rock.

In a lighter vein, 1977 saw the invention of a hugely successful all-boy bubble-gum Latin-pop band called Menudo. Their material was surprisingly sophisticated; even the legendary 'Tite' Curet Alonso wrote them a hit – 'CuCuBano'. 'It's a symbolic song about young love,' he explained, 'A Cucubano is a firefly.' When a Menudo reached sixteen he was replaced by fresh scream fodder. From the thirty or so Menudos, several succeeded in the adult world. Ricky Martin became a pop singer in Mexico and took a role in *General Hospital* – as a Puerto Rican pop singer. He shot into the European club charts in 1997 with the single *María* – a Caribbean pop take on flamenco – and in 1988 with a World Cup theme – 'La copa de oro'. Puerto Rico's other teen idol, Chayanne (not a Menudo), joined a New Kids on the Block copy band called 'Los Chicos' (The Guys), moved into Mexican tele-soaps and launched a singing career. A strong dancer, Chayanne found crossover success through the 1998 film *Dance with Me*, starring with Vanessa Williams.

Novelty aside, an explosion of native salsa bands was giving the New Yorkers a run for their money. Singers were the key commodities. One of El Gran Combo's most beloved and enduring vocalists, Andy Montañez – a stocky, sexy man with a gloriously clear and uplifting tenor voice – emerged from El Gran Combo to sing on the debut Puerto Rican All Stars album in 1976. He moved to Venezuela's leading band, Dimensión Latina, the following year – filling the vacuum left by the band's bass player and lead singer Oscar D'León, who had begun his sensationally successful solo career.

A new generation of back-up singers restocked the top bands, preparing them for their solo destiny in the following decades. A scrawny, shy boy called Frankie Ruiz joined La Solución in 1977. His incongruously mature, expressive voice filled the eighties and thrived on the vogue for salsa romantica and salsa erotica. Ruiz and another bantam-weight, Eddie Santiago, found their niche in a slew of hit records with corny, porny record sleeves.

Meanwhile, the school of classic salsa was maintained in the hands of the seniors: Sonora Ponceña, 'Papo' Lucca and El Gran Combo. Lucca revealed an insatiable musical curiosity and increasing fascination with Cuban salsa, particularly songs by Adalberto Alvarez which he covered on every album, smoothing their angular, Afro-Cuban rhythms to suit the Ponceña style. Like Ponceña, El Gran Combo circumnavigated the world, delivering polished songs and keeping a distance from erotic fashions.

More of a local secret were bass player Bobby Valentín's bands, which featured the soulfully bruised voice of local hero Marvin Santiago and the grainy sonero's voice of a partially blind albino singer called Cano Estremero, who came to Valentín from the underrated band Mulenze. El Cano fitted the Valentín 'classic Fania' mould and proved to be a great improviser.

In 1983 Rafael Cortijo died of cancer and the island paused. When Ismael Rivera died four years later, it stopped altogether as 70,000 people, including the Governor, followed the coffin to the old San Juan cemetery. A year later, a Park of Salseros was opened in San Juan in honour of the two musicians.

Towards the end of the eighties and all through the nineties Puerto Rican

FRANKIE RUIZ

Frankie Ruiz (1958–98), who died at forty after decades of drug abuse, is one of salsa's many tragedies. His legacy remains in timeless recordings of his throaty, increasingly husky voice with its endearing inaccuracies. Songs like 'Puerto Rico soy tuyo' (Puerto Rico I'm Yours) and 'Puerto Rico' are still anthems today. Ruiz began singing at 16 and went solo in 1985. A flow of songs filled the charts and his pained, romantic voice echoed through Latino neighbourhoods everywhere. Ruiz's live appeal was surprising: though he danced like a limp puppet, one small flick of his ring-studded hand brought screams.

EDDIE SANTIAGO

Singer Eddie Santiago (born 1961) was a contemporary of Frankie Ruiz and Lalo Rodríguez, co-leaders of the late eighties salsa romantica and erotica movements. His 1986 album, *Atrevido y diferente* (Daring and Different), produced by Julio César Delgado, clinched the style. The small, slight Santiago makes a surprising romantic, even erotic hero, in a world dominated by macho, hairy-chested tenors, but his sex appeal is never in doubt in live shows. His voice lacks the deep-soul pain of Frankie Ruiz, Luis Enrique or Héctor Lavoe, but has an appealing, taut, uneven edge, in theory too robust for 'salsa gorda' (limp salsa).

VICTOR MANUELLE

A late-nineties generation of young, old-fashioned Puerto Rican salseros is transforming the charts. In bright linen suits, singing jumpy salsa and soupy ballads, they are reacting to the gangsta-clad salsa-rappers. Ahead of the pack is Víctor Manuelle, a tall, engaging singer who made a mark at the age of 16 (in 1989) with producer Don Perigon. Manuelle's meteoric success as a soloist since 1993 has been assisted by a calculating, hit-making team: Sergio George's gold-fingered productions, Omar Alfanno's award-winning songs and the slick backing of New York sessioneers.

'Together for fun' – a magical mosaic of Puerto Rico's eighties vocalists (with Venezuelan Héctor D'León).

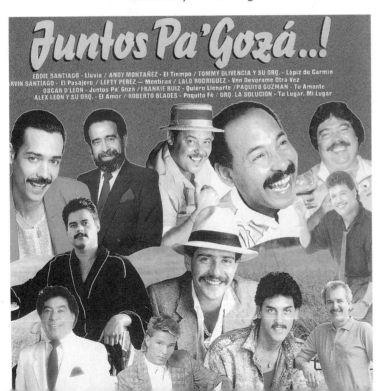

salsa scattered in several healthy directions. Merengue was swamping the charts of Latin America and many merengueros moved from the Dominican Republic to San Juan. The innovative Bonny Cepeda opened merengue to fresh outside influences which point to today's hit singers like Olga Tañón and Toño Rosario. Merengue made cracks in salsa's tight structures, and other topical Caribbean music also intruded: Roberto Roena's Apollo Sound had a hit with *Apollo Zuky*, a tropical cocktail of bomba, Martiniquan zouk and merengue. Even El Gran Combo included calypso on a 1990 album. But some musicians stuck more closely to the classic model: Andy Montañez returned from Venezuela and set up his own band, including his two sons, singers Andy and Harold.

A reassuring Festival of Soneros organized by a former timbales player called Don Perigon brought home bands from the world circuit, and a series of nineties supergroup albums asserted Puerto Rican salsa on the international scene, including, in 1990, *Príncipes de la salsa* (Princes of Salsa).

Of the younger eighties generation, Gilberto Santa Rosa towers above all other singers. This big, mustachioed man, decidedly of the pre-rap generation, possessor of a rich, dark, romantic tenor voice, has a track record in many significant bands, including the Puerto Rican All Stars. His voice is made for salsa romantica – as the 1990 hit 'Punto de Vista' proved – but he never stays still, keeping it fresh with bombas and merengues. In 1998 he delivered a solo show at the Carnegie Hall with a 14-piece band and string section.

By the nineties salsa's newest stars, Víctor Manuelle and Jerry Rivera, had leapt from singing coro with several key bands and were being guided to the top leagues by New York's leading producer, Sergio George. While MTV Latino reaches most houses on the island, it is hardly surprising that electro-salsa and rap-A-rengue are emerging. Teenage experimenters are modelling themselves on the black American scene. The teen group Limi-T XXX use merengue as a base, but others draw on the similarity between bass-heavy, repetitive bomba rhythms and electro-dance music.

An air of revivalism pervades some new salsa, as it does in Cuba. Puerto Rican Power, Plena Libre and the Jíbaro Boyzz (who play cuatros and dance) use plenas and bombas as their inspiration, driving towards the millennium with one ear to the island's traditions, the other to North American music. In the newly kindled Puerto Rican jazz camp, the globe-trotting saxophonist David Sánchez closed 1998 with an album called *Obsesión*. The lead tune was a sparkling bright version of Rafael Hernández's timeless ode to Puerto Rico, 'Lamento Borincano' – which doubly serves as a gesture to the island's pre-Columbian inhabitants.

Johnny Ventura
(third from left)
in a 1987 version of
one of merengue's most
dynamic show-bands.

SANTO DOMINGO: THE MERENGUE CAPITAL

Chapter 6

SANTO DOMINGO:
The merengue capital

MERENGUE IS THE national dance music of the Dominican Republic, the soundtrack to any visit to that country. There's no mistaking its crisp, zippy beat, hissed and scratched out on a metal grater güira in jaunty 2/4 time, or the bubbling triple beat roll of tambora rhythms and sharp twitter of inter-locked saxophone vamps.

Like Cuba's son and Puerto Rico's plena, this century-old music has been used to tell news and gossip and to spread political propaganda since the birth of the Republic. Its versatility has led to some surprising hybrids – smoochy bola-mengues, salsa-rengue, jazz-rengue – as well as to the nineties electronic mutants: mereng-rap, mereng-house and techno-rengue. In its big-band guise, it has emerged in various forms in different decades and different towns, including the exile communities in Miami and New York. Its country cousin, the bachata, a style formerly associated with dives and prostitutes' bars, brought the Dominican Republic to the world's attention in the late 1980s, when the guitarist and composer Juan Luis Guerra and his Grupo 4:40 erupted into the salsa charts.

AMERICA BEGAN HERE

The source of merengue is the island of Hispaniola (Little Spain), 75 miles west of Puerto Rico and 150 miles south east of Cuba. The larger part of the island is the French-patois-speaking Haiti, in the West; the rest is the Spanish-speaking Dominican Republic, sometimes known as Santo Domingo.

Santo Domingo is the New World's oldest city, founded in 1492 by Bartolomé Columbus, brother of Christopher. The island's original Indian inhabitants, who called their homeland 'Quisqueya' (Mother of the Earth), were systematically replaced by African slaves, who worked the plantations. Early Hispaniola tottered towards independence from the Spanish with the help of freed Haitian slaves, who had overthrown the French and occupied Santo Domingo from 1822 to 1844. But while Haiti developed into a Franco-African-Creole society with the strongest African traditions in the Caribbean, Santo Domingo's ruling class stayed closer to its Spanish ancestry.

The dictator, President General Rafael Leonidas Trujillo y Molina, in power from 1930 to 1961, obsessively stuck to a denial of Africa's part in Santo Domingo's history, even though his grandmother was a black Haitian. The merengue composer employed by Trujillo, Luis Alberti, wrote of the merengue: 'I don't believe there is any connection with negro or African rhythms. Merengue appears to me to be a mixture of Spanish with our rural tunes, from within the countryside...'

Most Dominicans today would disagree. The late Fradique Lazardo, founder of the National Music and Dance Company, traced the tambora drums to Madagascar; while Juan Luis Guerra made direct links with Africa in

105

General Rafael Trujillo, who ran the Dominican Republic from the capital Ciudad Trujillo (Trujillo Town) for over 30 years, commandeered merengue to bolster his regime. Alleged to have two left feet, he found merengue's fixed 2/4 beat to be the easiest of the island's folk styles, and elevated it from dirt-floor country dances to elegant hotel ballrooms.

his late 1980s recordings, when he introduced guitarist Diblo Dibala from the Congo-Zairean soukous tradition, completing a circle begun with the slave traders five hundred years earlier.

Merengue comes in many guises. Old-fashioned merengue tipico cibaeno (typical merengue from Cibao) is played on house porches, in bars and at cock fights, particularly in the northern country towns of Cibao province. The traditional line-up included the double-ended tambora drum, a scraped güira (the timekeeper), and a marimba box bass similar to the giant African thumb pianos used by the original Cuban son groups. The melody was carried on a guitar or banjo and from the 1870s on a lacerating button accordion. In time, the cumbersome marimba was replaced by a stand-up, then by an electric bass, and the modernist style was renamed merengue tipico moderno. Under the influence of imported American jazz in the thirties, an alto saxophone gave the sound even more clout.

A faster and more raucous version of traditional merengue has the dubious name of perico ripiao, which translates literally as 'ripped parrot', but is also slang for cocaine and prostitute – 'El Perico Ripiao' was a famous 1930s whores' bar in one of the merengue centres, Santiago de los Caballeros.

Another version of merengue, the pambiche style, has an intriguing history: the word is a Dominicanization of 'Palm Beach' – the local pronunciation of the drill cloth worn by the US Marines who occupied Puerto Plata in 1916. Pambiches are slowed-down merengues, retaining just verse and chorus, tailored for the Americans, who couldn't get the hang of the real thing.

> Palm Beach is better than drill,
> and it's better than cashmir.
> I'm going to enjoy myself with it,
> and I'm going to dance with my girlfriend.

The template for all merengue bands is a line-up like this 'merengue típico Cibaeno' outfit from the Northern province of Cibao, birthplace of the dance. The güiro, button accordion, marimbula and tambora are its crucial instruments.

Early versions of merengue can still be heard in the countryside and at folk festivals; their components have been absorbed into the outrageously camp showbands at the other end of the scale. A pioneer of the transformation was a singer called Johnny Ventura who in the mid-sixties launched his Combo Showband, which set off a wave of modern merengues in the wake of Trujillo's assassination in 1960. Ventura charged the music with rock'n'roll, Elvis Presley, The Beatles and soul music. A decade later, the trumpeter Wilfrido Vargas, with his Los Beduinos sextet, began to graft ideas from all around the Caribbean and Latin America onto the template. The third milestone in modern merengue was established in the late eighties and early nineties when Juan Luis Guerra and 4.40 transformed merengue and bachata under the influence of jazz harmonies and African music.

By the nineties, merengue's young club producers and DJs had forged a new lineage out of electronic crossovers with rap and house music, born in the barrios of Washington Heights and spread to San Juan and back to Santo Domingo. Many Dominican merengue bands had moved to neighbouring Puerto Rico, attracted by its higher standard of living and by the multinational record companies there. The invasion of MTV Latino also spread the electro-word. Juan Luis Guerra responded with his Mango TV and Mango Radio in 1997, to ensure Dominican music maintained its identity.

MERENGUE'S ROOTS

The first mention of merengue occurs around the 1850s, when the Dominicans overthrew the occupying Haitians and took their independence from Spain. To begin with, merengue was just another country dance music, with stirring, bawdy and often politically pointed or satirical lyrics. Songs were newsletters, love messages, humorous soap operas, accompanied by guitars and hand percussion. Merengue was made partially respectable by a number of classical composers who wove folk idioms into their pieces, as Bartók and Debussy were doing in Europe.

A song written by the clarinettist Juan Bautista Alfonseca, 'The Father of Merengue' (1881–1975), which survives only as the following lines, is an early written reference to merengue: 'Juan Quilina is going to cry/Because they take her to dance/the merengue...' Alfonseca's repertoire included not only merengues but also Christian masses and waltzes. Another pioneer was Esteban Peña Morell, a clarinettist who collected and published folk music, including merengues, and who worked in New York from 1930 to 1933 as an arranger for George Gershwin. The first officially published merengue, 'Ecos de Cibao' (Echoes of Cibao), was written in 1918 by Juan Francisco García.

AGITPROP MERENGUES

At the start of the twentieth century, merengue songs and their rowdy country dances created havoc in the newly independent Republic, whose high society still danced European waltzes and foxtrots. Merengue was strictly banned from society salons and dances, just as Africa-rooted son was in Cuba. But after the coup by General Trujillo in 1930, merengue's status underwent an astonishing elevation. Trujillo took a merengue quartet on his campaign trail and instructed the capital's hotel bands and the provincial brass bands to play merengues. It was said he relished the sight of the military and businessmen and their glamorous partners being forced to dance to music which previously only servants and peasants had enjoyed.

Trujillo took control in the middle of 'the Jazz Age' when Glen Miller's brand of Swing Jazz inspired him to speed up merengue and multiply the single saxophone to a full section. In 1936 he directed the pianist–composer Luis Alberti, who conducted his own orchestra in Santiago at the time, to move to the capital and work for him. For the next thirty years, Alberti composed and orchestrated songs that paid tribute to the General, his family and his policies. In the forties, he converted the original official merengue, 'Ecos de Cibao', to a new version, 'Compadre Pedro Juan', which became his theme tune. Alberti's hand-picked orchestra, which included the pianist father of Johnny Pacheco, was renamed Orquesta Generalísimo Trujillo and was launched in 1944 at the capital's most luxurious nightclub-casino

Out in the Dominican country villages, the traditional recreations were cock-fighting and playing and dancing merengue. This couple were photographed by US ethnomusicologist Verna Gillis, who recorded typical roots merengue in 1976.

inside the Hotel Jaragua on the seafront. They played in the hotel's elegant Patio Español – sedate and restrained music by today's standards, but at the time an infectious vehicle for propaganda.

When the Jaragua was demolished in 1985, Alberti's celebrated song, 'Luna sobre el Jaragua' (Moon above the Jaragua), was reworked as 'Réquiem sobre el Jaragua' by Juan Luis Guerra. 'It was a requiem for the hotel,' Guerra explained. 'At the end, we brought in the noise of the demolition as a background to the voice of Rafael Colón who had sung the original song.' A monstrous pink hotel complex rose from the dust.

Dominicans were bombarded with merengues. Trujillo's radio station, La

ABOVE: **Luis Alberti, pianist, composer and bandleader, who raised merengue from peasant entertainment to sophisticated dance band music.**
BELOW: **The National Folk Music and Dance Company, mid-1980s.**

Voz Dominica, run by the General's brother, sponsored competitions for tunes to be used in his campaigns – $1000 for a symphony and $200 for a merengue – and the music became irreversibly bound to a Dominican sense of identity. The General was obsessed with its 'purity' and forbade any references to jazz (Elvis Presley was the devil in disguise). Fradique Lazardo, who was regularly imprisoned under Trujillo, recalled, 'Some jazz bands did come here, but there was no opportunity to play jazz because that was "foreign music" and he didn't like anything foreign. You could hear Cuban and Mexican music on the radio, and mambo was very, very big here, especially Pérez Prado. Boleros were big too. But we only began to make Dominican records in the fifties; until then Columbia and RCA took our musicians to New York to record.'

It might be thought that after the assassination of Trujillo in 1961, merengue would have been thrown out and a new music installed to herald the People's Revolutionary Party. But merengue remains as strong a bond as it was in Trujillo's day. It *was* transformed, however. The first to pull the bricks from the wall was, ironically, a handsome young black vocalist called Juan de Dios, who had worked as a back-up singer in Orquesta San José, the in-house orchestra of Trujillo's radio station.

Sonia Silvestre (the Joan Baez of Dominican music) rose on a wave of late 1980s bachata songs. The electric production of her album, *Yo quiero andar* (I Want to Go), took these 'Songs of Bitterness' (*amargue*) to a sophisticated city audience.

Johnny Ventura is a most serious contributor to the modern history of merengue, but has always delivered his most radical changes with a broad smile and an X-rated hip-shake. His 'rich and tasty' penguin dance hooked the nation briefly in the mid-1970s.

MERENGUE'S ELVIS

In 1956 Juan de Dios organized a band inspired by American soul music and The Beatles. He changed his name to the more Americanized Johnny Ventura, cut down the line-up to a snappy 12-piece combo with just five horn players, and gave the band flashy soul-revue costumes and synchronized dance routines to match.

'When I started playing music in 1956', Ventura says, 'the musicians played sitting down and the people danced as if they were sleeping. We woke them up! The first singer to dance on stage was Joseo Mateo, the "King of Merengue", but he danced alone, in front of a full seated orchestra. With my band, all the musicians stood up, and all the singers danced. It was a revolution.' Ventura rewrote the rules of merengue. His weekly television show, *The Combo Show*, was compulsory viewing. 'People would listen to our songs on the radio during the week, then watch television on Sunday to see how to dance them! Each song came with different steps.' He added, with a sly grin, 'Our lyrics were slogans!' – they were also often raunchy double entendres.

Johnny Ventura pulled merengue from the society dancehall back onto the streets. But he never lost touch with the past. His television shows were platforms for the grandees of merengue, including saxophonist Félix Rosario, whose solos reveal their bebop origins, and the accordion players who were rapidly being replaced on stage by electric keyboards (and eventually synthesizers). Ventura watched as the studio was rocked by searing tunes from 'El ciego de Nagua' (The Blind Man from Nagua), the modernist Francisco Ulloa, and female virtuoso Fefita La Grande, whose solos fly like syncopated free jazz.

Ventura speeded up merengue, added a Cuban conga drum in the style of the New York-based conjuntos and proto-salsa bands, and boosted the tambora's beat. He brought back risqué lyrics and launched the fashion for erotic, hip-swivelling dance routines, performed like The Four Tops on speed. His audiences screamed like Beatles fans. For the next three decades, Ventura's huge-selling records preceded him on tours all over Latin America. He also made merengue a viable 'business', establishing a new 'pay-as-you-play' method of promoting records on radio. Known everywhere else as Payola, this is still a legitimate promotional system in Santo Domingo.

In 1964 Juan Bosch's democratically elected Revolutionary Party was toppled in a coup backed by President Johnson. After a brief civil war and a short occupation by the US Marines, rigged elections in 1965 installed a former Trujillo acolyte, General Joaquín Balaguer. Anti-Balaguer rallies drew crowds to the capital, and many leading singers joined the protest. One often-jailed activist was Rafael 'Cholo' Brenes, a guiding spirit of every new wave of Dominican music since the seventies. In that turbulent decade, Brenes studied in Argentina and Chile, where he hooked up with the protest singers involved in the nueva canción movement – Víctor Jara, Violetta Parra and Quilapallun. Back in Santo Domingo he recorded the first single for the young trumpeter Wilfrido Vargas, a samba called 'Como tú una flor' (A Flower Like You), and taught at the university. Former students were creating their own protest movement built around the bachata style of song. Its leaders were singer–songwriters Sonia Silvestre, Luis Díaz, and Víctor Víctor – a flamboyant, rebellious character who joined the Ministry of Culture in the nineteen. Their headquarters – a small bohemian club called Casa de Teatro – was a 'crucible for new music'.

In 1974 Brenes organized a festival called 'Siete Días del Pueblo' (Seven Days of the People) which united local bachateros with musicians from all over Latin America, including Cubans Silvio Rodríguez and Noel Nicolás, and Mercedes Sosa from Argentina, to name but a few. Nearly 40,000 people attended each night – until, by the end of the week, the police threatened to close it down. 'The consequence of the festival for me', says Brenes, 'was that every time I left the country and came back to the airport – straight to jail!' Also on the bill was the leading sixties protest musician, the bald-headed composer and singer Cuco Valoy, known as 'El Kojak de Merengue'. His hit songs, 'Páginas gloriosas' (Glorious Pages) and 'Himno de los rebeldes' (Hymn of the Rebels), had been rallying cries. Valoy launched his own radio station, Radio Tropical, in 1965, to make his opposition public. Johnny Ventura also exploited his popularity at anti-Balaguista and at 'Siete Dias' rallies – his satirical songs charted the country's political changes through to the late eighties, when he formally entered politics as a member of the House of Deputies, eventually becoming the mayor of Santo Domingo in the late nineties. But while middle-class bachateros played for the bohemian crowd, Johnny Ventura's audience cut across to the poor populations of the island's cities and towns. His songs and particularly his dance crazes obsessed the whole country. 'El Pingüino' (the Penguin), a craze of the early seventies, turned the Dominicans into strutting, arm-flapping birds.

THE MERENGUE CHEF

In the 1970s merengue was transformed by yet another magician. Just as Johnny Ventura had breathed rock'n'roll life into its lungs, the trumpeter, composer, singer and bandleader Wilfrido Vargas linked Santo Domingo with music from the Caribbean and South America.

Vargas had surfaced on the jazz-club scene in the 1960s, and in the mid-1970s had made his mark in a local band, Los Beduinos. They called their music Mini-Jazz, a name taken from the Haitian dancebands of the time. Their bass player Chery Jiménez described the band as follows: 'We were six guys from university – bass, guitar, trumpet, tambora and piano, plus a singer, and we had a violin too because we worked in an Arab nightclub and needed one to play their music.' The band started out playing topical bossa novas and jazz until Vargas suggested they play merengue. He took over the band and took up the harmonica – 'to get the accordion sound'.

Wilfrido Vargas's 1978 album *Punto y aparte!* (Full Stop!) was a turning point for merengue, featuring the hit song 'El barbarazo'. His 1984 compilation album, *Evolución*, reveals the prototype for new merengues in his eclectic range of crossovers with snappy Trinidadian soca horns, electric guitar solos

Cuco (Pupo) Valoy (born 1937), worked as a gardener until he and his brother Martín formed a guitar duo, Los Ahijados (The Protégés), and had hits with Cuban son classics. In his long career he has mixed merengue and salsa and delivered many thoughtful, catchy and often humorous songs. The 1979 salsa hit 'Juliana' was reborn in storming mereng-house style by DLG in 1994, with Valoy's warbling, operatic voice upfront.

WILFRIDO VARGAS

ABOVE: Trumpeter Wilfrido Vargas (born 1949) is merengue's most significant modern producer and composer. He made his name with his own spirited big bands and with a chain of youthful protégés – Los Hijos del Rey (The King's Sons), Las Chicas del Can (The Good-Time Girls), the Altamira Band Show (named after his hometown), and the New York Band (his first mainland venture). With these slick and poppy eighties line-ups he nurtured a generation of young singers – particularly Sergio Vargas, Sandy Reyes and Ruby Pérez, who became the most popular solo voices for most of the nineties. With his own showband, though, Wilfrido Vargas delivered complicated, musical cocktails with a slapstick, vaudevillean flare, charging around the stage with his silver trumpet hanging on his arm. It was a stark contrast to the supercharged, voguish, erotic dancing of his contemporaries.

Wilfrido Vargas's most successful creations.
ABOVE RIGHT: Sergio Vargas (centre), with Los Hijos del Rey, live on children's television in 1987.
RIGHT: Las Chicas del Can, caught in a mutual grooming moment before going on stage. Their giggling singing voices were heard to perfection in their greatest hit, 'Juana la Cubana'.

and hissy hi-hats, borrowed from the Haitian Mini-Jazz dancebands and from America's doowop, Platters' harmonies, New Orleans brass and Glen Miller saxophones. The pushing thud of a bass drum paved the way for the electronic drum beats of the nineties. He even incorporated Bach piano riffs.

By the seventies and eighties Vargas was the most inventive Dominican composer. He also ran an auxiliary band of protégés called Los Hijos del Rey (The King's Sons), a hotbed of teenage talent. Their records contain several Vargas trademarks, including his silver mambo trumpet, a falsetto vocal lead and a funky Spanglish proto-rap. The original members have almost all remained central to the merengue story: falsetto lead singer Fernandito Villalona and back-up singers Raulín and Rasputín, and in the next generation the soulful Sergio Vargas – all top soloists today; the Kenton brothers, whose dance routines were based on their passion for karate; pianist Bonny Cepeda, who introduced synthesizers into merengue in the eighties and exported merengue to Puerto Rico in the nineties; and the studious tambora drummer Catarey, who systematically reworked its rhythms. Another Vargas production was Las Chicas del Can (The Good-Time Girls), a competent, fun-and-glamour girl-group whose every single and album brought novelty-act glamour to the charts.

In the eighties, Vargas cast further into the Caribbean and Latin America, pulling into his own full-size showband the sparkling electric guitars and splashing cymbals used by Haitian bands, the lilting horns and brass of Martiniquan zouk, and Colombia's closely related accordion-led cumbias and vallenatos. His 1984 hit *El jardinero* (The Gardener) was a turning point for merengue, a fusion of all those ingredients. Vargas's guest appearances with the Fania All Stars spread his infectious, innovative music all over Latin America and spawned many local changes. He incorporated Jamaican dancehall reggae into merengue in the smash hit song 'La chica de los ojos cafés' (The Girl with Coffee Eyes), and launched a trend in Colombia when Grupo Kerube covered the song in an electronically more extreme version.

While Wilfrido Vargas's Beduinos were creating ripples with their first album in 1974, the young classical music prodigy – and medical student – Michel Camilo was hanging out with a bohemian crowd in bars and small theatres. 'I had long hair and a beard, and we played jazz: that's what hippies did

Juan Luis Guerra y 4.40

The six-foot-four-inch son of a Dominican baseball champion, Juan Luis Guerra has little in common with most salsa or merengue stars. His middle-class background and education in jazz guitar at Boston's Berklee College, and his taste for The Beatles and Manhattan Transfer harmonies, Pat Metheny's fusion-jazz guitar, and the South African vocal group Ladysmith Black Mambazo, all single him out from the merengue pack.

4.40's original, most perfect line-up: Juan Luis Guerra (left, in trilby) with Maridalia Hernández, Mariela Mercado and Roger Zayas-Bazán.

Guerra founded Grupo 4.40 (named after the 'A' tuning at 4.40) in the early eighties with friends Roger Zayas-Bazán, Maridalia Hernández and Mariela Mercado. Their 1985 record, *Mudanza y acarreo* (Moves and Changes), was a mellow performance of studiously copied Manhattan Transfer style harmonies. From there they adventured into unfamiliar Dominican rhythms, unearthed by their restlessly curious percussionist, Catarey. Then, in the late eighties, as a frenzy of insanely fast merengues shook the Latin world, 4.40 delivered a shockingly different series of records based on a softer, more poetic version of merengue and a rural Dominican drinking music called 'bachata'.

In 1987 Guerra had written a song for a TV commercial for coffee called 'Ojalá que llueva café' (Let It Rain Coffee) which became an anthem for the island's impoverished peasant coffee growers. It was the basis of an album of the same name which launched 4.40 into the Latin world. *Bachata rosa* (Pink Bachata) followed, bringing merengue its first Grammy in 1991 and selling five million copies. Guerra's disarmingly charming, romantic and surreal songs, and his clever, guitar-led tunes converted young middle-class Dominicans from rock to the music on their doorsteps. They also sold Spanish audiences on salsa and merengue for the first time.

All through the nineties, Guerra's records contained enough surprises to earn golden sales. *Fogarate* (Sudden Fever), in 1994, turned to country merengue; the 1998 release, 'Ni es lo mismo, ni es igual' (Neither the Same Nor Equal), included some merengue-raps, doowop harmonies and the now trademark African guitars.

Guerra produces music as slowly and thoughtfully as he talks. But on stage he leaps into a new role: 'The band grows to a 12-piece with four dancers,' he says with sudden enthusiasm, 'There's so much choreography, we're all dancing and moving around, it gets really fiery.'

4.40 in full flight: five dancers in a merengue blur out front, and the static, bearded figure of the band's leader and songwriter, Juan Luis Guerra (right), serenely supervising the animation of the poems which set Latin America alight.

then,' said the clean-cut pianist two decades later. Camilo joined the avant-garde bachata clan at the Casa del Teatro. His group, Baroco 21, was influenced by the Modern Jazz Quartet and The Swingles Singers. 'There were twenty-one of us, all students. Jazz was in, then merengue became popular, and we had dancers, then we got too big for the club. We performed at the National Theatre – and even played one night to President Balaguer in the Capitol building.'

The clique was the starting point in the career of Juan Luis Guerra, who was by then also writing and recording advertising jingles with his friend Roger Zayas-Bazán. The lanky jazz guitarist and musical all-rounder who had studied in the US teamed up with singers Maridalia Hernández and Mariela Mercado to form 4.40, and sang sambas and Manhattan Transfer harmonies ('We spent weeks practising their songs,' said Guerra), Beatles-influenced tunes and jazz classics.

EMCA STUDIOS, THE MERENGUE POWERHOUSE

EMCA studios was responsible for about 80 percent of all merengue albums in the eighties and was also used for recording radio and television jingles. The nucleus of 4.40 spent most of their teenage years there, making hit jingles. Only Vargas and Ventura took their own bands into the studios; the other chart bands sent their lead and back-up singers, and the bands mimed on stage.

The backbone of the sessions was a group known as 'the core', intense musicians with classical and wide-ranging backgrounds: former salsa and Latin Jazz saxophone supremo Crispín Fernández, who published two merengue saxophone tutors and today plays flute in the Santo Domingo Symphony Orchestra; trumpeter Kaki Ruiz, whose nickname is 'El Alicate' (The Pliers); Catarey, the tambora drummer; Sonny Ovallo, the keyboards player with a passion for Bach; arranger Manuel Tejada, who became the key merengue producer of the late nineties and whose Minilab studios eventually overtook EMCA; studio engineers Salvador Morales and July Ruiz (whose interest in world music led to future crossover productions in New York and Miami); and the keyboards player Ramón Orlando (son of Cuco Valoy), who moonlighted from his father's band and his own hit Orquesta Internacional.

In the summer of 1988, a few weeks after recording songs for a new album, Los Hijios del Rey were on tour in Venezuela with Juan Luis Guerra's 4.40 when their tour bus crashed, killing Catarey and two local musicians. Wilfrido Vargas wrote an obituary in the national newspaper; EMCA studios posted a wall of tributes from the musicians. Outraged criticisms appeared alongside poems, since 4.40 had flown the journey while Catarey and the 'boys' went by bus. Guerra paid tribute in the moving song, 'Angel para una tambora' (Angel of the Tambora).

Catarey's death sent merengue society into crisis. The Ministry of Tourism and ACROARTE – the nearest thing to a musicians' union – set up a conference to discuss 'The State of Merengue'. Ex-president Juan Bosch, hoping to return to power, ranted about the decline in standards, dirty dancing and sexy lyrics. Modernists clashed with purists who refused to recognize modern merengue. Johnny Ventura recited examples of lewd traditional merengue classics; Ramón Orlando pulled out a portable electric piano and demonstrated the connections between merengue cibaeno and the big-band styles. And the media lapped it up.

'CHICHI' PERALTA

Percussionist Pedro 'Chichi' Peralta became a merenguero as a four-year-old when he made a small tambora drum. In his teens he recorded percussion parts for television and radio jingles and anonymously backed chart records. He joined Fernando Echavarría's eclectic samba-rengue band, Familia Andre, and in 1988 moved into Juan Luis Guerra's 4:40 for a six-year blaze of stardom and breathless experimentation. In 1996 he leapt into the unknown with his own big band, La Familia, which includes singer–songwriter Jandy Félix. Félix's 1997 hit, 'Amor narcótico', is a quirky salsa-merengue hybrid which rides a seductive techno-reggae groove and is dramatically drenched by strings. Peralta refers to his 'dream mix' of bachata, bolero, blues and jazz with local voodoo rhythms (ga-ga) as 'Cutucupla Cupla'.

Singer Kinito Méndez (left) makes no bones about his heroes in this 1998 top-selling album, *Homenaje al caballo* (Homage to the Stallion – nickname of the veteran merenguero, Johnny Ventura [right]). Singing with Pochi's Cocoband was a rehearsal for Méndez's own solo career. Already on their fast, bubbling, poppy collections, his auctioneer's speed of delivery and his facility with long, chanted lines were just showy gimmicks around a strong, versatile voice.

BUBBLES OF LOVE

The tragic Venezuelan tour coincided with the start of Juan Luis Guerra mania in Latin America and Europe. 4.40 stopped the traffic in the centre of Madrid every night for a week during their concerts. 'Ojalá que llueva café' (Let It Rain Coffee') became their signature tune. 'The audiences all took out umbrellas and opened them when we played,' Guerra recalls. Just as Rubén Blades had broken salsa's pattern of tired love songs, so Guerra transformed merengue and bachata with his poetic and surreal stories of everyday life. 'The farmers began to sing that song like a plea – "Let it rain coffee!" – while they were doing their crops,' he said. 'It had a great impact everywhere we went in Latin America because all Latin Americans have the same reality. The song is like a hymn.' His other explosive hits included 'Bubujas de amor' (Bubbles of Love), a surreal, erotic poem, and 'Bilirubina', a bizarre love story on the unlikely subject of bile pigments. The battle for purity was forever lost.

All over Latin America, imitators of 4.40 included 4-part vocal harmonies, breathy children's choruses and electric guitars in their songs. The most blatant copyist was Alex Mansilla, a former backroom musician for 4.40, whose group Cañaveral plundered 4.40's trademarks – and got away with it. The 4.40 mothership also launched an original: the former conga player Pedro 'Chichi' Peralta, whose ambitious big-band project was supported in 1997 by a new free-spending label, Caimán. Peralta incorporated lurching dancehall reggae rhythms, brassy skippy soca beats, techno beats, rock guitars, African guitars, acoustic guitars and a string section into an irresistibly dynamic first album, *Pa'otro la'o* (To the Other Side).

In spite of the richness of the music emerging from Santo Domingo in the late eighties and early nineties, imported salsa romantica threatened the market. When the Gypsy Kings unleashed a craze for flamenco, everyone from

Merengue's purity was dissolved in the eighties and nineties crazes for Brazilian lambada, Nicaraguan punta, hiphop, rap and reggae. With the Cocoband, lead singer Pochi ushered in a determinedly tropical fusion of merengue with all these ingredients; the Coco sound included 'swing' brass; short, jolting choruses and percussive breaks; and choruses that played with the latest black Dominican street-slang.

Gloria Estefán to Celia Cruz recorded 'Bamboleo', but Sergio Vargas's flamboyant flamenco-rengue version topped them all. A new input into Latin music came to salsa from the non-Spanish Caribbean and some clever new flavours appeared in merengue. The Cocoband, led by singer Pochi (Alfonso Vásquez), produced breathless merengues and cool bachatas threaded with traces of soca, soukous and cumbia. Dance crazes like the Central American punta and the macarena, with their brisk, commanding rhythms, pulled salsa couples apart and into sexy Latin line-dance formations. Their rhythms merged easily into merengue's formulae. Jamaica's X-rated dances such as the bogle and butterfly were incorporated by many new groups, especially in New York. The singer Kinito Méndez sang in reggae-influenced Spanglish raps and scored a hit with 'El suero del amor' (The Love Serum), which turned back to the Dominican Indians for inspiration. His use of the bandoneon (accordion) and traditional drumming behind a girls' chorus produced a charming effect.

The arriviste who is taking merengue into the new century is sultry Puerto Rican singer Olga Tañón. Her first solo album, *Sola*, in 1992, struck an alliance with Mexican singer–songwriter Marc Anthony Solís, who tailored songs to her disarmingly mature voice with its penchant for strident flamenco outbursts.

Merengue's seemingly infinite versatility was proved yet again in the late nineties crossovers with electro-dance music. Much merengue today moves to an electronic pulse. Launching the trend were Proyecto Uno and Los Ilegales, who gave it a new twist; fast-talking rappers Sandy and Papo; and two late-nineties boy bands, Fulanito and Sancocho, both versed in their family's music, who acknowledged that musical boundaries are for crossing, not fighting over. Former Wilfrido Vargas band member and musical inventor Roy Tavare introduced sequencers and mereng-house to Santo Domingo, then moved to Miami in 1997. His intelligent productions veer from harsh electro-merengues and upbeat reworkings of various Latin rhythms with a nod to rock music, to poetic bachatas. One of his regular accomplices is merengue pianist Ramón Orlando, who pioneered rap-a-rengue with a clatteringly exotic late-eighties single *Toma! Toma!*.

While merengue is still thoroughly Dominican, what counts as merengue at the end of the century would be virtually unrecognizable to those musicians who performed for General Trujillo in Santo Domingo's elegant palm-court hotels in the thirties. Many Dominican musicians moved to San Juan, following in the wake of former Wilfrido Vargas protegée Bonny Cepeda. By the late nineties, merengue's axis had tilted: the capital had become San Juan, its superstars Puerto Ricans – Manny Manuel and Toño Rosario, and the latest 'Queen of Merengue', the wonderfully arresting contralto singer Olga Tañón, whose repertoire ranges from downright funky, racing merengues, to deep, throaty, soaring flamencos. Merengue's most valuable mouthpiece at the end of the nineties is the long-haired, rock-styled Elvis Crespo, who emerged as a soloist from Grupo Mania in 1998 with the near-million seller *Suavamente*. In 1999 he drove unapologetically hard merengue, sung in Spanish, straight into the US top fifty with *Píntame* (Paint Me), more proof that Latin music is today, once again, universal.

MIAMI: NINETY MILES TO CUBA

Chapter 7 MIAMI: 90 miles to Cuba

I started out to go to Cuba,
Soon I was at Miami Beach.
There, not so very far from Cuba,
Oh, what a rhumba they teach.

So I never went to Cuba,
But I got all its atmosphere,
I'll save Havana for mañana,
Meanwhile I'll have them in my reach.

I found all the charm of Old Havana,
In a rhumba at Miami Beach.

OPPOSITE: **The Calle Ocho Festival, held every March in Miami's Little Havana, attracts bands and fans from all of Latin America – except Cuba.**
ABOVE: **'So near and yet so foreign'. A 1930s poster enticing visitors from Miami to Cuba.**

THE KING OF KITSCH, Xavier Cugat, recorded 'Miami Beach Rhumba' during his heyday as purveyor of rhumbas and mambos for Miami dancers, movie soundtracks and the world's gramophones. The lyrics are even more apt today than they were in the twenties and thirties, when Prohibition made Havana an offshore drinking haven for North Americans. Today, Miami has its own sound, its own stars, and is a centre of the expanding Latin American music business.

The majority of Cuban-Americans living in Miami will have to 'save Havana for mañana' because they can't or won't go back under the present regime. But the tide is turning fast and Miami Cubans have been forced to accept that the rest of the world thinks Castro's Cuban music is deeply hip. The major American record companies are poised in their Miami Beach offices to sign the new generation of singers and bands just as soon as Washington drops its trade embargo.

For musicians like Gloria and Emilio Estefán and others in the local super-star clique, whose politics do not allow them to trade with Castro's Cuba, it is doubly painful to watch as Europe and Latin America revel in the music being produced ninety miles from their power-boat's landing dock. Since the late nineties, the enemy has arrived in the camp: the Havana salsa idol Issac Delgado performed in the Nostalgia club in Miami's Little Havana – and survived; the leader of Los Van Van visits his family there. In the autumn of 1998, MIDEM's Latin and Caribbean music trade fair ignored local opposition and invited a super-group of Cuban musicians, including Grammy winners Compay Segundo and Chucho Valdés. About three hundred people demonstrated outside. The following day singer Omara Portuondo and pianist Valdés were photographed in Havana looking at their performance pictures on the front page of the *Miami Herald*. The ninety-mile gap was indeed getting narrower.

Today, almost half the population of Miami has family roots in Cuba. The city has had a right-of-centre Cuban mayor on and off for several years. Xavier Suárez was in power in the 1980s, and won back his seat in 1997; he was the only American mayor who refused to greet Nelson Mandela during his nationwide 'Freedom Tour', because of the latter's endorsement of Fidel Castro. Miami's uniquely Cuban tinge starts at the airport. The city speaks with a Cuban accent and moves to the clave beat. Cuban Miami – once restricted to the district around Calle Ocho (8th Street), known as Little Havana – now fills the whole city. English is still the official language, but most people flick between the two, with the musical hybrid Spanglish in between.

But Miami is more than just a Cuban city: it houses an estimated 1 percent of the Caribbean's population (legal figures) and a third of all US Nicaraguans (an estimated 200,000 legals). Other recent arrivals have come from Central America and Mexico. The city has been likened to an unstirred paella, whose ingredients simmer together, absorbing each other's flavours, but remaining separate.

Miami, 1940: Gangsta chic for bandleader José Curbelo (right) and his newly discovered teenaged drummer, Tito Puente (left). The pair were photographed against Curbelo's first car, bought from the proceeds of playing at local hotels. They drove the car home to New York.

'LA FLORIDA'

Miami's history is as old as that of the continent: the land was first settled in 1565 by Spain's Juan Ponce de León, who called the settlement 'La Florida' (The Flowery Place). The region passed between Spanish and English hands and was finally dealt to the Americans in 1814. But Miami only developed from a collection of scattered fruit orchards in the Everglades at the turn of the twentieth century: the first tourists followed the new railroad laid down the coast in 1896, and Miami was born, sold from the outset on its climate.

The early winter travellers, known as 'snowbirds', arrived from New York, Boston, Philadelphia and Baltimore for sun, sea and dancing in the first resort, Miami Beach, which was built at the height of art deco magic in the 1920s and 1930s on a long, narrow spit of land off the mainland. What became Little Havana grew up around the axial 8th Street (Calle Ocho) – acres of Spanish-tropical ranch-style bungalows with wrought-iron verandas and tropical gardens. In stark contrast, the 'new city' of Downtown Miami, constructed on eighties drug revenues, is a colony of fantastical postmodern structures which illuminate the city's skyline at night with a neon son et lumière.

In the 1930s, Miami Beach rang to the youthful voices of Northern tourists and the beat of the rhumba bands. By the fifties and sixties it had slumped into retirement, a final destination for Jewish couples and widows who had danced there decades earlier. They were joined by Latin American newcomers, welfare survivors at the base of the drug pyramid and a smattering of tourists. Business thrived at the Cuban coffee shops, Jewish delis, beauty parlours and all-night restaurants.

Entertainment was provided by tea-dances and socials, a handful of country music bars catering for 'Southern' white Americans, and a few Cuban clubs. By the late 1970s, when the Miami Beach Preservation Society began its rehabilitation of the crumbling art deco hotels, the city had stirred back into life. The elderly Jewish sunbathers and the mongrel junkies were eventually ousted from South Beach, replaced by tourists and local Yuppies and Yucas (Young Urban Cuban Americans). The new soundtrack is a heat-hazy collage of pumping rock and reggae and hissing salsa, screeching tyres and conversations in Spanish and English.

The roots of the so-called Miami Sound lie in the 1930s when the first wave of migrants arrived in town from Cuba. Among them was the family of the mayor of Santiago de Cuba, Desi Arnaz Senior, who fled the violent revolution against General Gerardo Machado. Arnaz traded a sophisticated life in Cuba for a backwater. During Prohibition, the Mob occupied Havana, built, ran and stocked the city's nightclubs, casinos and hotels and set up their luxury family mansions in Miami, just half-an-hour's plane ride away. One of Desi Arnaz Junior's schoolfriends was Sonny (son of Al) Capone. While Old Miami was built on moonshine and smuggled rum, the modern city was paid for by drug dollars, and in both instances music was the cover and beneficiary.

In full-blown rhumba shirts, Desi Arnaz's first band gave Miami's modest new Cuban population a taste of home with their showbiz congas and rhumba dancing act. Arnaz (with the guitar) already revealed the boyish charm that would beguile viewers to his long-running *I Love Lucy* shows.

In the 1930s the hotels and nightclubs in Miami were only just beginning to feature on the books of New York agents and the 'snowbirds' were starting to fit Miami into their winter schedules after summer in the Catskills. Their presence attracted the same bands that played for them in New York and in the mountains. This hedonistic period throbbed to Xavier Cugat's rhumbas and lured Desi Arnaz Junior back to town. Arnaz had worked briefly with Cugat's band in New York but left for Miami in the winter of 1936, saying 'If there are Cubans there, I'll give them Cuban music.' When he arrived he found very few Cubans. Moreover, hardly anyone knew how to dance to his rhumbas, and his non-Latino musicians could barely play them. So Arnaz came up with an idea that captivated his audience and spread way beyond Miami. While his mother sewed a batch of rhumba shirts with frilly sleeves, he coached the band in the simplified Cuban carnival routines he had danced as a child, in the hope that this would hide their musical inadequacies. In his autobiography, *A Book*, he

Gloria Estefán

Gloria Estefán is Miami's Golden Girl, the singer who put her city on the world's music map and introduced millions of rock fans to Latin music. Her dual cultural passport has allowed her to slide between American rock and ballads and Latin American salsa and boleros without stumbling or missing a syncopated beat; her dramatic changes of image – from girl rocker to disco flame, flamenco singer to Cuban diva – were coordinated with hugely successful hit songs which followed the latest music fashions and filled the world's dance charts.

The mid-eighties Latin disco hit 'Conga' launched a string of million-selling rock songs so salsa audiences had to wait until 1990 for the next upbeat Latin dancer, 'Oye mi canto!' (Listen to My Song!). They took to the dancefloors en masse with the sparkling 1993 album *Mi tierra* (My Land), a full-tilt salsa collection played by Cuban American alumni including Cachao and Paquito D'Rivera. Her voice – in Spanish – had found its natural home. In 1995 the Colombian songwriter Kike Santander produced *Abriendo puertas* (Opening Doors), which coaxed Estefán into an irresistible Nashville-Latin twang and led her into fashionable vallenato accordion music territory.

Behind Gloria Estefán's career is the sharp and imaginative business manager and record producer – her husband, Emilio. He helped turn the reluctant, podgy teenager who preferred studying psychology to performing with his Miami Cuban Boys into the supremely confident, relentlessly entertaining personality who has performed for two American presidents, received eight Grammies, opened two Olympic ceremonies (Seoul and Atlanta), and sung and danced on every major stage in the world. In 1993 Gloria Estefán followed fellow Cubans Desi Arnaz and Celia Cruz onto Hollywood's Walk of Fame.

The Estefáns' story is a classic rags-to-riches, immigrants-in-the-USA tale of (Cuban) children growing up in a poor, marginalized community and becoming one of the country's richest couples. Admittedly the story was interrupted by a series of horrendous accidents – a tour bus crash which left Gloria temporarily paralysed, a powerboat accident which killed a young jet skier – but these appeared only to toughen her ambitions and deepen her involvement with other people's problems. Gloria Estefán's rooms of gold discs, her waterside house on Miami's exclusive Star Island, the couple's modernist studios and offices *and* their obviously happy marriage are convincing proof to fellow *Latin* Americans that the American Dream occasionally works – and that Cubans are Americans too.

The Miami Sound Machine's 12" remix of 'Conga!' by Puerto Rican DJ Pedro Flores is an everlasting dance hit. Its main attractions are Emilio Estefán's conga drumming, Gloria Estefán's animated chanting, and the show-stopping piano solo by Paquito Hechavarria.

explains that because there were no good percussionists, he strapped a conga drum over his shoulder and played as he danced, leading them like carnival drummers. He got the band drunk on Bacardi, handed them percussion instruments and led them round the club to a conga rhythm. The audience rose from their seats and followed. A craze which spun around the world was launched – though it was actually Miguelito Valdés, 'Mister Babalú', who launched the conga in New York and Arnaz who took it to Miami. It was Arnaz's '1-2-3, KICK!' which spread both his name and the dance around the war-torn world, and led Miami's visitors in exuberant, high-kicking conga lines.

After World War II most musicians avoided Miami and stayed with the excitement of the great mambo and cha-cha-cha bands in New York. Castro's victory in Cuba in 1959 and his adoption of Communism in 1962 would transform the city – thousands of families landed at Miami airport complete with baggage, cash and children. They were mostly doctors, lawyers, office workers and business managers, but there were also scores of musicians, who feared that socialism might dry up their opportunities. This exodus formed the basis of the Cuban population which dominates Miami today. At that time, the city was still a backwater and many musicians passed straight through. In 1959 the singer Roberto Torres stayed just one day: 'There was no money there – only water and palms! I moved to New York – the capital of the world. I needed a big city to start in.' Torres founded Orquesta Broadway with friends from home and returned to Miami with his own record company in 1982. Broadway's flautist Eddie Zervigón stayed longer but admitted, 'There were no jobs, no tourism and only three or four nightclubs.'

The Cubans who arrived in Miami as children are today running the city. The musicians among them created 'The Miami Sound'. The most significant players in the early fusions were Emilio Estefán, husband and manager of Gloria, real-estate developer, record producer and founder of the Miami Sound Machine; Willie Chirino, bass player, singer, songwriter and band-leader who carved a Beatles-and-salsa-influenced style and a rock'n'rollers' image; Carlos Oliva, whose band Los Sobrinos del Juez (The Judge's Nephews) stayed closer to Latin rock; and Joe Galdo, former Miami Sound Machine drummer, now a record producer.

Both Estefán and Chirino had to provide money for their families while they were still at school, though Chirino was already earning good dollars as a nightclub drummer when his parents followed him from Cuba. Emilio Estefán worked in restaurant kitchens. Their friend the drummer Tony Soto, a working musician in Cuba, was luckier: his mother bought a hotel which had a piano. Chirino adopted the place as his second home and rehearsal room. As teenagers, Estefán, Chirino and Co. called themselves the 'We're Missing Cuba Team' (Añorado Cuba). Soto reminisced, 'We used to dance and play music – twenty or thirty of us – in the street and at youth centres, playing the carnival music we played in Cuba. Our favourite weekend hangout was the El Farito Park, South of Miami. We'd go there and jam in our swimsuits. Our big song was Celo González's 'Vamos pa'la playa, caliente el sol' (We're Going to the Beach, the Sun's Hot).'

Throughout the 1960s, tourism was still virtually non-existent, and immigration was limited to sporadic arrivals from Haiti or Jamaica. But the young generation of Cuban-Americans were brewing something that would erupt in the following decade. Disco music had a major impact in Miami; it seems to

ROBERTO TORRES

Roberto Torres is one of Miami's elder statesmen whose evocative songs and nostalgic record covers have nurtured thousands of exiled Cubans since the early 1960s. His shy, tuxedoed figure is a familiar sight at the city's most lavish parties and glitziest launches; his hits and distinctive, neat vocals have been used since the 1980s in radio jingles selling everything from real estate to coffee. Following his sixties success in New York with the charanga Orquesta Broadway, Torres carved a niche with productions for his SAR and Guajiro labels, reworked Cuban classics played by musicians from Havana's heyday bands. In early eighties Miami, his jaunty new Cuban-Colombian fusion of flute and accordion known as charanga-vallenato brought him unexpected gold discs and a new image – his schoolfriend and record sleeve artist José Esposito painted him in the picture above on horseback, wearing a Colombian straw hat. Esposito described Torres's voice as coloured by the smell of herbs washed by the waters of their childhood river, the Mayabeque.

Willie Chirino at the Sheraton Hotel in 1977. Within a few years the wide lapels and flares had been swapped for black jeans and leather jacket – and the mellow guitar songs for rowdy, rock-influenced salsa. He performed at an unforgettable late eighties wedding reception wearing all black with leopard-skin brothel creepers and matching tie.

have originated there. The white American singer H. W. Casey (K. C.) insists that his Sunshine Band made the first musical moves with their funky, guitar-led dance tracks peppered with Cuban beats. K. C. was part of a local multiracial soul music scene featuring the underrated Latin r'n'b guitarist Little Beaver and singer Timmy Thomas, who boosted their deliciously laid-back soul songs with a light conga beat. The gospel singer Betty Wright took two Latinized disco songs, 'Clean Up Woman' and 'Pain', to the UK charts.

In the bloom of discomania, the local band Foxy reached the charts and launched several key musicians. Foxy's drummer, Joe Galdo, joined Emilio Estefán's Miami Sound Machine, playing in the backing band, The Jerks. He left when Gloria Estefán went solo. Foxy's Latin percussionist was Ritchie Puente, son of the Mambo King, Tito, whose first significant gig had taken place in Miami in 1934. Foxy's pin-up lead singer was Ish Ledesma, a Cuban who moved from a brief solo career to producing Latin hiphop songs for his girl group, Company B, in the late 1980s. Unlike the Estefáns or Joe Galdo, Ledesma's productions rejected Cuban music, just occasionally adding a cowbell's ring as 'a people mover'.

The eighties belonged to Gloria Estefán and the Miami Sound Machine, who coasted through a succession of massively successful, wonderfully appealing Latin-flavoured pop and dance music songs – and multiple Grammy awards. By then, Willie Chirino, Miami's most dedicated crossover Latino, had established a key position in the city with his Cuban-percussion-led salsa-rock band. His most lucrative work came from wedding parties and local festivals and he rarely ventured abroad. Chirino crafted a distinctive singing style to match his musical experiments with electronic drums and synthesizers, merengue beats, voice-manipulated ballads, soca, reggae and rap, but never deserted the salsa framework. Increasingly, traces of influence from the new Cuban bands (particularly Los Van Van and N.G. La Banda) appeared in his songs – music he heard on the radio from Havana.

Chirino played electric bass guitar and wore black leathers. Except for the core of conga players and Cuban percussionists, his band resembled a rock outfit. His conga player – Tany Gil – was a crucial element and a connection to the purer Cuban music scene in the city. In his spare time, Gil ran the Tania label from his Coral Gables home, which was something of a Cuban musicians' social club where eminent musicians turned up to drink coffee and rum and listen to music. From those gatherings emerged some significant but overlooked recordings. The legendary mambo bass player Israel 'Cachao' López lived round the corner and survived by playing in the Miami Symphony Orchestra and at barely advertised Happy Hour sessions in the city's more sophisticated Cuban bars. Gil organized a series of sessions along the lines of Cachao's influential late 1950s albums of descargas recorded in Havana just before the Revolution. He brought along Miami's most versatile pianist, the dandified Paquito Hechavarría, who was responsible for the funky solo which burns the heart of the Miami Sound Machine hit 'Conga!', and the trumpeter Walfredo de los Reyes, who played on the original descargas. *Cachao y su descargas* contains some of the most exhilarating, varied music in Cachao's career and is a dazzling display of awesome technique with the double bass.

Not all of the sixties generation deviated from the true Cuban line. Charanga 76 was founded by the percussionist Felipe Martínez and singer Hansel Martínez as a classic Cuban flute-and-violins formula with a modern edge. Martínez left in 1980, having met his perfect vocal partner in Raul Alfonso. As Hansel y Raul, harmonizing to a charanga backing, they created a special niche in Miami's salsa aristocracy. Their hit records were interrupted briefly in the late eighties when Martínez was jailed for cocaine trafficking.

The next significant wave of immigrants arrived after 1981 as part of a 125,000-strong exodus from the Cuban port of Mariel (hence Marielitos). Many were unskilled and black, or political or criminal outlaws. Some were musicians. They were temporarily housed in a tented city under the main I-95 Highway which looms over Little Havana – today's location for the main stage at the annual Calle Ocho festival. The eighties also saw waves of immigrants from Colombia, Nicaragua, Honduras and the Dominican Republic. By the time Reagan boosted the Contra armies, and the not-unconnected Colombian cocaine cartel intensified its operations in the city, Miami was being dubbed 'The Capital of Latin America' – Spanish was the language of business and salsa the language of pleasure.

Many successful musicians moved to suburban high-security estates divided by nationality. The former Nicaraguan rock star Alfonso Lobo ('The Wolfman') arrived in Miami on a stretcher, having been shot up in a hijacked plane. He eventually moved into a Nicaraguan enclave in Kendal and started releasing mildly political songs. He launched a band called Wolfman and the Pack, playing metal guitar to a Chicano and salsa backing. The short-lived all-star band included Carlos Santana's percussionist and Wolfman's old school friend, Chepito Arreas. Wolfman sent a copy of his first single, *Freedom Fighter*, to President Reagan. For the record sleeve, he wore a guerrilla's bandana around his head, a sash of bullets across his chest, and held his Fender guitar like an Uzi.

HANSEL Y RAUL

Not all sixties Miami musicians deviated from the Cuban line. In 1976 percussionist Felipe Martínez founded a classic violins-and-flute charanga, Charanga 76. The seductive, grainy-smooth voice of Hansel Martínez took the band's first song, 'Soy', written by Willie Chirino, to charts beyond Miami. In 1980 the addition of singer Raul Alfonso launched one of the great harmonizing duets in salsa. Four years later they set up alone as Hansel y Raul, a more modernized charanga. Their stream of hits was interrupted in the late eighties when Martínez was jailed for trafficking cocaine; a temporary inconvenience – he released an album from inside jail, having done the business over a pay-phone.

Alfonso Lobo, 'The Wolfman', studied agriculture in the UK in the sixties and hung out with Jimi Hendrix. He returned to Nicaragua to become a Latin-rock star, driving around in a bright pink Mercedes.

CALLE OCHO – LATIN CARNIVAL

A perfect introduction to Miami's rich Latin music scene is the world famous Calle Ocho Cuban Carnival. This major event in the calendar was founded in 1978 when a group of Cubans calling themselves the Kiwanis Club of Little Havana (named after a tribe of Cuban Indians) held a street party on 8th Street. Twenty years later it is a 23-block extravaganza stretching from sleepy suburbia at one end of the street, to urban chaos below Interstate I-95 at the other. Normally 8th Street is a typical Latin American high street providing most things to support a Cuban lifestyle – from beans and rice and yucca and yams to magnetic saints to pin to the car's dashboard. A couple of family record stores cater for the Cuban music nostalgia trade, along with up-to-date salsa, while botánica shops provide spiritual counsellors and artefacts for the santería religion. Halfway down the street, close to Celia Cruz Way, is Freedom Park, with the Bay of Pigs memorial, an eternal flame burning in a vast metal bowl above the street, supported by a ring of waist-high rockets. In José Martí Park, rows of old men play dominoes and shoot the breeze while waiting to go 'home'.

The Cuban country music look – dungarees and diamanté – for the Queen, Celina González, and her eighties protégée, Albita Rodríguez, photographed in 1987.

Every March Calle Ocho attracts over a million people, all crushed together to see their favourite bands. The high point of the week is the Sunday parade and the coronation of the King or Queen. Past carnival monarchs have included the Cuban divas Olga Guillot and Celia Cruz, 'The Dominican Elvis' (merengue master Johnny Ventura) and local girl-made-good, Gloria Estefán. In the year of Estefán's triumph, 1988, Gloria and Emilio led a conga line down Calle Ocho and broke the record in the *Guinness Book of Records* with more than 119,000 people wriggling behind them. The event coincided with the start of Gloria Estefán's astounding conquest of the non-Spanish-speaking world. Increasingly, other music has been included on the programmes alongside the familiar salsa, cumbias and merengues: rootsy accordion vallenato music from the Colombian valleys; raucous Mexican mariachi bands, and Nicaragua's sensationally erotic 'Punta' bands, whose winding and grinding dancers outdo even the salsa crowd.

Booming above the street's salsa beats are the bass-heavy concoctions from the youth scene. Hybrids of salsa-rap, mereng-house, Spanish dancehall reggae and other Spanglish mutants attract crowds of dynamic leaping and dipping kids who spurn the salsa stages where their parents and elder sisters and brothers are twirling and clapping in clave.

Calle Ocho is a carefully controlled showcase of music supporting a rigid anti-Castro policy. Any musician suspected of collaboration with Cuba is banned, regardless of his or her status in the wider Latin world. The leading Puerto Rican salsero Andy Montañez was cast out one year for singing in Cuba; the Venezuelan mega-star Oscar D'León was similarly punished for visiting the Cuban grave of his idol, Beny Moré; even Julio Iglesias suffered in his early years after confiding to a radio interviewer that he would like to visit Cuba. Rubén Blades was banned not only from the Calle Ocho Festival but from performing anywhere in the city, and his records were banned on the radio and in record shops. Even in the more liberal late 1990s, only the community station WDNA played his music. By that time, however, Cuba's new salsa generation was already performing in other US cities.

ALBITA

Albita Rodríguez says she left Cuba because she could no longer function as a musician. From 1990, she spent three years performing in Colombia, had a massive hit with 'La parranda se canta' (The Revellers Are Singing), then, rather than return to Cuba, she and her band crossed the US-Mexican border and flew to Miami. Like a snake emerging from an old skin, the new Albita appeared: 'I was never a guajira,' she laughed; 'I can't even plant a tomato. My parents [singers in the country controversia style] are the true guajiras.' In her act at the upmarket Yuca club today, she wears pinstripes and waistcoats, slicked-back bleach-blonde hair and blood-red lips. In her show she breaks the ultimate rumba taboo: strutting the stage with pumping elbows like a funky chicken – dancing the male steps – to the delight of the knowing crowd.

THE MIAMI SOUND

Miami calls itself 'City of the Future' but is also preoccupied with the past. Yet Miami Beach is America's hippest southern city, pulsing to a collision of rock, reggae and tropical music. For four years between 1986 and 1990, the refurbished Cameo Theatre presented futuristic programmes which had more in common with European world music festivals than with conservative Miami events – rock bands alongside Latin, Caribbean and world music performers, and, most significantly, local salsa bands found an opening beyond the Latin circuit and lured young Latinos from Miami's Cuban districts to the cosmopolitan South Beach for the first time.

Today, former Cameo director James Quinlan exercises his catholic tastes on Miami Beach's music from his office in City Hall. Miami's musical identity has shifted yet again. Defections from Cuba have slowed – though they are always greeted with a triumphant fanfare. The most surprising newcomer was the country music guitarist and songwriter Albita Rodríguez, who was reborn in Miami as the cabaret diva Albita. On arriving in 1993, she received the leg-up most singers can only dream of when Madonna slipped into one of her shows at the Centro Vasco supper club in Little Havana and then invited her to sing at her birthday party in New York. Emilio Estefán rushed in with a contract and recorded Albita's first album for his Crescent Moon label. Their 1998 album together, *Una mujer como yo* (A Woman Like Me), took her to the Grammy nominations, but the Miami party (the Estefáns and Albita) had to watch as the Cuban *Buena Vista Social Club* veterans took the prize.

Today, Miami is being pincered into change from all directions. In 1997 the Latin and Caribbean Music MIDEM trade fair visited Miami Beach. Sixty-five countries represented every imaginable shade of salsa, merengue, cumbias, vallenato and son, and the UK label TUMI Records set up shop brazenly with their catalogue of modern Cuban music. Many traders criticized the absence of Cuba at the show, though its ghost drifted through the proceedings all week.

'Save Havana for Mañana' may be an appropriate slogan for those waiting for Castro to 'go', but it could turn this vibrant city into a backwater as the European music industry and many American companies trade with the enemy. While an official city-wide boycott exists among record companies, radio stations and most Latin music venues, visiting Cuban musicians are already playing to tense gatherings of progressives in other, unadvertised parts of the town. Some Little Havana restaurants have seen awkward and aggressive meetings between the legends-who-left and visiting islanders who appear to have the best of both worlds. Such situations reveal the ridiculous impasse which Washington and Havana will have to solve. It is mainly the established local musicians who are most vociferous in their opposition to Cuban music's arrival on US soil. Willie Chirino's captivating 1998 album *Cuba libre*, named after the Cuban cocktail referred to in the title song, is actually a rallying cry from the elite of the exile community (including new Miami resident Celia Cruz): their response to the success of the forgotten veterans of Havana's musical heyday, when Cuba and Miami were still Siamese twin towns.

Colombian buses are like mobile discotheques as they careen through the streets. Los Tupamaros — named after the revolutionary sixties group — broadcast their bright, tropical Atlantic coast salsa from their unmistakably gaudy tour bus.

Chapter 8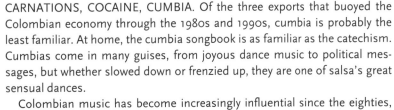

COLOMBIA:
Continental connections

CARNATIONS, COCAINE, CUMBIA. Of the three exports that buoyed the Colombian economy through the 1980s and 1990s, cumbia is probably the least familiar. At home, the cumbia songbook is as familiar as the catechism. Cumbias come in many guises, from joyous dance music to political messages, but whether slowed down or frenzied up, they are one of salsa's great sensual dances.

Colombian music has become increasingly influential since the eighties, when boundaries began to blur and the all-pervasive MTV Latino shrank the differences between countries, and when Colombia's most popular singer, Joe Arroyo, delivered his ebullient tropical salsa to the Latin world. Salsa was popular in Colombia before it was called salsa, when it was still a collection of Cuban rhythms. In the twenties, records by the great Cuban trios such as Trío Matamoros were as influential there as everywhere else. The octogenarian Cuban singer Laito described Colombia as 'the land where no Cuban feels a foreigner'. La Sonora Matancera made an impression in the forties and fifties and introduced two of their premier vocalists, Celia Cruz and Roberto Torres, who remain icons today. Since the late sixties and particularly the seventies, New York salsa bands have been a major draw at the annual carnivals in the coastal music centres of Baranquilla and Cartagena, even winning the prestigious prizes over the locals. But Colombia has its own impressive star system and a dance music which is more musically versatile and open-minded than in many other regions. It is lighter and more jaunty, with tropical – that is to say, Caribbean – airs, and built around melodic bass lines drawn from the traditional cumbia and vallenato rhythms.

Colombia was named after Columbus, though he never even went there. The first Spanish ships landed in 1499 in search of gold, and throughout the first centuries of Spanish rule, the region was governed as part of 'Nueva Granada', along with Venezuela, Panama and Ecuador. The four fought for independence from Spain under the Venezuelan leader Simón Bolívar. In 1819 Colombia and Panama were declared independent – as Gran Colombia – and remained a bloc until 1903, when the US government intervened on Panama's side against the Colombians, established a border, and set about building the canal. Panama was the birthplace of accordion-led cumbia dance music, but by the time of the separation this was as much Colombian as Panamanian.

After Independence, the Colombians continued to make war in various guises, including the brutal civil war known as 'La Violencia' (1948–57), battles between Marxist guerrillas and government forces and clashes between marijuana and cocaine cartels. Throughout the most tumultuous years, the record company Discos Fuentes has been a constant. Founded in 1934 by Antonio Fuentes, a clarinettist and sound engineer, it started out in a small premises in Cartagena, but expanded in 1948 to an all-purpose pressing plant/ recording and radio studio complex in Medellin. Since that time, the Fuentes label has recorded every band of note in the country.

Fuentes's in-house producer, bass player and multi-instrumentalist Julio Ernesto Estrada Rincón, known as 'Fruko' (after a tomato in a TV advertisement), has directed a tight team of studio musicians since the seventies and created the sound identity for vast numbers of Colombian chart records. Of paramount importance in his team has been the trombonist Alberto Barros, who contributed to the soft, trombone-heavy sound of many bands.

The languid Caribbean sugarcane lands around the ports of Cartagena and Baranquilla house a large black population descended from slaves. These two towns are famous for their riotous carnivals, which draw hundreds of thousands of Costenos (coastal people) for sleepless nights of tropical salsa and cumbia, sweetened with Caribbean soca and jolted by reggae's latest dance crazes which have crashed through the coastal borders. The tropical rainforests sprawling along the Eastern Pacific are home to isolated communities of Indians and descendants of slave runaways from the coastal plantations, the most truly Afro-Colombian people, known collectively as the 'Choco'. Their version of salsa is understandably influenced by Cuban music. In the wide Andean valleys of the rivers Cauca and Magdalena, the music capitals of Cali and Medellin support the country's cumbia, salsa and vallenato industries. Up in the north-eastern corner, nudging onto Venezuela's coastline, is the desert region of César and La Guajira provinces, the heartland of vallenato, where every April hundreds of visiting accordionists fill the streets with screaming, pulsing melodies.

Colombia's musical identity can be reduced to two main dance styles: the cumbia and the vallenato. When the Nobel-prize-winning writer Gabriel García Márquez arrived in Norway in 1982 to receive his award, he took a vallenato accordion group with him to serenade his success. Cumbia and vallenato both started life as accordion-led acoustic folk music. Cumbia was initially a slow and sensual courtship dance, performed by the slaves and

Cumbias and closely related gaitas are Colombia's national dances, still played in the countryside by small groups on percussion, bass, accordion and a hand-made bamboo or sugarcane flute (gaita). On the Night of Cumbia (right), celebrants with lighted candles dance to the music's side-winding rhythms. The striped straw hat (far right of picture) was originally a gaucho's accessory, but is now worn as a national symbol by Colombians everywhere.

Fruko & Joe Arroyo

Julio Ernesto Estrada Rincon, aka 'Fruko', is the lynchpin, the so-called Godfather of Colombian salsa. His great-grandfather, a Cuban engineer who migrated to Colombia, bequeathed the young Fruko a life-long love of Cuban music. Fruko started work at the age of 12 in the Medellin studios of Discos Fuentes and in his teens played timbales and toured with old-fashioned, big-band Los Corraleros de Majagual, playing covers of Cuban songs.

While performing in New York, he was transfixed by the tough, trombone-led experiments with Cuban music he heard from Fania's bands and in 1971 switched to bass guitar and founded Los Tesos (The Treasures), featuring two trombones. The head of Fuentes then donated to the group a new, confident, sharp-voiced 17-year-old from Baranquilla, Alvaro José Arroyo González – aka Joe Arroyo. Their early hit with an upbeat version of Celina González's 'Yo soy el punto Cubano' (I Am the Soul of Cuban Music) launched a procession of songs whose rhythms zig-zagged around the Caribbean.

ABOVE: **Fruko (front) with his protégée India Meliyara.**
BELOW: **Joe Arroyo, Colombia's longest-loved singer, still maintains a down-to-earth lifestyle.**

From 1974 Fruko also converted The Latin Brothers – an erratic four-trombone salsa band – into an impeccable salsa orchestra flavoured with Caribbean rhythms. His third acquisition, in 1977, was a flagging cumbia outfit called La Sonora Dinamita (Dynamite Sound), founded in 1960. In Fruko's hands it became the definitive, effervescent, modern cumbia-salsa band, playing compulsive dancers' music.

In 1981 Joe Arroyo left Los Tesos and formed his own band, La Verdad (The Truth). Following their first hit, in 1981 – his autobiographical 'Tumbotecho' (The Roof's Falling In), about the antics of a drunkard – he was repeatedly in the charts with songs and rhythms of his own invention which won him six Golden Congo awards. Arroyo's life reads like a soap opera – from singing as a child in strip clubs, to golden success, then to collapsing in 1983 into a drugs-and-exhaustion-induced coma for a week, as the country held its breath. He made a startling comeback, moving straight back into the charts with hits like 'Rebelión' and 'La noche', songs which are political history lessons, covering the slave experience and colonialism. In 1998 Fruko produced the world's catchiest football anthem, 'La pachanga del fútbol', though it had no effect on Colombia's performance in the World Cup.

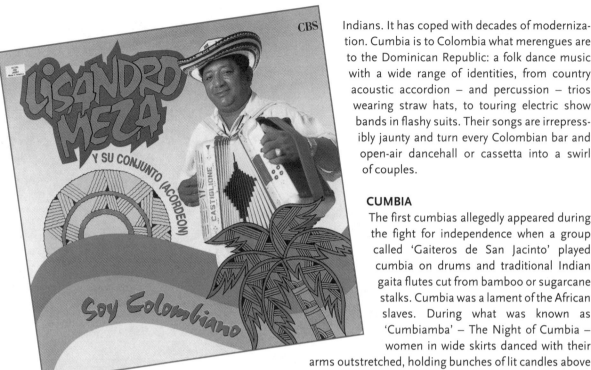

Lisandro Meza, king of the cumbia accordions since the 1950s, is a most versatile, virtuosic player and possesses a soaring yodeller's voice. He graduated from the veteran sixties band Los Corraleros de Majagual, whose cumbias were led on clarinet and accordion.

Indians. It has coped with decades of modernization. Cumbia is to Colombia what merengues are to the Dominican Republic: a folk dance music with a wide range of identities, from country acoustic accordion – and percussion – trios wearing straw hats, to touring electric show bands in flashy suits. Their songs are irrepressibly jaunty and turn every Colombian bar and open-air dancehall or cassetta into a swirl of couples.

CUMBIA

The first cumbias allegedly appeared during the fight for independence when a group called 'Gaiteros de San Jacinto' played cumbia on drums and traditional Indian gaita flutes cut from bamboo or sugarcane stalks. Cumbia was a lament of the African slaves. During what was known as 'Cumbiamba' – The Night of Cumbia – women in wide skirts danced with their arms outstretched, holding bunches of lit candles above their heads. The Fiesta de la Virgen de la Candelaria, every February, is still celebrated in the northern coastal regions where the cumbia was born, and Colombians everywhere still alternate their couple-dancing with free-form moments when the dancers raise their outstretched arms in the air, holding imaginary candles.

In the thirties, cumbia bands fell under the spell of American Swing; horn sections were installed and arrangements matched to the local rhythms. La Sonora Cienaguera worked the saxophones as one wildly bucking unit, while the solo trumpeter or gaita player shot the breeze. Early modern cumbia recordings in the fifties included racy songs like 'La pollera colorá' (Little Red Skirt) by Los Trovadores de Baru (The Troubadours from Baru, a largely African district of Cartagena), which remain essential ingredients in every respectable cumbia menu today. The top sixties band led by clarinettist Lucho Bermúdez – 'The Benny Goodman of the Tropics' – mixed his love of Swing with a passion for local flute-led gaitas. Bermúdez's most successful song was 'La gaita de las flores' (The Dance of the Flowers). His young timbales player for many years was Roberto Pla, who would become the UK's leading Latino musician. Other veterans include Los Cumbiamberos de Pacheco, who play a classic accordion style, and Los Guacharacas, a roots group from the Atlantic coast who use the traditional Indian gourd scraper known as a güiro in salsa and merengue but called a guacharaca in Colombia.

The most enduring veterans are Los Corraleros de Majagual, in business since 1961 and a nursery for young talent. Fruko was one of their early bass players and Alfredo Guttiérez and Lisandro Meza, the two most decorated accordionists in Colombia, also passed through the band. The prolific songwriter and singer Calixto Ochoa provided this group and others with scores of hits which are covered not only by every other cumbia band in the land but by many salsa bands abroad. In the nineties, Alfredo Guttiérez's sons, Dino and Walfredo, also accordionists, took honorary membership. Cumbias –

Corraleros style – are a sensual interplay of muted trombones, spiky accordions, and even clipped reggae guitars, backed by a characteristically hopping bass-line and interspersed with copious yodel-yelping and girlie choruses.

In 1955, during the Baranquilla carnival, the trumpeter Pacho (Francisco) Galán concocted a crush made from merengue and cumbia called 'El Merecumbe'. His theme tune, 'Ay, cosita linda!' (Hey, What a Gorgeous Little Thing!), was a national hit, a catchphrase and a dance which spread beyond Colombia. Both Nat 'King' Cole and La Sonora Matancera had hits with it. Galán cultivated a sturdy, mixed-up sound; his singers even had to adopt the nasal tones of the old-fashioned folk singers, and the brass section swung like Count Basie's band.

The salsa meteor hit Colombia in 1968, the year two flamboyant and unconventional New York salseros – pianist Richie Ray and singer Bobby Cruz – snatched the coveted Congo de Oro prize from the local bands at the Cali carnival. Eddie Palmieri's wild piano style and his trombone-led charanga were another obvious influence on Fuentes's recordings, and particularly on arrangements by trombonist–producer Alberto Barros. In 1977 the salsa icon Héctor Lavoe made an historic visit to Bogotá in the wake of his separation from Willie Colón. His poignant, melancholy, nasal style influenced many Colombian singers; his percussionists stressed the Cuban accent.

In 1977 Fruko took charge of La Sonora Dinamita (The Dynamite Sound), a Fuentes cumbia band which was in decline. Fruko accelerated their beat and introduced ideas from the Fania sound. One surprising fan was Daniel Ortega, former president of Nicaragua and leader of the Sandinista Party, who interviewed the band live on Radio Managua in 1989. Their secret weapon is their singer and founder, Lucho Argain, who provided a steady flow of hooking hit tunes. While most Fuentes bands blend popular dances – cumbia, salsa, merengues, porro and vallenatos – Argain stayed with cumbias. The instantly recognizable electric piano threads a bright, tinkly trail through his songs, the horns steer clear of the complexities of Swing and mambo and tend to work in unison, emphatic but soft, with a distinctly Mexican mariachi flavour. La Sonora Dinamita was the first cumbia band to hire female vocalists – flirtatious singers who could hold their own against the noise of a big band. The most outstanding were the throaty, joyous 'La India Meliyara' (Melida Yara Yanguma), who moved on to a successful solo cumbia career, and Margarita, who left to form the Cocoloco Band.

Colombia is home to hundreds of cumbia bands, traditional and ultramodern. Rodolfo Aicardi – an expressive tenor with a gritty vibrato – unwittingly introduced cumbias to the UK when his song 'La colegiala' (The College Girl) was used by Nescafé in a cinema coffee advertisement in 1989. The song's walking bass line, whirling saxophones and jaunty 2/4 beat captivated Londoners and contributed to the nineties explosion of interest in salsa.

VALLENATO

'The music of the valleys' – vallenato – has emerged from the shadows of cumbia and today enjoys success all around the Latin world. Vallenato originated in the north-eastern states of La Guajira and César, closest to the Venezuelan border. Traditional vallenato was played by trios: button accordion (imported from Germany), a single bongo-like drum called a caja and a guacharaca scraper. Sometimes, to enrich the melodies, an acoustic Spanish guitar was added to the wooden gaita flute. Some bands, most notably

ALEXIS MURILLO

Alexis Murillo Londoño is a native of the Pacific coast jungle town of Quibdó – best reached by helicopter or canoe. Through his group, Los Nemus del Pacífico, and through his songs, he represents the Choco people, descendants of African slaves and local Indian populations. A delicate guitarist, he accompanies his songs about the Choco lifestyle and political issues with an imposingly deep, soft voice, tuned to the style of Cuban son – his major inspiration. He describes his music as possessing 'A little bit of everything with a touch of madness'. The music begins with son but draws in many other influences, particularly local folk rhythms, and his lyrics reveal his skill at recreating humorous (and often scandalous) bar-room conversations between men about their women, sung in whiney, nasal caricatures.

NICHE

MC HUELE A MATRIMONIO

Grupo Niche, Colombia's most popular salsa band, was the brainchild of Jairo Varela. His quintessential Cali salsa has smooth, addictive melodies and is weighted with trombones. Varela established Niche in 1980 with lead trombonist Alexis Lozano, another child of the Quibdó region.

Binomio de Oro, founded in 1979, add an electric guitar, whose crisp bright notes and delicate finger-picked mariachi-flavoured solos are a delicious foil to the screeching of light-fingered accordions and keening vocals. Some find the val-lenato formula too sentimental, but this is Colombia's country music, after all.

What makes vallenato so irre-sistible to dancers is the combina-tion of the pulsing, angular rhythms of the accordion and the jumping bass line which lends a lurching sideways beat. In the modern versions, an electric bass gives the essential drive to the dancers' feet; its ambling beat emphasizes the swaying of the 2/4 rhythm.

The high point in the vallenato calendar is April, when thousands of musi-cians and fans crowd into the desert towns of the North East for a jamboree of accordion duelling. Valledupar's week-long Fiesta Vallenata fills the town with the tumbling, screaming melodies of hundreds of accordions. The classics blend with freshly minted songs which compete for prestigious awards. The winning songs stay in the repertoires throughout the coming year. The climax of the week is the coronation of El Rey del Vallenato (always a king, never a queen). At the height of the drugs wars the festivals were controlled by the barons; the kings and princes would receive cars, apartments, jewelry, women and recording contracts in return for being at the barons' beck and call and playing in their clubs and parties.

As with every other style of Latin music, vallenato has surrendered to change. One successful hybrid came from outside, when in 1981 the Miami-Cuban Roberto Torres transformed a vallenato classic, 'Caballo viejo' (The Old Stud), by merging it with a charanga formula. He arranged the Cuban violins and flute in magnificent clashes with an accordion. Torres's career enjoyed a new lease of life in the early eighties through several hit albums in the same hybrid mode. Another Cuban legend, Celina González, enjoyed an unexpected comeback in 1984, when she appeared to 50,000 overjoyed carnival-goers in Cali. She has been immortalized in the Cali dance bar Celina y Reutilio's, named after the duo with her late husband.

Vallenato was in for more remodelling in the nineties when the dimple-chinned former telenovela star Carlos Vives launched a rock-vallenato band,

La Provincia, and targeted the young, international Latin audience. His first album, in 1993, *Clásicos de la Provincia*, was a tribute to the great vallenato composers. Vives swung between the yodelling style of the homey vallenatos and a husky Cuban tone. For the 1997 album, *Tengo fé*, he incorporated flavours of Trinidadian soca, Martiniquan zouk drumming, salsa percussion, rock guitar solos, funk bass, merengue tambora drums, as well as the local vallenato classics. In 1995 Gloria Estefán was steered towards Colombian music by former Miami Sound Machine band member Kike Santander, who produced her underrated album *Abriendo puertas* (Opening Doors). Estefán's voice had never sounded so strong, so natural. Santander followed it with a record by another inhabitant of the Estefán stable, the Cuban country singer Albita, whose vallenato, 'El amor llegó' (Here Comes Love) is a high point of the 1997 Grammy-nominated album *Una mujer como yo* (A Woman Like Me).

SALSA, COLOMBIA STYLE

Today's Colombian salsa is both mellow and sensual, closer to the Puerto Rican sound of El Gran Combo and La Sonora Ponceña, less heavily arranged and complex than anything coming out of Cuba, and upbeat and electric.

The music of the Pacific coast is quite different from that of the Caribbean-influenced northern coastal territories. Representing the local Choco people is a guitarist, singer–songwriter, former dancer and footballer, academic and journalist called Alexis Murillo. His salsa band, Los Nemus del Pacífico, is named after the local music gods, the Nemus. But his inspiration is absolutely Cuban son. His lyrics air the issues affecting his people, carried on a groove of seductive, guitar-based dance music. His voice carries the jaded, strained quality of an authentic Cuban sonero.

This London-produced collection of rough, rural vallenatos is a riot of careening accordions, the spirit voices of the style. These master accordionists were captured on tape by the roaming Globestyle director Ben Mandelson, at remote festivals in the North East.

Television soap pin-up Carlos Vives (at left) began his career as a drama student in Bogotá, and switched to music in the mid-nineties, by which time he was a familiar face all over Colombia. A lifelong passion for accordion music led him to vallenato. He hooked up with accordionist Egidio Cuadrado and a bunch of maverick experimenters called La Provincia. With their long hair, cut-off shorts and sandals, they resembled a rock band, but their first album, *Clásicos de la Provincia* (1993), was an accordion feast of tributes to the great vallenato composers and performers, played *almost* straight.

In the mid-seventies, Fruko devoted his attention to his mould-breaking group Los Tesos (The Treasures), whose songs reveal both his deep understanding of hit-making and his wild sense of adventure. At the same time, the Fuentes hit factory also included the straight-ahead salsa of The Latin Brothers, which crystallized the careers of both Joe Arroyo and co-singers the late Piper Pimiento and Wilson Saoco. Arroyo developed a distinctive vocal style which included high-pitched whinnies and screeches in imitation of Beny Moré. With his breakaway band La Verdad (The Truth), formed in 1981, he paraded a continuous flow of clever, uptempo songs in the charts, original fusions of cumbia with salsa which he called 'cumbión' and 'joesón'. He remains Colombia's favourite son who crossed all social divides. After he had won the coveted 'Congo de Oro' trophy at the Cali festival six times, a 'Super-Congo' was created for him. Many of Arroyo's songs serve as pointed political or historical commentaries. His 1980s classic 'Rebelión' fitted perfectly into the 1992 compilation *América 500 años*, which undermined the anniversary of Columbus's arrival in Colombia with a showcase of nationalistic songs such as La Sonora Dinamita's 'Cartagena heroica'.

Colombia's best-loved and most influential pure salsa band is Grupo Niche from the self-styled 'Capital of Salsa', Cali. Their evergreen song 'Cali pachanguero' is resurrected every year for the seven-day Cali Christmas carnival spree. An exceptional singer emerged in the seventies – a tiny woman with the penetrating voice of a Cuban sonera – Arabella (Margarita Pinillos). During the height of her success in Colombia, and later in her new home in Miami, she was promoted as 'the next Celia Cruz', but though she wrote and recorded many hit songs (still powerful movers), she never penetrated the New York Fania or RMM shield, or received appropriate marketing.

The future of Colombian salsa is safe in the hands of hundreds of bands, many influenced by the New York and Puerto Rican models, but mostly by Grupo Niche. The slick, smooth, infectious hit songs that fill the charts in the late nineties include regular appearances from Orquesta Guayacán, La Misma Gente and latterly Grupo Gale, formed by the prolific songwriter and percussionist Diego Gale. A fashionable neo-Cuban retro movement is led by Alcemia, whose repertoire includes the same songs by Celia Cruz and La Sonora Matancera that drove their parents and grandparents around the dirt floors of the country's cassettas in the fifties.

Throughout the nineties, Colombian dance music became ever more influenced by the Caribbean, with newly invented fusions such as soka (Colombia's version of Trinidadian soca), son caribeño (tropical salsa), salsa-rap and salsa-reggae, and the creation of local, new, bass-heavy styles known as 'terapía' and 'champeta'. The 'tropical sound' matured into a recognizably Colombian style. Nineties milestones guaranteed that the rest of Latin America was taking note of the music from this corner of the continent: Carlos Vives had unimagined success in the overall Latin charts with his electric guitar vallenato. Grupo Kerube hit gold with rap, reggae and African-guitar band crossovers. New rock-inspired dance music groups acknowledging vallenato and cumbia are headed by the Aterciopelados (The Velvety Ones) and Carlos Vives's breakaway band, Bloque de Quesada. All point – with an electronic baton – to the future.

Chapter 9 SALSA IN LONDON:
From Edmundo Ros to Snowboy

THE ORIGINS OF today's fanatical interest in salsa music and dancing in the UK lie in the 1930s, when a band called the Lecuona Cuban Boys introduced their strange ethnic instruments, ruffle-sleeved rhumba shirts and irresistibly catchy rhythms to London. 'The Rum Rhythms of the Real Rumba' was how the *Melody Maker* summed up their first concert in 1934, describing them not only as 'a slap-up authentic Cuban band', but also as 'a queer outfit who introduced the new dance, the Conga'. Infatuated local danceband musicians learned to play the music by studying these exotic visitors and their records, and tried to get 'that Cuban look' by slipping on lurid rhumba shirts, slicking back their hair and adding an -ez or an -o to their surnames. Today salsa is a respected part of Britain's uniquely eclectic music scene; clubs span the UK and homegrown bands race up and down the motorways to join the local DJs and dance teachers.

OPPOSITE: A kaleidoscope of salsa in the UK, from Edmundo Ros through the pioneering eighties Sol y Sombra club to today's professional, slick, home-grown bands. BELOW: 'He came, he saw, he conga'd' – one of wartime London's great headlines – described Edmundo Ros's success in London's swankiest nightclubs, such as the one below (Ros, right, in bow tie).

The Latin performer who first captured London's attention and held it for several decades was the Venezuelan classical musician Edmundo Ros, who arrived in London in 1937 to study at the Royal Academy of Music. He was twenty-seven. On his first night in town, he was hired as a singer and drummer by the Cuban bandleader Don Marino Barretto, who was performing in the West End's supper clubs. Their repertoire included rhumbas and congas picked up from the Lecuona Cuban Boys and their sister group, the Havana Cuban Boys. At the high-society Embassy Club in Mayfair, guests included the Prince of Wales, a great fan of the music.

After six months Ros left Barretto to form his own band and built a smooth, diluted version of Cuban dance music, tailored to suit British dancers. Suddenly the whole of London was side-kicking and chanting in snakey lines to his congas. The bandleader Victor Sylvester published a *Modern Ballroom Dancing* manual to provide strict rules and footprint charts for the crowds that flocked to the new Palais de Danses springing up all over the UK. When the cha-cha-cha swept the world in the fifties, Ros simplified that too, and gave his songs clever, tongue-twisting wordplay titles and catchy, casually swinging and polished arrangements. 'I introduced something they could move to,' he recalled later.

In the fifties American bebop shattered the calm of London's bohemian clubs. As tenor saxophonist Pete King, cofounder with Ronnie Scott of the world famous Soho jazz club, explained: 'For progressives like us, bebop and the early Cuban jazz, the cubop, were the things. Ronnie and I opened our first club as somewhere for us to play them.' King and Scott sowed the seeds of Latin Jazz in Soho at that time, three decades before their Frith Street premises became its European headquarters.

The rock generation began its Latin love affair in the sixties with Carlos Santana's psychedelic guitar version of Tito Puente's 'Oye como va' on his *Abraxas* album, and a few years later the Rolling Stones dropped a conga solo into *Sympathy for the Devil*. Ray Barretto's rocking soul number 'El Watusi' stormed the UK pop charts in 1963 and London got its first taste of live salsa in 1976, with the appearance at the Lyceum Ballroom of the Fania All Stars. The guest singer was pop star Stevie Winwood.

The eighties saw the enthusiasm for Latin music explode. Interest was sparked in 1981 by a concert by Tito Puente's formidable Latin Jazz Sextet. The jazz buffs, New Romantics, champion ballroom dancers and watchful musicians were mesmerized. 'I think we've finally opened the door for all the Latin bands to come,' Puente declared triumphantly – and accurately – after the show. Within a couple of years he returned with his queen, Celia Cruz, in a unforgettable night of love. The golden couple fed the salsa boom with their annual appearances over the next decade.

Following Puente came his rival from the Palladium, Machito. Ronnie Scott's club cleared the tables and chairs for dancing. By the late eighties Ronnie Scott's was a centre for Cuban jazz, following Scott's life-changing visit to the Havana Jazz Festival in 1982, and the first Soho Festival of Cuban jazz in 1983, which introduced to the UK the three key jazz pioneers: Afro-Cuba, Grupo Rubalcaba and Irakere. Ronnie Scott's 25th anniversary in 1985 coincided with the Cuban Revolution's quarter century, and provided an excuse for another Soho Cuban Festival.

While the focus was on visiting bands, a homegrown scene was emerging, led by Spiteri, Paz and Cayenne, who constructed their own blends of salsa, jazz, fusion and funk. Club DJs rehabilitated lost hits from the fifties and sixties and created boogaloo, Latin soul and jazz revivals at their new underground venues. A uniquely British Latin Jazz dance scene was born above the Electric Ballroom in Camden Town, where young black dancers in braces, baggy trousers and two-tone shoes, cut mambo steps with advanced breakdancing moves to music provided by ground-breaking DJ Paul Murphy.

The action spread from Camden to Soho's WAG Club (former sixties in-place, Whisky-a-go-go), where Murphy was joined by the precocious, enthusiast DJ Gilles Peterson. This new headquarters of Brazilian and Cuban jazz was also a residency for jazz dancers – now professionally organized as 'Jazz Dancers' and 'IDJ' (I Dance Jazz). Rival dancers from Birmingham, Bristol and Brighton fought it out in Soho and took Latin music byond London.

The eighties pop scene flirted with Latin music, and Latin percussionists and horn players found themselves on BBC television's *Top of the Pops* backing hit singles by Fun Boy Three, Blue Rondo a la Turk, Havana and Animal Magnet, all swinging to some kind of Cuban beat. Modern Romance's hit, 'Everybody Salsa!', gave ruffle shirts a new lease of life and scored a surprising success in New York. The UK music press wondered aloud if 'the Latin thing' would catch on. In 1985 it did: a Cuban-flavoured dance meteor called 'Dr Beat' landed in the charts, and its creators – Miami Sound Machine – appeared on *Top of the Pops*. Britain's love affair with the shy young lead singer Gloria Estefán had begun. Their follow-up, the remixed 12'' Latin-pop single *Conga*, is still a floor-filler.

In 1986 the burgeoning Latin music community found refuge in several new West End venues incuding the Sol y Sombra, run by the eclectic DJ Dave Hucker. In the basement of this Colombian drinking club, Hucker and DJ Paul Murphy stoked the jazz and Brazilian fires, and mixed salsa, African, jazz, reggae and funk. Hucker initiated the dancers in Colombian salsa, and his mission was boosted by the Nestlé coffee advertisement which featured an infectious accordion-backed cumbia called 'La colegiala'. Quickwitted World

LEFT: Sheet music such as this was essential for England's rhumba musicians who covered the songs off imported 78'' records. BELOW: In 1934 The Lecuona Cuban Boys brought rhumba to the UK. The band's creator, Cuban pianist Ernesto Lecuona, never actually played with them, but composed material in Havana which entertained all of Europe in the thirties and forties.

Circuit Records issued it on a compilation of Colombian music, *Cumbia, Cumbia*. Mango Records followed with a stream of releases. Within weeks the jumpy bass lines and jaunty melodies of cumbias boomed out of clubs and bars all over London. Their sidewinding 2/4 beat were easy going for non-Latin dancers confused by salsa's riot of cross rhythms.

The East London Bass Clef club programmed by DJ Dominique became the leading venue for live Latin music. Oscar D'León's world famous 12-piece salsa band squeezed onto the club's table-sized stage in front of about fifty people one cold winter night in 1987. Other guests included the Cuban conga player Daniel Ponce and pianist Charlie Palmieri, both of whom served as tutors for the local players who backed their music. By the end of Palmieri's week of mesmeric music, littered with his gloriously rhythmic piano solos, London's musicians had graduated to a new level. By that time several Latin bands had emerged in the capital, in imitation of the then New York idols. Free of the constraints of Edmundo Ros's rhumba shirts and playing customized Latin music, percussionist Robin Jones launched King Salsa, led by the flamboyant Venezuelan singer Víctor Hugo.

The genuine Latin American musicians – particularly Colombian timbalero Roberto Pla, Uruguayan bass player Andy Lafone and later Ray Barretto's trombonist Joe de Jesús and Cuban violinist Omar Sosa – were in demand by visiting bands. They raised the standards in bands like Valdez (the first genuine salsa outfit), El Sonido de Londres (The Sound of London), La Clave, Cayenne, and later Salsa y Ache and Raíces Cubanas. One unlikely Latin music fanatic emerged from Southend-on-Sea: Mark Cotgrove, known as 'Snowboy', is a multi-percussionist with an encyclopaedic knowledge of Latin music who was taught the secrets of Latin percussion by Robin Jones.

The harmony and unity of the scene was brief: divisions grew between jazz and salsa audiences, fans of Cuban music attracted by the politics, and the Colombians living in London who had strict tastes (they would boycott the dancefloor if the 'wrong' tune came up and walk away from 'gringas' who couldn't dance properly). At another extreme, gangs of weekend-happy tourists and office workers demanded Gypsy Kings' records and lambadas in the eighties and the handful of salsa tunes they heard at dance classes in the nineties. For those who discovered salsa through politics, Club Sandino was a magnet: what began as a fundraiser for the Nicaraguan cause in London turned into a missionary force for salsa which

LEFT: **Cuban band Irakere in front of Big Ben, during one of their first 1980s residencies at Ronnie Scott's Soho Jazz Club.**
RIGHT: **During one tour, the local Colombian percussionist Roberto Pla invited Chucho Valdés to join the cream of London's Latin music sets on this 12" single. Pla is a veteran of the eighties bands who did the groundwork for the thriving Latin scene today, including Cayenne and El Sonido de Londres.**

BELOW AND LEFT: **London's first rhumba bands had to be versed in the whole range of Latin music: tangos and sambas as well as Cuban rumbas and congas.**

spread to other cities, from Dublin to Edinburgh, Bristol to Brighton. One of the most influential and eclectic clubs was the Mambo Inn in Brixton. DJ Gerry Lyseight explains its significance as follows: 'Our range of music was so wide – Latin, African, jazz and all huge interrelated categories – and the atmosphere so seductive, that many people were drawn deeper into the music they discovered there, particularly salsa.'

The new passion was also fed by glitzy shows by the top salsa bands at Stuart Lyons promotions for the Empire Ballroom, Leicester Square. Local councils and the G.L.C. funded salsa summer carnivals after the success of 'La Gran Fiesta' in 1989, which introduced the Cubans Elio Reve and Celina González in a big top on the South Bank.

The ultimate stumbling-block for non-Latin fans of Latin music has always been learning how to dance. Edmundo Ros solved the problem by simplifying the music; four decades later, thousands of people take dance classes. The first, in 1989, were run by the Cuban Nelson Batista with English salsa musician Daniella Rosselson, and Colombian Xiomara Granados, who offered the Colombian angle. By the late nineties every sizeable town in the UK boasted salsa classes and the burning issue was the adoption of salsa by the ballroom dancing set. By then, the English were no longer wallflowers.

The new appetite for salsa was also fed by a new generation of record labels. Peter Gabriel's Real World label, Virgin's Earthworks, World Circuit and Island's Mango all opened the window on Cuban and Colombian salsa, while Charly and Globestyle Records both hired local DJs to rifle the back catalogues of Fania and Caiman's New York classics. In the nineties TUMI Records' irrepressible Cuban music fan Mo Fini released a breathless stream of Cuban music from Cuba's EGREM label.

Today London's Latin scene is vast, but live music has been overtaken by dancing. Dance DJ Dominique, who organizes the 'Divine Diva' nights with female DJs at Club Havana and also manages her husband Roberto Pla's Latin Jazz Orchestra, says regretfully, 'Salsa's popularity is great for the clubs but not for the musicians. Live music has been virtually abandoned.' DJ Jo Shinner adds: 'By the end of the nineties, the scene was virtually segregated: the Colombians and the rest – Cubans, tourists, English. The Colombians don't want to be pushed about by the twirling of mad English people; they dance more compactly – it's not like rock'n'roll. And they want 100 percent Colombian music.'

The most progressive evolutionary line since the eighties has been in the area of 'New Latin Jazz', where both musicians and fans have reinvented themselves and supported the reappearance of jazz albums from salsa artists Ray Barretto, Eddie Palmieri and Tito Puente. The 1997 visit by the NuYorican Soul project spelled out the latest generation's take on Latin music, born into an atmosphere of rap, drum-and-bass music and r'n'b. The projects director Gilles Peterson says: 'NuYorican Soul makes the important connection between Latin music and disco and future Latin. Hip-hop comes from Latin, the SalSoul label's crossovers in the seventies flirted with Latin artists, and now these musicians are making connections between modern dancefloor music and the history of salsa.' Ironically, in the very same year, the Latin Grammy went to the *Buena Vista Social Club* album and rock promoter Harvey Goldsmith turned his back briefly on Rolling Stones productions to import the cast of the Tropicana nightclub from Havana to the Albert Hall. Among a forest of palm trees, he built a tropical haven in Kensington – the Lecuona Cuban Boys would have been very much at home.

In 1983 Mark Cotgrove, aka 'Snowboy', took conga classes with former Edmundo Ros drummer Robin Jones. Within a decade, he was the capital's most in-demand bongo and conga player. He appeared on many Latin pop and soul chart experiments, Brazilian jazz and Cuban crossovers.

SALSA IN LONDON: FROM EDMUNDO ROS TO SNOWBOY

LEFT: Merengada's slick merengue 'Un mensaje de London' (A Message from London) is backed by the surprise hit salsa version of Bob Marley's 'No Woman, No Cry' – sung half in Spanish. Merengada includes saxophonist Nina Jaffa, who designed the cover, and members of London's Latin establishment.
BELOW: Nico Gómez (French, left), Wilmer Cifontes (Venezuelan, centre), and Néstor García (Canaries, right), together with Venezuelan lead singer Lino Rocha, constitute the London-based Tumbaito.

3 Crossing borders

Chapter 10 Latin Jazz, Afro-Cuban Jazz

As a child, Luciano 'Chano' Pozo y González (1915–48) was renowned throughout his Havana tenement block for his rumba dancing, singing and conga playing. From drumming with his prize-winning carnival band Los Dandy's in the thirties, he joined the outdoor nightclub Sans Souci in 1940, entertaining American tourists with his frenzied, flamboyant conga solos. In 1946 he moved to New York, invited by childhood friend Miguelito Valdés, and was hired by Dizzy Gillespie in 1947. Gillespie described Pozo's revolutionary style to Harry Belafonte: 'He stripped to the waist, oiled his body, and strapped on the drum (a single conga), played long solos, sang and danced; he looked as if he was looking for the gods.' In 1948 Pozo was shot dead in a Harlem bar as 'Manteca' played on the jukebox.

PRECEDING PAGES: **The face of New Cuba –** Bamboleo, with the first shaven heads on the island, photographed against a backdrop of traditional Old Havana, 1996.

THE HISTORY OF LATIN JAZZ was a well-kept secret for much of the twentieth century, but the merest hint of syncopated rhythm, swaying horn riff or jolting conga solo gives it away. Ragtime pianist Jelly Roll Morton linked the twin ports of Havana and New Orleans when he described jazz as possessing a 'Spanish tinge'. Certainly the funeral processions and carnival parades of New Orleans, with their jaunty rhythms and brash clarinet and trombone tunes, were cousins to Cuban comparsas. Yet while bookshelves sag with tomes on African-American jazz, European jazz, even Polish and Russian jazz, Latin Jazz barely gets a mention.

For the sharp-eyed and -eared, though, a Spanish name or music title gives the clue: Duke Ellington's 'Moon over Cuba' in 1941, and 'Perdido', written by his Puerto Rican trombonist Juan Tizol in the early thirties; Art Blakey's work with Cuban percussionist Sabu Martínez; Charles Mingus's collaboration with conga player Candido on *Cumbia and Jazz Fusion*.

Benny Goodman launched the craze for big-band Swing in 1935 with its anthem, 'It Don't Mean a Thing, If It Ain't Got That Swing'. At the Savoy Ballroom in Harlem, the movement was buoyed along by the tiny, tubercular power-drummer Chick Webb. Audiences flocked to see the young singer Ella Fitzgerald and the Five Horsemen – the nickname for the fiery horn section which included the band's musical director, saxophonist Mario Bauzá. Through the gig with Chick Webb, Bauzá met Dizzy Gillespie, then playing trumpet in the warm-up band with Cuban bandleader Alberto Socarras. In 1939 Gillespie and Bauzá (by then playing trumpet too) moved together into Cab Calloway's orchestra, where Bauzá was able to introduce Latin flavours into the arrangements to suit the fashion of the time. At the downtown Stork Club, Puerto Rican pianist Noro Morales was playing a programme of Latinized American standards and simplified Cuban classics to an elegant American crowd. The first American big-band leader to pick up on Cuban music was Stan Kenton, who in 1947 hired Jack Constanza – 'Mr Bongo' – to play bongos (their first appearance in jazz) in a rendering of 'Peanut Vendor'.

Amid the frenzy of forties bebop, Dizzy Gillespie was most interested in merging Afro-Cuban rhythms into the new anarchic formula. When Mario Bauzá introduced him to the brilliant rumba drummer Chano Pozo, he hired him on the spot. Pozo spoke no English, but they communicated through music: 'We spoke "African",' Gillespie said later. Pozo transformed Gillespie's experiments with 'Cubop', and left a terrible void when, in 1948, he was shot dead in a Harlem bar over a dope deal.

Gillespie's records inspired generations of Latino musicians. Ray Barretto first heard him during his army service in Germany. 'Someone played me a Dizzy record with Chano Pozo,' he told New York musicologist Max Salazar. 'The following night, I sat in with one of the jazz groups and played the back of an old banjo, trying to imitate him.' Back in New York, Barretto took up congas and became one of several 'jobbing' Latin percussionists who joined Harlem's jazz sessions and live shows alongside Charlie Parker, Max Roach

Mario Bauzá & Chucho Valdés

Mario Bauzá was a tiny, mischievous man with a huge, infectious grin. He was the first musical director to successfully merge Cuba's dance rhythms with American jazz horns to create a third entity – Afro-Cuban jazz. The identity was established with the Afro-Cubans band, a tight, brilliant, family affair run by his brother-in-law Machito and his sister, the big-voiced, warm-hearted, scat-singing Graciela. Their first recording, *Sopa de pichón* (Pigeon Soup), was an appropriate theme for a family whose exuberant musical dinners were a magnet for visiting Cuban musicians. In the jazz-dance scene which erupted in eighties clubland Britain, Bauzá's original tracks enjoyed a new lease of life, though the seventy-something Bauzá was by then musically silent and had been unacknowledged for years. By the end of the decade, however, he had won a Grammy for the surprising best-selling comeback album, *Afro-Cuban Jazz: Mario Bauzá, Graciela and Friends*, and was back on New York's stage with musician friends from three generations.

The 1992 CD *The Legendary Mambo King Mario Bauzá and his Afro-Cuban Jazz Orchestra* paid warm homage to Bauzá's career. It opened on a five-movement jazz suite, 'Tanga' (Marijuana), a sophisticated big-band adaptation of his 1943 composition, and closed with 'Chucho', a typically brass-loaded affair featuring a knotty saxophone solo by Paquito D'Rivera and others by old collaborators from Bauzá's heyday.

'Chucho' is named after Jesús 'Chucho' Valdés, the composer-bandleader who took Bauzá's template to a new evolutionary level as pianist and helmsman of the Havana-based band Irakere. Valdés entered the wider jazz consciousness around the time of Bauzá's death in 1996. Irakere was Cuba's most lucrative export during the eighties, but its gruelling, six-month tours prompted the two original co-leaders, Paquito D'Rivera and trumpeter Arturo Sandoval, to give up on the restricted contacts with the rest of the Latin Jazz world, and flee to the US where they catalysed a gentle revolution in Latin Jazz. Chucho remained with Irakere, nurturing a second generation of young Conservatory graduates.

An immensely tall, slow-moving bear of a figure, Valdés plays piano like no one else: at the height of a fast and rolling, twisting, rhythmic pace, his long, thin fingers roam the keyboard with the ease of a very tall basketball player scoring a goal. While playing, he turns to face the audience, casting his eyes slowly around the room, smiling at familiar faces, and letting the seamless flow of music reformulate the stories of his exceptional lifetime.

ABOVE: **Chucho Valdés in a late 1980s line-up of Irakere.** LEFT: **Mario Bauzá, triumphant over his 1986 Grammy-winning comeback album, *Afro-Cuban Jazz.***

GRACIELA

Graciela Pérez (born 1915) (left) and brother Frank 'Machito' Grillo (1909–84) (right) moved to New York on the urging of their brother-in-law, Mario Bauzá. By 1943, they had organized Machito's Afro-Cubans, the band which shaped Latin Jazz. Graciela brought a sharp, picante texture and a confident edge to Bauzá's forceful, swinging arrangements. Her first hits, including the coquettish mambo 'Si, si, no, no', reveal the influence of idols Sarah Vaughan and Ella Fitzgerald. Machito, a virtuoso maracas player, exuded gentle, charming charisma in his lead role. The 1975 split of Graciela and Mario Bauzá because Machito pared down the band's brass section was a family tragedy, never fully repaired.

RIGHT: In 1955 Armando Peraza joined the band of London pianist George Shearing alongside Dave Brubeck's former drummer, the Swedish-American Cal Tjader. Tjader had turned to vibes and established the 'cool' West Coast sound in a band with his 'Pals' – percussionists Peraza, Mongo Santamaría (right on the sleeve) and New Yorker Willie Bobo (left).

and others. Several percussionists moved West and laid the foundations for the West Coast Latin Jazz scene, which still exists today.

AFRO-CUBAN JAZZ

While Gillespie was cooking up the abstract sounds of Cubop, the Cubans were drawing on big-band jazz. Mario Bauzá launched his dream orchestra in 1943, after summoning to New York from Havana both his brother-in-law, the singer 'Machito' (Frank Grillo), and Machito's sister Graciela, lead singer with the all-women dance orchestra Anacaona. Machito and his Afro-Cubans would become the fountainhead of Afro-Cuban jazz. While Graciela provided the vocals alongside her brother, Bauzá shared the arrangements with pianist Rene Hernández and their friend from Havana, Chico O'Farrill, who already had a reputation for his work with Count Basie, Stan Kenton and Dizzy Gillespie by the time the Afro-Cubans got in their stride. O'Farrill's compositions for the Machito band included the sophisticated 'Afro-Cuban Jazz Suite' with Charlie Parker on saxophone. The band landed a residency at La Conga club in Manhattan and released *Tanga* (Afro-Cuban for marijuana), Bauzá's first radical experiment in powering every instrument with Afro-Cuban rhythms.

The turning point for the Afro-Cubans came at the Palladium Ballroom on 52nd Street, where, from 1947 through to its peak in the fifties, Machito's band was one of the lead attractions at this mecca for mambo and cha-cha-cha with its emphasis on improvisation. The line between Latin and jazz became increasingly blurred, but Latin Jazz was always danceable, unlike the bebop further down 52nd Street which was defiantly against dancing and for listening. The three leading mambo bands, 'The Mambo Kings', were led by Tito Puente, Tito Rodríguez and Machito, each of whom had a symbiotic relationship with the jazz being played up the road. Rodríguez's *Live at Birdland* (1963) is a timeless example of how well American standards like 'How High the Moon' respond to Latin arrangements, though few American soloists

(with exceptions such as Flip Phillips and Charlie Parker) could adapt to Cuban cross rhythms. Competition between bands was furious; just as jazz bands at the Cotton Club, the Savoy and the Apollo set up 'cutting contests'. Mambo solos were high points of the night for the educated audience, who sometimes stopped mid-dance to follow the 'musical conversations' on stage.

Percussionists were vital to Latin Jazz and mambo bands, hired like strikers for a football team. Mongo Santamaría, who originally worked with Tito Puente, became one of the most widely known Latin musicians in jazz and also struck gold with Latin versions of American songs, including Herbie Hancock's 'Watermelon Man'. Of all the Palladium graduates, Puente took Latin the furthest into the mainstream with a series of hits over the following decades. His forties instrumental 'Ran Kan Kan' has been repeatedly revamped; in 1997 Puente's percussionist son, Tito Puente Jnr, included his father and the Latin soul singer La India in a Latin-Jazz club version.

CUBAN JAM SESSIONS IN MINIATURE

" DESCARGAS "

Panart RECORDS HIGH FIDELITY 107 - 28037 STEREO

CACHAO y su Ritmo Caliente

For bass players, Israel 'Cachao' López (born 1918) (far left) is the leading role model: 'One half of the genius of his great bass playing is as a totally schooled classical musician; the other is he's the funkiest street bass player around,' asserts his greatest fan, NuYorican Andy González. Not quite as tall as his instrument, Cachao embraces it like a lover, smiling as he draws from the depths of the wood deep, earthy sounds and long, husky groans which no electric instrument could parody.

LET LOOSE, LET RIP
In the late fifties, a new concept of improvised Cuban jazz emerged in after-hours sessions in Havana. Some of the greatest innovators of the decade, who normally played the tourist clubs, flocked to late-night sessions where improvisation and free-form structures were tested. The inventive pianist Bebo Valdés, who was directing the Tropicana Orchestra in 1952, rustled together some of his band at an after-hours bar, and produced five singles, including a free-form jam called *Con poco poco*. A couple of years later, the double bass player and co-inventor of the mambo, Israel 'Cachao' López, organized his own after-hours sessions and called them 'descargas' (letting loose, letting rip). These were immortalized in a five-volume set of *Cuban Jam Sessions* for Panart records recorded in 1955 and 1957. *Cuban Jam Sessions in Miniature* were released as 3-minute singles, musical haikus which still fill dancefloors today.

Most musicians involved in the descargas moved to New York after the Revolution and took the descarga bug with them. Al Santiago organized sessions in imitation of Cachao's, featuring many of the same players. He called the pool 'The Alegre All Stars' and installed pianist Charlie Palmieri as musical director. Santiago's descargas were perhaps more commercial and less intrepid than Cachao's, but no less interesting and they have equally stood the test of time.

In 1977 Cachao leapt back into the fray with *Cachao y sus descargas Volume I* and *Dos* (volume two), featuring several of the original descarga team with young Alfredo de la Fé on electrified violin and veteran charanga fiddler Pupi Legaretta. More structured than before, they still exhibit the unrivalled brilliance of Cachao's double bass style.

Through the seventies and eighties, as Fania set the standard for Americanized Cuban music, jazz promoter Jack Hooke established Monday nights at

Tito Puente

'The Mambo King', 'The King of Latin Jazz', 'El Rey del Timbal' (King of the Timbales) – Tito Puente's titles are based on a phenomenal career, decorated with Grammys and gold discs, honorary degrees, star-studded concerts and more than one hundred albums. He is a central figure in the story of twentieth-century American music, from the Swing-band and rumba-crazed thirties through the mamboing fifties to the eclectic Latin Jazz which currently spills into salsa and dance music, and back again.

Born in 1923, Puente planned a career as a dancer, but a torn ligament turned him to music. He eventually conquered piano, percussion, vibes and saxophone, composition, production and arrangement. Through the GI Bill, he attended the Juilliard School, which put him streets ahead of most percussionists – and many bandleaders. His career began in 1937 when the Cuban bandleader José Curbelo talent-spotted him. He formed The Piccadilly Boys in 1948, renamed it the Tito Puente

Orchestra, and rode into the mambo storm with a crossover hit 'Abaniquito' in 1949. Dancers from the American and Latino camps crowded to his shows. *Dancemania* in 1958 is one of the lasting memories of those heady days, featuring one of his favourite singing partners, Santos Colón.

On stage, Tito Puente is a comic showman, joking with the audience, but when he fires the first timbales shots, the mood changes: trebly shards fly from the metal-rimmed drums while his fiddly cowbell beats fill in between the mosaic of precisely interlocked brass and saxophones. He plays vibes with the same forceful attack as he drums. In rehearsals, Puente is serious and workmanlike, driving his mathematically complex arrangements home until they are perfect and polished and ingrained in the band; only then can the improvising fun start. On stage with his long-standing partner, Celia Cruz, he manipulates the orchestra to chase her every vocal need.

Puente's forties and fifties mambo and cha-cha-cha records still work magic on dancers today, but so do his rattling guest solos on many fusions of jazz and rap in the NuYorican Soul project (1996). The spectacular 3-CD tribute *50 years of Swing* in 1997 drew together tunes by a 41-strong cast, including his leading ladies (La Lupe, Graciela and Celia Cruz) and the men who have dominated Latin music this century. Its fifty tracks include an unreleased 'I'm Going Fishing' – an unlikely hobby for such a restless dynamo of Cuban rhythm.

ABOVE: **In typical high spirits during the 1997 NuYorican Soul recordings.**
LEFT: **Puente's revolutionary performing style: standing front of stage to play melodic solos.**

HILTON RUIZ

Hilton Ruiz is typical of Latin Jazz's new eclectic pianists and shares many qualities with the similarly bebop-inspired Cuban, Gonzálo Rubalcaba. Ruiz's early years ranged from a debut classical piano concert at Carnegie Hall, aged eight, to a seventies diversion into jazz-blues with singer Mary Lou Williams and five years with freestyle reedsman Rahsaan Roland Kirk. His return to Latin Jazz was crystallized in a 1987 gig with 'Papo' Lucca and Eddie Palmieri and three successive hit albums, *Something Grand*, *Strut* and *El camino*, anchored in Latin rhythms but drawing on bebop and blues.

MICHEL CAMILO

Michel Camilo Morel is the most joyously rhythmic, physically energizing pianist of the nineties generation. Like Hilton Ruiz, he was a child prodigy reared on classical piano and captivated by the folk music of his home country (in his case, Dominican merengue). Camilo's Caribbean background is unfailingly conjured in his buoyant solos but his deep, religious faith is at work as well. In the nineties, Camilo broadened his base in collaborations with the experimental Spanish flamenco band Ketama, and in minimalist duets with Puerto Rico's imaginative young conga player Giovanni Hidalgo.

the Village Gate in Manhattan for 'Salsa meets Jazz' bouts. A prestigious jazz soloist would jam with the leader of a top salsa band. Hooke admitted that at first he hadn't believed in this mix of 'fish and fowl', but the 'experiment' lasted until the late nineties. 'The musicians were very brave – there are no rehearsals', Hooke enthused. He recalled some of his favourite moments, including the night when pianist Eddie Palmieri 'fought' with McCoy Tyner, and when Tito Puente and Mario Bauzá were pitched against Dizzy Gillespie in the forties hit tune 'Manteca' (Bauzá remembered every note of Dizzy's original). Another of Hooke's favourites is, surprisingly, the Puerto Rican salsa band El Gran Combo, not often considered as Latin Jazz. 'Whenever they play, I hear the Basie Band,' Hooke said. 'The horn sections really *swing*, and have their own [Puerto Rican] rhythms which enhances it for me. You *have* to move your feet.'

NEW CUBA, NEW JAZZ

The reopening of Cuba in the late nineties gave American players their first full idea of what had been cooking on the island since the revolution and the mass exodus of so many players. Behind the scenes, a major emphasis had been on investigating African rhythms and the concepts enshrined in rumba and santería. Cuba's most sophisticated jazz band, Irakere, even employed the unsanctified batá drums normally used in santería rituals, and were copied in New York by the younger generation of experimenters.

For much of the eighties and into the nineties, three groups – Irakere; former Irakere trumpeter Arturo Sandoval's high octane bebop-influenced trio Afro-Cuba; and the young piano prodigy Gonzálo Rubalcaba's trio, Proyecto – had relentless touring schedules, earning dollars in Europe for the nation. Drummer Steve Berrios talked in New York of his relief at being expelled in the 'Mariel' exodus in 1981 and recalled how American jazz was banned in the sixties and seventies: 'We used to listen secretly to Dizzy Gillespie and Art Blakey, wrapped in Beny Moré sleeves,' he said. Tapes were passed around like samizdats and sowed seeds for new ideas. By the eighties, attitudes eased – a 1979 visit to Havana by CBS musicians, including Weather Report, had a dramatic influence. Irakere's part in the show led to a first solo album on CBS from Chucho Valdés, Irakere's pianist and leader.

Many musicians defected during tours of Europe, and Irakere was particularly leaky: lead 'voices' – saxophonist Paquito D'Rivera and trumpeter Arturo Sandoval – moved to the US, as did several lesser-known members.

On his arrival in New York in 1980, D'Rivera soon found himself at the 52nd Street Soundscape loft sessions run by Andy and Jerry González with producer Verna Gillis. These heady nights were structured more or less on jazz lines, with themes as a basis for improvisation, and ranged from solos to group work. The Cuban escapees, including conga master Daniel Ponce and percussionist Orlando 'Puntillo' Ríos, stirred up the locals like ants in a kitchen. The battle of the clave wars were fought in wild, lengthy jam sessions with an undertow of nationalism – between the NuYoricans and the Cubans, whose takes on jazz, salsa and Afro-Cuban music were very different. Pianist Michel Camilo, who cut his teeth there, recalls playing open-ended solos with three batá drums. He considers the sessions to have contributed to the music

153

LATIN JAZZ, AFRO-CUBAN JAZZ

PAQUITO D'RIVERA

Francisco 'Paquito' D'Rivera (born 1948) abandoned Chucho Valdés's Irakere at Madrid airport on 6 May 1980 and defected to Spain. Arriving in New York in 1981, he jumped into the brewing American Latin Jazz movement at the milestone Soundscape jam sessions between prestigious NuYorican, Dominican and Cuban soloists. As musical director of Dizzy Gillespie's United Nations Orchestra, he reconnected with former Irakere sideman Arturo Sandoval, heir to Gillespie's exhibitionist, high-octane trumpet style, then turned to producing carefully chosen recording groups – playing in combinations he dreamed of in Cuba. Most memorable are *40 years of Cuban Jam Sessions* (1993), in which three Cuban generations met in Miami for a mighty descarga; *Cuban Jazz – 90 miles to Cuba* (1996), which reunited pianists Bebo Valdés and son Chucho for the first time since 1962; and the two-volume *Cachao Master Sessions* (1993), where the two men relished every note of their passionate stroll through Cuban music, and classical and jazz history.

he plays today. Hilton Ruiz, fresh from seven years with the jazz genius Roland Kirk, and Argentine pianist Jorge Dalto who was then playing with George Benson, laid the foundations for an entirely new school of Latin piano jazz. But around the pianos and percussion was a clan of horn players – refugees from the borderlands salsa-jazz bands run by Eddie Palmieri, Ray Barretto and Manny Oquendo – and the pioneering Grupo Folklórico Experimental Nueveyorkino, a pool of players around the dedicated González brothers, Andy on bass and Jerry on congas and trumpet. Paquito D'Rivera's presence at the sessions galvanized fast changes and a rush of recordings from a slew of new band configurations. D'Rivera announced his arrival in the US with *Blowin'* in 1981; Dalto, Ruiz, Camilo, Ponce and the González brothers all released records which featured many Soundscape members and which launched American Latin Jazz into a new era. Two *Soundscape Sessions* albums released in 1998 reveal a set of dramatic pieces, in which solos fly between

Dizzy Gillespie's 15-piece United Nations Orchestra was the dream accompaniment to his last years: 'Talk about music as the international language – man, this is IT!', he yelled after the London debut (shown here). His trumpet solos, scat-singing and nifty mambo steps were accompanied by three generations of top Latin musicians. The orchestra's conga player was Puerto Rican Giovanni Hidalgo (right of photo).

continents and countries, time and space, and the exhilaration is tangible. From those groupings Dizzy Gillespie hired the dream team for his United Nations Orchestra which launched in London in 1989. When the trumpet master died in 1993, D'Rivera inherited the project.

For Irakere's leader, Chucho Valdés, each departure heralded a new direction. Valdés had an encyclopaedic repertoire of twentieth-century music; the band collectively excavated their roots in Afro-Cuban rhythms and were fired with ideas.

By the mid-nineties, Cuba's doors were opening wider. The elite dollar-earning musicians could record and perform almost anywhere and keep dollars earned abroad. And they could play with whomever they chose. Chucho Valdés began to loosen his ties to Irakere and was soon the most desired player in world jazz. In 1996 he was appointed president of the Havana Jazz Festival and invited the young American trumpeter Roy

DAVID SANCHEZ

Latin Jazz was rooted in Cuba but several Puerto Ricans have contributed to its eclectic stock along the way. Saxophonist David Sánchez (born 1968) arrived via an exceptionally musical family in San Juan and an American music-college education. His obsession was John Coltrane. Late eighties sessions with the NuYorican brothers Andy and Jerry González, and Cubans Daniel Ponce and Paquito D'Rivera led him into Dizzy Gillespie's United Nations Orchestra (1991–93). His repertoires are calculatedly broad – from boleros to plenas, strings and simple tunes, collaborations with the pioneering master-pianist Chucho Valdés and American jazz icon Brandford Marsalis, producer of the 1998 album *Obsesión*, which he packed with Puerto Rican classics by Rafael Hernández and Boby Capo.

Hargrove with his group, Crisol. He joined the unit, which included guest percussionists 'Changuito' from Los Van Van and ex-Irakere conga player Miguel 'Anga' Díaz. Hargrove's regular line-up featured the prodigious Puerto Rican saxophonist David Sánchez. Crisol's Grammy-winning 1998 album *Habana* was a big-band feast with a Cuban theme. On Sánchez's solo album that year, *Obsesión*, he broke the Cuban stranglehold on jazz by weaving Puerto Rican classics and rhythms into the North American and Cuban idioms.

The other major US influence in the late nineties came from the New York M-Base collective's brash new metallic jazz creations of saxophonist Steve Coleman. Coleman visited the Havana Jazz Festival in 1996 and recorded *The Sign and the Seal* with several local musicians, including members of the dynastic family Los Terry. The following year he returned to record with roots rumba group Afro-Cuban de Matanzas, and hired Boston-educated Yosvany Terry on saxophone. Coleman's influence is obvious in the exciting new eclectic rush of music from former Irakere members César López (saxophone) and 'El Indio' (trombone), who regrouped in 1997 as the César López Ensemble. Their influences range from Indio's penchant for Jamaican ska and reggae to López's crush on M-Base, but both are hand-reared in the Irakere school.

Latin Jazz today is being stretched and twisted into exciting new configurations and is entering new territories. Chucho Valdés is a loose cannon, stirring up changes wherever he plays. In 1998 he gave a tie-and-tails solo concert at the Lincoln Center in New York, revealing to attentive New York jazz lovers not only his extraordinary technical range and imaginative powers but also the state of modern Afro-Cuban jazz. In the same city, the futuristic young NuYorican Soul project, built from a pool of inventive young Latin dance DJs, producers and musicians with a passion for jazz, is making alliances with soul and salsa and its members are anchoring themselves with the legends of American Latin Jazz. Tito Puente is the key to their new experiments: he has proved for half a century that innovative, ground-breaking jazz can (and should) also be dance music.

Chapter 11 AFRICANDO: Cuban music returns to African soil

In sixties Dakar, Cuban music rather than local, traditional Senegalese music bewitched young dancers at clubs and parties. Malick Sidibe was typically obsessed with imported pachanga, cha-cha-cha and Latin twist records and he carried out a documentary project with his stunning black and white photographs of friends, which are now a unique record of that era.

THE GENETIC CONNECTIONS between salsa and African music are revealed in markets all over West Africa, where cassettes by Johnny Pacheco, Ray Barretto, Roberto Torres and the charanga orchestras Broadway and Aragón sell alongside the local superstars Youssou N'Dour, Salif Keita and Baaba Maal. Cuban music and salsa have had an enduring impact in the region – spread from Cameroun to Congo by local radio stations, in particular the uniquely powerful Radio Brazzaville, founded in the Congo in 1949. The music's greatest effect was felt in French-speaking countries such as Congo, Senegambia and Mali, which had surrendered so many of their people to Cuba through the slave trade. The music was returning to its roots, still recognizable in the rhythms.

Cuban records by the son groups of the twenties and thirties had as much impact there as elsewhere in the world. Don Azpiazu's 'El manicero' (The Peanut Vendor) and Trío Matamoros's 'Son de la loma' (Song of the Plains) both sparked a Cuban craze locally. Their soft, sweet tunes and winding rhythms hooked local musicians into imitating them on acoustic guitars, often homemade from chunks of wood, and bottle percussion. They sang in a mixture of languages, including phonetic Spanish. By the forties, jazz and big-band Swing prompted expanded line-ups, but because piano keyboards were generally unavailable in Africa, their part was played by guitars. Many modern African bands use not one but a whole line of electric guitars, playing densely layered and repeated patterns of hypnotic delicacy, in imitation of the horns.

Baaba Maal's searing voice has much in common with the high, keening Cuban sonero's style, but his influences are exceptionally catholic. Maal has made extensive trips around Senegal with his childhood friend, the guitarist Mansour Seck, in search of local musical styles. Youssou N'Dour's Wolof music greatly influenced him as a student in seventies Dakar, but his overriding passion was Latin music.

In the late fifties and early sixties, as Independence movements swept through Africa, imported music took a knocking as 'Africanization' policies encouraged or dictated a return to traditional music and dancing, instruments and languages. The unofficial national anthem of newly independent Congo-Zaire was, ironically, a seductive electric guitar band tune called 'Independence Cha-Cha'.

Johnny Pacheco first played in Africa in 1965, in the Ivory Coast capital of Abidjan (a capital of salsa). The city turned out in force to hear him perform in the elegant Grand Ballroom; dancers in ornate traditional robes travelled from all over Africa and knew his songs by heart. 'When I got out of the plane,' he recalls, 'about five thousand people were chanting "Pacheco! Pacheco!" and the streets from the airport to the hotel were blocked. The people had an incredible knowledge of our music – they knew who played with who and in what year, and even what colour suit I was wearing!'

Since those days, Pacheco and the Fania set and Cuba's Orquesta Aragón have become icons in Africa for every subsequent generation of musicians. In 1974 Kinshasa-Zaire was the host to a series of starry concerts running alongside the 'Rumble in the Jungle' fight between George Foreman and Mohammed Ali. James Brown and B. B. King played on bills with Ray Barretto, Pacheco and the Fania All Stars, and local superstars Franco and Tabu Ley Rochereau, who played their African versions of Cuban music known as 'African rumba'.

AFRICAN RUMBA

An African development of Cuban music was launched from Congo in the fifties by a pioneering showband called Africa Jazz. Its fusion of Cuban music and Congo sounds – known as 'African Rumba' – was the invention of a Zairean guitarist known variously as Kabaselle or Le Grand Kalle (family name: Joseph Tschamala), whose influence was felt all over Central and West Africa; wherever he played, local musicians turned to Western instruments and added Spanish to their local song lyrics.

In 1956 a teenage guitarist in Leopoldville (later Kinshasa) formed L'Orchestre Kinois Jazz (or OK Jazz) which rose to rival Le Grand Kalle. Franco – real name L'Okanga la Ndju Pene Luambo Miakiadi – would become Africa's most influential and most magnificent musician, the 'Sorcerer of the Guitar'. He developed Le Grand Kalle's rumba into an infectious new dance fusion with Cuban music known as 'soukous', using electric guitars and building in traditional African elements. His expanded version of the band was named TP (Tout Puissant – All Powerful) OK Jazz. For decades it supplied the charts with songs that could be heard in bars, cafés and dancehalls over wide swathes of Africa.

Franco was a vast man who played electric guitar with the delicacy of an embroiderer. His music moved huge audiences, who danced as if hypnotized. In full flight, the guitar sections rippled and shimmered, Franco's solos rising above them, while the horns harmonized like a gospel choir. At the front of the stage, the dancers led adoring audiences in new steps which became overnight crazes. Many young guitarists and singers, graduates of TPOK Jazz, carried the Cubanized soukous bug to world music audiences in Europe and the US; both Kanda Bongo Man and Sam Mangwana still fly the Latin flag with their own bands.

Sixties Congo band Ry-Co Jazz followed in the wake of Le Grand Kalle with a sharper style than Franco's. They were notable for their taut combination of electric guitars, congas, maracas, and a biting r'n'b saxophone tone. Another line of musicians followed a mellower route, using thumb pianos (known locally as sanzas) rather than guitars. Franklin Boukaka was the doyen of this genre, working with two other sanza musicians, a saxophonist and a double bass player, in a set of loping, languid songs closer to the velvety texture of bossa nova than to the stirring sound of salsa.

The sharp charanga sound of Orquesta Broadway has been popular in Africa from the early seventies. The 1972 album *African Soul, Alma Africana* includes the hit 'Pa'Africa', released in advance of the band's debut trip to the Ivory Coast.

The sanza or thumb piano is one of Africa's most ubiquitous melody instruments. In the hands of Franklin Boukaka and his group (below), it is used to play tumbling, overlapping melodies to an accompaniment of thick, warm bass-lines.

THE WEST AFRICAN CONNECTION

From the fifties, Senegal's capital, Dakar, was a stronghold of Cuban music and salsa aficionados. In 1960 the influential Star Band de Dakar was founded to mark Senegal's Independence celebrations. A seventeen-year-old Youssou N'Dour joined them in 1973, singing mambos, cha-cha-chas and rumbas in phonetic Spanish (with no clue as to the meaning of the lyrics) and dancing pachanga like Pacheco. He possessed the raw, keening tone of the best soneros.

With his own band, Etoile de Dakar, formed in 1979, N'Dour added the sharp chatter of a traditional tama talking drum to the Cuban congas and timbales to create Senegal's first modern, electrified music which he called mbalax (meaning 'rhythm'). It had its own leaping dance steps. In his 1979 album, *Absa Gueye*, N'Dour welcomed the independent government's 'Africanization' policies and paid a last tribute to Cuban music in two tantalizingly beautiful songs, 'La última rumba' (The Last Rumba) and 'El hombre misterioso soy' (I Am the Mysterious Man). Even so, strains of 'The Peanut Vendor' and other Cuban classics continue to waft like ghosts through his songs.

Youssou N'Dour's influence reached a seventeen-year-old art school student called Baaba Maal, who moved to Dakar from Northern Senegal. Maal was captivated by Cuban music and was a fan of Cuba's Orquesta Aragón, which he heard on the radio and in the clubs. He assumed the music was from somewhere else in West Africa because bands from Guinea and other regions played the same thing. 'People in my village danced African dances to it,' he says. With his own band, Maal drew heavily on the Cuban repertoires: 'Some of the top bands in Dakar sang in Spanish but we were singing in Fulani and improvising at the same time. I was using a Western acoustic guitar and playing things like "Guantanamera". We didn't know what the lyrics were saying, but the instruments talked to us, and we just transposed whatever they said.'

Newly independent Guinea established ties with Castro's Cuba in the sixties, and its musicians fell under the spell of Cuban music when Le Grand Kalle visited the country with his band, Africa Jazz. The most persistently Latin local band was Bembeya Jazz, a full salsa showband except for the line of shimmering electric guitars played in Zairean style.

The ancient Kingdom of Mali produced some outstanding bands during the sixties and seventies, including a group of students who attended a Havana music school in 1965. The flute player Boncana Maiga launched a charanga band, Las Maravillas de Mali (The Mali Miracles), who became local celebrities in Cuba. When Maiga moved to New York years later, he performed with Orquesta Broadway, a cult band for many African musicians.

From 1970 onwards Mali's hippest nightspot was the Railway Hotel in Bamako, where the government-sponsored Rail Band was led by a sharp-voiced young albino called Salif Keita. In 1973 Keita launched his now legendary band, Les Ambassadeurs du Motel. Inspired by Orquesta Aragón, whom he saw perform in Abidjan, Keita sang cover versions of Cuban songs in both Spanish and local languages. The band copied Aragón's charanga

The Zairean guitarist and godfather of big-band Zairean guitar music was fond of saying 'Cuban music has one root – Africa', but the revolutionary soukous that Franco creates with his legendary TPOK Jazz band clearly owe as much to the Cuban songs he was weaned on as they do to local African music.

formula, but substituted electric guitars for Aragón's soaring violins. 'I was hearing charanga and "Guantanamera" on Radio Mali,' he says, 'And through Cuban music, we discovered modern instruments.'

THE AFRICANDO PROJECT

Ties between Latin and African music were consolidated in New York in 1992 through a unique project called 'Africando', meaning in Wolof (the Niger-Congo language of the Senegalese) 'Africa Reunited'. Its inventor was the leading Senegalese record producer Ibrahim Sylla, who set up operations in a New York studio. The hand-picked salsa 'names' included members of Orquesta Broadway and the Fania All Stars who joined the Malian flautist Boncana Maiga and a group of leading Senegalese and Malian vocalists. At the helm was Youssou N'Dour's original singer, Pape Seck, whose gritty voice charged the music with a vigour that defeated any potential sweetness.

When Pape Seck died suddenly in 1995, Sylla broadened the group's base beyond Cuba by introducing the guitarist and singer Roger 'Shoubou' Eugene, a lifelong fan of Cuban music from the Haitian-New York band Tabou Combo, and Zaire's soukous master Tabu Ley Rochereau, who had begun his career singing Cuban songs. The cast also included former members of Rubén Blades's band, the new African superstar Sekouba 'Bambino' (Baby) Diabate and veteran Cubanophile singer Gnonnas Pedro. For the fourth album, *Baloba* (Let Them Speak), Sylla stretched Africando's musical territory further with a mesmeric Latino version of Edith Piaf's 'La Vie en rose' and a salsa cover of a Cuban-Algerian hit 'Aicha' by the Paris-based rai singer Khaled.

When the Senegalese record producer Ibrahim Sylla starts work on the latest album for the Africando project, he has a collection of over six thousand Latin records to draw on for inspiration. Africando has notched up a set of extraordinary albums.

The album's release was tied to the 150th anniversary of the abolition of slavery. In the recording studio, conversations flitted effortlessly between Spanish and English, Wolof and Mandingo, as the music soared across political and geographical boundaries and contacted the deep-rooted memories which bind Caribbean music to Africa.

Chapter 12

From here to

mañana

'FAMILIA – this is our decade!'

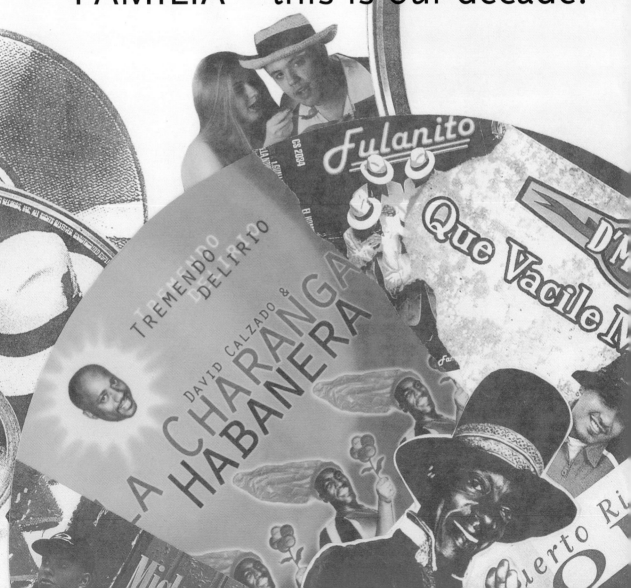

'FAMILIA, THIS IS OUR DECADE!' New York journalist Jessie Ramírez has used that sign-off for years; it could equally apply to the twenty-first century as Latin music of all shades overflows into the rest of the world. 'Salsa' is moving faster than the politics which try to control it; even the name-tag is more nebulous than when it was invented in the 1960s.

Today, there is a beautiful symmetry at work as bands of old, frail, grey-haired Cuban men fly between the capitals of Europe to perform songs they made popular in the earliest years of their careers, while at the same time young futurists are deconstructing the century's Latin music into sampled fragments and rethreading them with electronic beats into sounds which the originators would hardly recognize.

All eyes are again on Cuba. It is once more a fantasy destination for tourists, a backdrop for fashion shoots and travel stories, and a haunt of record company talent scouts on the lookout for potential hit-makers, new – and old. The future of Latin music will be decided politically in Washington and Havana but the forty-year embargo is already being bypassed in New York and the West Coast by record companies eager for some of the action stirred up by Europe. The signs are that they have already been left trailing behind, but this will probably change when the multinationals' dollars start kicking in. For those US record labels which dominate the salsa charts every week, particularly RMM, EMI, Sony and WEA, the game is how legally to outwit the embargo and sign some of the musicians before Europe's small-fry independents seal them all up.

But, despite the sensational worldwide success of the *Buena Vista Social Club* projects, the future of Latin music will not be counted in retro-remakes of eighty-year-old rhythms – though the discovery of those gems has been a revelation for vast numbers of non-Latins and has spawned an industry of fabulous reissues and tributes. Latin music has entered a post-modern, post-salsa age, with unimagined fusions invigorating Latin dance and jazz. American salsa is being stirred up by the new Cuban sounds which are freshly available. New-wave salseros like Marc Anthony and the three young musical guerrillas known as DLG (Dark Latin Groove) have incorporated the sinuously jiving songo rhythm which propels Cuban salsa – timba, as they call it – into their US hits. The visionary producer Sergio George (behind both Anthony and DLG) freely mixes funk, reggae and hiphop beats with songo and salsa and ignores the old rules of rhythmic purity. Clave comes and goes but the dancers don't miss a beat; they don't even dance in couples half the time. In reverse, young Cuban musicians like the singer Paulito F. G. and groups Bamboleo, N. G. La Banda and Charanga Habanera are hungry for the rap and reggae, jungle and house music they catch on Miami radio and MTV. And for the first time, bands like Cuba's Dan Den are revelling in the possibilities of polished, classic salsa from New York and Puerto Rico.

New alliances in the Latin hiphop community are editing together a soundtrack for the millennium. Two former club DJs now known as 'Masters at Work' – Louie Vega and Kenny 'Dope' González – delved into all corners of the city's mosaic of music for their mammoth, eclectic project *NuYorican Soul*. They effortlessly mixed the music of jazz fusion legends George Benson and Roy Ayers and Latin Jazz percussionist Tito Puente with salsa newcomer India and soul diva Jocelyn Brown, and linked into the salsa mainstream with a dedication to Vega's uncle, the salsa icon Héctor Lavoe.

The new salsa stars have as much in common with rock stars as with

PRECEDING PAGES: **The clash of the past against the future: the most exhilarating rule-breakers from around the continent, whose music is already providing clues to the sound of the new century.**

Marc Anthony & India

Marc Anthony Muñiz and Linda 'India' Caballero are the figureheads of late nineties salsa. Born in 1969, they took the long road to salsa, Marc Anthony through sessions with his folk-singer father, Felipe; India through opera classes. Their teens coincided with the birth of Latin New York's electronic 'free-style' dance music, but while most singers mimed to their studio-enhanced hits, these two sang live back-ups. India's first solo record, *Dancing in the Fire* (1986), was a belting collision of hiphop and soul. Marc Anthony's solo debut, *When the Night Is Over* (1990), was also more hiphop than salsa, but was peppered with solos by Tito Puente, Louis 'Perico' Ortiz and Eddie Palmieri.

Among the icons of young salsa-rock, Marc Anthony (left) and La India (below) are the most privileged – signing to salsa's dominant RMM label offered them dream collaborations with the great names of the RMM family. For Marc Anthony, his hit records are a springboard to acting roles; La India has her eye on a diva throne, but definitely one in a Latin American setting.

In the nineties, both singers were drawn into the RMM Records salsa royal family – Marc Anthony cherry-picked by the experimental producer Sergio George, India on the arm of Eddie Palmieri. *Llegó La India, via Eddie Palmieri* (Here Comes India with Eddie Palmieri) revealed her tremendous potential in searing hit-and-miss vocals. Her voice has an instinctive power with a tendency towards undisciplined shrieks, all of which benefitted from Palmieri's anchoring piano backing. The title track's modern soul-boogaloo is her lasting legacy. On stage, her extraordinary charisma can ignite a stadium. She keeps her hiphop crowd sweet with projects like her back-ups on Tito Puente's electronic remix of his forties hit 'Ran Kan Kan' (1992) and the eclectic NuYorican Soul experiment.

Marc Anthony had no problems finding his voice or making it fit the music. His first solo albums, *Otra nota* (1993) and *Todo a su tiempo* (1995), were startling debuts for a versatile new voice. He is a free-flier, switching from soaring flamenco to doowop falsetto and hunky soul ballads, between Spanish and English lyrics. On stage, he has the magnetic, easy-going presence of a world-class rock star and a casual, rap-chic image to match. Rubén Blades pioneered the deal between rock and salsa audiences and Marc Anthony is clinching it. In 1997 he played lead role with Blades and fellow twenty-something salsero Frankie Negrón in Paul Simon's *The Capeman* musical on Broadway.

Through the short years of their salsa careers, India and Marc Anthony have led their generation away from the all-consuming culture of rap and American music and turned them towards salsa, enabling a new, late-nineties posse of professional young singers – Michael Stuart, Frankie Negrón, Jerry Rivera – to take over the charts.

DLG: Dark Latin Groove

Huey, Fragrancia and Da Barba are the nametags of the three musical guerrillas who operate under the name of DLG – Dark Latin Groove. Since their first album, *DLG*, in 1996, they have redefined Latin dance music by effortlessly weaving into salsa and merengue the rap, reggae and house music clichés familiar all over the world. DLG's image and packaging is a hip composite of rap and ragga style with an inimitable Latino cool. Only the lead singer, 25-year-old Huey Dunbar, speaks Spanish (the others are learning) and all are darker skinned than the conventional Latin pop front-liners.

The key player in the DLG story is its fourth member – creator of the group, and its producer and keyboards player, Sergio George. He brought a track-record of hit productions for some of salsa's top bands and in the late nineties focused his eclectic past and futuristic vision on the fresh generation of salsa figureheads, India and Marc Anthony, Víctor Manuelle and Jerry Rivera. With DLG, he really let loose.

ABOVE: **The group's most prominent voice is the falsetto tenor of Huey Dunbar (at front), the only Spanish speaker among them.**

ABOVE RIGHT: **Representing the face of new Latin dance music, Dark Latin Groove (DLG) wear an image light years away from the conventional salseros' look.**

Sergio George first heard Huey Dunbar's soaring falsetto tenor at a talent contest; Wilfredo 'Fragrancia' Crispín bowled up at his office with a demo tape and a reputation for quick-witted vocals with the prototype mereng-rap duo Sandy y Papo. George already knew James 'Da Barba' DeJesús's growling bass from his back-ups with former Conjunto Clásico singer Tito Nieves, on the English-language boogaloo-rap hit 'I Like It Like That'.

Through George, the trio are edging closer to salsa and merengue. The magnificent 1998 album *Swing On* includes a cover of the Cuban salsa-son hit 'Juliana' by Dominican legend Cuco Valoy. 'Magdalena, mi amor (Quimbara)' is a rap-and-salsa remake of Celia Cruz's raunchy hit. *Gotcha*, soundtrack to the summer of 1999, hooked back to the source with guests Johnny Pacheco and Wilfrido Vargas.

DLG strike a universal chord with young Latinos reared on the cacophonous soundtrack to Latin American life. They represent Latin youth in all its extraordinary hues of nationhood, skin tone and economic status. Their music is not, however, for the salsa purist.

salseros. Traditional qualifications like perfect pitch and an intuition for improvising, which used to separate a coro singer from a leader, are no longer essential. Gone are the showstopping moments for the instrumental solos; the singer is now the show and the image is all-important. Marc Anthony is salsa's first rock star, cast in the mould of the original crossover success story, Rubén Blades. He darts around the stage in a designer suit, clapping clave, singing in English and Spanish, rapping in Spanglish, but also delivering straight salsa. A lead role in Martin Scorsese's 1999 film, *Bringing out the Dead*, introduced to the wider world the man who singlehandedly filled Madison Square Gardens with 20,000 screaming fans.

For many young continental Latin Americans, Latin rock is the new salsa. Afro-Cuban rhythms have little reality in Argentina, the country which spawned the 'movement'. But in Colombia's wildly eclectic music scene, rock is just one of many elements being sewn into the mix of genuinely new dance music. Former television soap star Carlos Vives hit the charts in the late 1990s with his avant-garde, rock-influenced vallenato which set off accordions in many unexpected places (Gloria Estefán, Julio Iglesias). Then his band broke away to form an experimental venture called Bloque de Quesada, signed by David Byrne to his eclectic Luaka Bop label, and their subsequent fusion of traditional flutes and drums, with synths and electric guitar, vallenato accordion and whacking drum-and-bass beats places them at the head of the new wave. The pioneers of such adventures – a laconic duo with the magical name of Aterciopelados (The Velvety Ones) – reveal more allegiance to left-field British dance music (Tracey Thorne and Ben Watt spring to mind) than to salsa, but still the ghosts of Cuban and Colombian rhythms thread through the songs. Colombia was also the starting point for the London band Sidestepper, a minimalist dance trio of Roberto Pla's timbales with trumpet and synthesizers, which stretches and fattens the bassy vallenato beat and injects it with Jamaican dub. Such projects make reference to salsa, sampled and actual, but only as a springboard for new possibilities.

A key question is how does salsa fare in the face of such crossovers and fusions and brand new styles? It is reassuring that hardcore salsa, with its characteristic risk-taking solos, still survives today. The great Cuban innovator, bass player Cachao, continues to run a touring band in his eighties. Two graduates from the Bronx 'University of Manny Oquendo', otherwise known as Orquesta Libre, are proving that dancing is not the only criterion of perfect salsa; trombonist Jimmy Bosch and multi-instrumentalist Wayne Gorbea both leave wide-open spaces in the music of their bands for improvised solos, the legacy shared with Latin Jazz and also the great salsa of the Fania heyday. And they also create stomping good dance music.

The Puerto Rican scene, traditionally blessed with more than average numbers of distinguished vocal stylists, continues to feed the charts. And just as Cuba has rediscovered its old son champions, so Puerto Rico has witnessed a renaissance of bomba and plena styles and neo-traditionalist bands (Plena Libre and Descarga Boricua), and also the birth of the tellingly rap-tagged Jibaro Boyzz.

The potential danger ahead for salsa is that the heritage would be lost to the twin forces of capitalism, which panders to the white crossover audiences, and the undemocratic technology of the Internet. When a cheap mixer can create new sounds which no longer have any linear connection to tradition, then the musical heritage would be atomized. But, miles away from Havana, young musicians with no contact with Cuba apart from their parents' stories and dreams are creating music of the future which does acknowledge the connections to their heritage in Colombia, Puerto Rico and Cuba. Two bands on the cutting edge of Cutting Records, a label run by former Latin hiphop name Aldo Marín, are making music which matches New York's crazily mixed-up daily reality. Fulanito – five Dominicans in white suits – add 'live' instruments in vigorous electronic interpretations of the Latin rhythms (from merengues to bombas to cha-cha-cha), rapping in Spanglish, dancing to pumping techno beats. Sancocho, from the same label, play heavy, unrelenting, techno-free-style Latin with sampled salsa breaks, but open their album with an abuelita (a grandma) giving the recipe for Puerto Rico's national dish, sancocho. Whichever unpredictable dance crazes emerge in the new century, whichever whims of the North American record industry are suggested to their Latin artists, salsa's powers of reinvention, its energy and wit, will survive – even in the face of dilution by The Spice Girls, its irrepressible soul will shine through.

Not forgetting...

Omar Alfanno: Panamanian dentist-turned-Grammy-winning songwriter, particularly popular among Puerto Rican salseros.

Tito Allen: New York salsero, veteran from Ray Barretto's band, Típica 73, Conjunto Clásico and Puerto Rican All Stars.

Johnny Almendra: Former timbalero, leader with Mongo Santamaría of **Jovénes del Barrio** (Kids from the Block), a successful, jazz-influenced New York charanga featuring students from Johnny Colón's East Harlem Music School and fellow teacher Louis Bauzo, with singer Jillian.

Paulina Alvarez: The Empress of Danzonete, adored Cuban soprano who inspired Celia Cruz.

Asere: Dynamic, young, baseball-hat-generation Cuban band, playing son.

Camilo Azuguita: Panamanian whose mercurial tenor enlivened Rafael Cortijo's Combo and Roberto Roena's Apollo Sound. Based in Paris.

Batacumbelé: Significant Afro–Puerto Rican super-group formed in early eighties by former members of Louis 'Perico' Ortíz's band; pivoted around percussionist Angel 'Cachete' Maldonado and young conga genius Giovanni Hidalgo, and produced by Frank Ferrer, who evolved the band in the nineties into **Descarga Boricua**.

Bongo Logic: Los Angeles-based, classically inclined charanga, led by percussionist and composer Brett Gollin.

Borincuba: Influential Puerto Rican band. Founded in 1979 by singer Justo Betancourt; passed to Tito Rojas who renamed it **Conjunto Borincano**; then passed to singer Luisito Ayala as **Puerto Rican Power**; and finally, with Borincano's conga player Pedro López, became **Pedro Conga y su Orquesta Internacional**.

Cachaoíto: Bass player from Cuba's dynastic López family. Long track record in Cuba and central to Afro-Cuban All Stars.

Eddie Calvert: Trumpeter who fed UK obsession with cha-cha-cha with his version of Pérez Prado's 'Cherry Pink, Apple Blossom White'.

Angel Canales: Bald-headed, Puerto Rican, avant-garde singer and timbalero, his wackiness acknowledged in his hit 'El diferente'.

Candido: Showy Cuban conga player, often plays shirtless; shone with George Shearing and Stan Kenton in the West Coast Latin Jazz scene.

Carabalí: Late-eighties New York cult salsa-jazz group, formed by conga player Raul 'Primo' Alomar. Featured vibes player Valerie Naranjo.

Celínes (Celínes Pagan Montalvo): 'La flor de merengue', a drama school graduate and Puerto Rican singer of hit girly merengues.

Jesús Cepeda and Grupo ABC: Short-lived Puerto Rican bomba revivalists, former members of Rafael Cortijo's Combo and their offspring.

Andy Colé: Director and songwriter for popular Cuban trumpet-led son band.

Conjunto Chaney: Puerto Rican band founded in 1980 by bongosero Nicolas Vivas, after El Gran Combo. Launched singer Eddie Santiago.

Jack Constanza: 'Mr Bongo' – Italian-American, first bongo player in jazz; played Stan Kenton's *Peanut Vendor* (1947), in Nat King Cole's classic trio, and in the soundtrack of Orson Welles's *Touch of Evil*.

Cruz Control: New York band specializing in revamps of heavy Palladium-era standards, led by timbalero Ray Cruz.

Cuarteto D'Aida: Cuba's first girl group, founded in 1952 by pianist Aida Diestro. Sang American-influenced four-part harmonies and made a name for future solo singers Omara Portuondo and Elena Burke.

Cuarteto Patria: Veteran Cuban group led by lyrical guitarist–singer Eliades Ochoa; in 1998 created interesting r'n'b son with African saxophonist Manu Dibango.

Jorge Dalto: Argentine pianist, member of Tito Puente's 1981 Latin Jazz Ensemble and central figure in the new Latin Jazz scene of eighties New York.

Miguel 'Anga' Díaz: Exceptional Cuban conga player, ex-Irakere; plays Afro-Cuban, songo-influenced jazz on five tuned drums.

Jordano D'León: Son of Venezuela's super-sonero Oscar D'León. With his orchestra, launched his rapping and break-dancing act and now sings solo salsa hybrids.

Luis Enrique: Nicaraguan singer, guitarist and percussionist; leading light in eighties craze for salsa erotica.

Las Estrellas d'Areito: Cuban super-group (featuring future members of Afro-Cuban All Stars) based on Fania All Stars and conceived by Ivory Coast's Raul Diomande.

La Familia Valera Miranda: Six-piece family son group from Eastern Cuba, run by tres guitarist Félix Valera Miranda.

Roberto Faz: Cuban guajira-style singer and bandleader who influenced New York Fania keyboards player Larry Harlow.

Frank Ferrer: Creator of Puerto Rican nationalist projects **2010** and **2013**, whose singers included Héctor Lavoe soundalike/lookalike Van Lester.

Henry Fiol: New York singer (hypnotic guajiro's voice), songwriter, painter, teacher; director of traditional son band Saoco and subsequent solo projects.

Kenny Graham: English saxophonist who directed London's fifties Cubop band **The Afro-Cubists**, featuring saxophonist Pete King (now director of Ronnie Scott's Club) with African and Caribbean percussionists.

Olga Guillot: Cuban diva, contemporary of Celia Cruz, famed for rich, operatic voice and beehive hairdos; now a Miami-Cuban aristocrat.

Tata Güines (Aristides Soto): Cuba's most influential modern conga player (born in 1930) who invented new techniques, including use of finger-nails. An unrivalled improviser, featured on Cachao's *Cuban Jam Sessions*, *Estrellas d'Areito*, and in sessions with today's young Cuban singers and jazz pioneers.

Hanny: Young Havana singer, 'discovered' busking by UK entrepreneur Mr Bongo (Dave Buttle) who recorded his 'son casino' style in London, and the Cuban hit 'Sexo, dinero y fantasia' (Sex, Money and Fantasy).

Andy Harlow: Miami-based brother of Larry, flute and saxophone player; seventies hit album *Sorpresa la flauta*.

Kike Harvey: Colombian singer who resurrected pachangas in early-nineties recordings and made improved hit of Madonna's 'La Isla Bonita'.

'Havana Jam': Milestone 1979 visit to Havana by US super-groups, including Weather Report, Fania All Stars and Típica 73; resulted in CBS album *Havana Jam*. Deeply influential event for local musicians.

Víctor Hugo: Flamboyant Venezuelan singer who brought exotic South American style and professionalism into the UK with Robin Jones's King Salsa and his own Salsa Picante.

Jovénes Clásicos del Son: Vibrant, young, traditional Cuban son sextet, led by double-bass player Ernesto 'Palma' Reyes Proenza.

Karis: Puerto Rican merengue group, massively popular in late nineties following the hit *El poder del swing* (The Power of Swing).

Raphy Leavitt: Pianist and leader of veteran Puerto Rican band La Selecta, founded in 1971, and player of solid, brass-led music.

The Lebron Brothers: Veteran Puerto Rican New Yorkers whose soul-tinged songs reflect local collision of African and Latin-American sounds.

Ernesto and Margarita Lecuona: Sibling piano prodigies, Cuba's most significant 20th-century composers, equally successful with hit dance songs and classical pieces. Ernesto was an international concert pianist.

Ricardo Lemvo (and his band, Makina Loca): Los Angeles-based Congo-Zairean singer, creator of salsa-soukous with Cuban partner, Ninjo Jesús Alejandro (tres, piano, flute).

José Mangual Jnr: Master percussionist; starting with Willie Colón, he moved through other leading New York salsa outfits and became keystone producer of solid salsa, particularly revered in Colombia.

José Mangual Snr: New York-based bongo player, 'El Buyu'; created in Machito's band a new language for bongos, using fast, intricate fingerwork.

Sabu Martínez: Powerful conga player who replaced Chano Pozo in Dizzy Gillespie's band in 1948, and subsequently shifted between roots Cuban music and jazz.

Joseíto Mateo: Dominican accordionist, strong influence on the young Johnny Ventura; specialized in traditional Cibao country style.

Celeste Mendoza: Cuban singer, 'The Queen of the Guaguancó' (rumba queen); popularized and modernized Afro-Cuban traditional styles.

Gunda Merced (Julio): Adventurous Puerto Rican trombonist who wrote hits for Roberto Roena's Apollo Sound; formed exhilarating splinter group Salsa Fever in 1978. Successful producer for MPI Records.

Mulenze: Classic Puerto Rican eighties salsa group, influenced by Swing-jazz and led by Edwin 'Mulenze' Morales. A selling-point was Pedro Brull's vocal improvisations.

Tommy Olivencia: Puerto Rican singer, trumpeter and entertaining bandleader who has adopted many stage identities, including Sheik. Nurtured young singers, including Paquito Guzman, Lalo Rodríguez, Frankie Ruiz and Gilberto Santa Rosa.

Louis 'Perico' Ortíz: Puerto Rico's most significant trumpeter, arranger and producer; graduate of PR Conservatory and Fania Records, leader of bands in New York and San Juan.

Los Papines: Traditional Cuban rumba group founded in 1963 by four Abreu brothers, playing a conga apiece. Long-term Tropicana favourites.

Pello 'El Afrikan': Quirky Cuban percussionist, popularizer of the mozambique, given to wearing eccentric outfits while playing congas.

'Lefty' Perez: Puerto Rican salsero and former Venezuelan soap actor whose solo albums have been produced by PR ace Carlos 'Cuto' Soto.

Peruchín (Pedro Justiz): Distinctive Cuban piano stylist, his rhythmic playing drove leading cha-cha-cha band Orquesta Riverside and featured in *Cuban Jam Sessions* albums. Major influence on Chucho Valdés.

Giraldo Piloto: Young Cuban singer, leader of innovative band Klimax.

Daniel Ponce: Brilliant Cuban conga player who hit New York's new Latin Jazz scene in 1980. Brought an exotic voice to albums by Mick Jagger, Nona Hendryx and Laurie Anderson and made two moderately successful solo records, *Chango te llama* and *Arawe*, but burnt out and disappeared.

Pucho (Henry Brown) (and his Latin Soul Brothers): Harlem-raised timbalero who took up Latin music on hearing Tito Puente. Made a name with boogaloos and Latin soul.

Tito Puente Jnr: Miami-based son of the maestro of Latin percussion; salsa-house pianist, singer and percussionist, he included his father's classic, 'Oye como va', on his debut record, *Guarachando*, in 1996.

Puerto Rican All Stars: Super-group launched to rival Fania All Stars; sprang key producer Jesús César Delgado onto Puerto Rican scene.

Domingo Quiñones: Popular Puerto Rican singer, hand-percussionist and composer; back-up for José Alberto, Conjunto Clásico and Roberto Roena. As soloist, made first video to deal with HIV issues.

Manuel Ramírez: Afro-Peruvian singer, guitarist and tres player, emerged as a salsero in Colombia.

'Rasputín' (July Mateo): One of merengue's long-serving singing stars; introduced merengue to Panama and Central America.

Johnny Rivera: New York romantic salsero, graduate of Johnny Colón's East Harlem workshops and Conjunto Clásico. His back-up singers included Michael Stuart.

Mario Rivera: One of the original Dominican New Yorkers, a perennially sought-out reeds player and flautist with long, varied track record in salsa and Latin Jazz. His first solo album (1993) and a part in Juan Luis Guerra's *Fogarate* (1994) took him back to his roots.

Niño Rivera: Cuban tres guitar stylist, veteran of many great son groups including Septeto Bolona. His modernized sound features distorted, amplified solos.

Alfredo Rodríguez: Cuban pianist influenced by Peruchín and decades of working out of Paris (hence his nickname, 'Monsieur Oh La La'). Impressive, profound recordings with Afro-Cuban congosero 'Patato' and 'Totico'; a guest member of Jesús Alémany's Cubanismo.

Bobby Rodríguez: New York flautist, clarinettist, leader of La Compania; from 1974, created experimental clarinet-led salsa, flavoured with Dixieland jazz and funk.

Willie Rosario: Puerto Rican radio journalist, singer, bandleader, guitarist and saxophonist. Formed his first band, Coamex, in 1958 and with it forged his characteristic heavy brass style. Many top singers, including Tony Vega and Gilberto Santarosa, started with his bands.

Gonzálo Rubalcaba: Son of Cuban pianist Guillermo who broke the family's danzón piano dynasty and moved into bop-influenced jazz, supervised by Dizzy Gillespie. His trio Proyecto and his solo work feature awesomely complex, technically brilliant solos.

Bobby Sanábria: New York percussionist, graduate of Mario Bauzá and Mongo Santamaría bands; leader of Afro-Cuban jazz outfit Asunción.

Marvin Santiago: Puerto Rican singer who passed through Rafael Cortijo's Combo and Bobby Valentín's band. In 1977 he recorded a solo album from gaol, then became a community worker. His long-lasting popularity relies on witty, controversial, nationalistic ad-libbed songs.

Jon Secada: Miami-Cuban, Latin-pop singer–songwriter; his aunt Moraina Secada sang in sixties girl group Cuarteto D'Aida.

Charlie Sepulveda: Puerto Rican salsa-jazz trumpeter with a fast, clean sound; trained in left-field Puerto Rican bands with Eddie Palmieri. Led important early-nineties group which launched future Latin Jazz aces Danilo Pérez (piano) and David Sánchez (saxophone).

Ray Sepulveda: NuYorican singer 'discovered' by Ray Barretto; likened his voice to a 'hoarse woman's'. Performed as hit eighties duet Johnny (Zamot) and Ray.

Sidestepper: London-based minimalist trio (trumpet, timbales, synthesizers) led by world music producer Richard Blair – a 'rappasonic' collaboration influenced by his three years in Colombian recording studios.

Sintesis: Cuba's first salsa-jazz fusion, synth-rock band; founded in 1976 and modelled on Yes and Genesis. Summed up in the two-album *Ancestros* (Ancestors).

Michael Stuart: New-wave salsero and dancer who emerged through late nineties hit 'Cuentos de la vecinidad'

Ned Sublette: Texan New Yorker, head of Qbadisc records, specializing in modern Cuban music. Released a quirky country-and-western merengue album *Cowboy Rumba* (1999).

Terapía: Colombia's new-wave coastal dance style, led by King Trigger and Anne Zwing, influenced by vallenato, ragga and house.

'Tiburón' (Shark): Charismatic Cuban country singer Eduardo Morales, who co-founded Cuba's most significant modern son group, Son 14, with songwriter Adalberto Alvarez.

uan Pablo Torres: Eclectic Cuban trombonist and producer; his five-record set, *Estrellas d'Arieto*, produced in five days in 1979, was reissued in 1999. Lives in New York and Italy.

Nestor Torres: Virtuoso Puerto Rican classical flautist, ex-New York Symphony Orchestra. Moved to Miami and joined local charanga and jazz scene. Has performed with David Bowie and Chick Corea.

Steve Turre: Trombone stylist and virtuoso conch shell player. Turre's background includes playing with Rahsaan Roland Kirk and Art Blakey, and Puerto Rican salseros Libre – his solo work reflects that unique mix.

Francisco Ulloa: Dominican accordionist and songwriter; his accordion zips at spectacular speeds. Guest on Chi Chi Peralta's new merengue sessions.

Alfredo Valdés Jnr: Cuban pianist from dynastic family (his father was a leading son pianist). His light, bright style appeared on Ray Barretto's hit 'El Watusi' and in Roberto Torres's charanga-vallenato fusions.

Carlos 'Patato' Valdez: Veteran Cuban congosero with a sweet, melodic style and a track record stretching across the century – from La Sonora Matancera, through Dizzy Gillespie and Johnny Pacheco, to Cachao.

Bobby Valentín: Inventive Puerto Rican bass player, played trumpet with Tito Rodríguez and Charlie Palmieri; arranged for Fania All Stars and nurtured singers, including Marvin Santiago and Cano Estremero.

Dave Valentín: Flute player with vast collection of ethnic instruments, a former member of New York band Libre, he slots effortlessly into Latin Jazz and salsa line-ups, turning live shows into full-scale entertainment.

Orlando 'Maraca' Valle: Cuban flute player who operates from Paris with his flautist wife Céline Chaveaux. A prolific member of the scattered ex-Irakere and Cuban salsa set who are transforming Latin Jazz.

Tony Vega: Romantic salsero, discovered in Raphy Leavitt's La Selecta. His nineties songs reflect his born-again Christian faith.

Discography

Perfect dancing soundtrack records, as recommended by London's original salsa teacher **Nelson Batista**: 'Old, slow **Johnny Pacheco** classics for beginners; Latin Jazz such as **Louie Ramírez** for fast fancy footwork; **Oscar D'León** for the most refined salsa; **Joe Arroyo** for tropical Colombian, and **La Sonora Dinamita** for cumbias. Merengue classics by **Johnny Ventura**, African-influenced merengues by **Juan Luis Guerra**, and giddying fast ones by **Jossie Esteban**.'

Chapter 1 Cuba: The roots of salsa

Paulina Alvarez, *La emperatriz de la danzonete* (EGREM)

Arcano y sus Maravillas, *With Miguelito Cuni* (EGREM); *Danzon-Mambo* (EGREM)

Don Azpiazu and His Havana Casino Orchestra, *New York 1930* (Harlequin/Interstate)

Celina y Reutilio, *Desde la habana te traigo (early songs)* (TUMI, 1998)

Félix Chappotín y Sus Estrellas, *Perlas del son* (EGREM); *Estrellas de Cuba – with Miguelito Cuni* (Antilla)

Compay Segundo with Omara Portuondo, Silvio Rodríguez and Pio Leyva, *Lo Mejor de la vida* (East West/Warner, 1998)

Cuarteto Las D'Aida, *Cuarteto Las D'Aida* (EGREM, 1995)

Xavier Cugat with Miguelito Valdés, *Rumba Rumbero* (Tumbao Classics); *The Early Years, 1933–38* (Harlequin/Interstate)

La Familia Valera Miranda, *Cuba – Son et bolero* (Ocora, 1997)

Joseito Fernández, *Y su guantanamera* (EGREM, 1992)

Celina González, *Fiesta guajira* (World Circuit, 1993)

Grupo Oba-Ilu, *Santería, Songs for the Orishas* (Soul Jazz Records, 1998)

Antonio Machín, *El Manicero* (Tumbao)

Mambo Kings, *Los Reyes del Mambo – José Curbelo, Tito Puente, Tito Rodríguez* (Carino Records)

Beny Moré, *Beny Moré de verdad* (EGREM, 1996); *Canto a mi Cuba* (EGREM, 1996); *Golden Years: Beny Moré, Perez Prado and Orquesta Aragón* (RCA)

Los Muñequitos de Matanzas – The Rumba Originals, *Cantar Maravilloso* (Ace Records, 1990)

Eliades Ochoa y El Cuarteto Patria, *Sublime Illusion* (Virgin, 1999)

Orquesta Aragón, *Best of Aragón* (Eden Waves); *The Heart of Havana, Vols I and II* (RCA Tropical, 1992–93); *Orquesta América y Orquesta Aragón* (EGREM)

Orquesta Casino de la Playa, *Memories of Cuba* (with Miguelito Valdés) (Tumbao); *Todos los barrios* (with Arsenio Rodríguez) (Harlequin, 1994)

Orquesta Enrique Jorrín, *Todo cha-cha-cha* (EGREM, 1992)

Orquesta Neno González, *Danzones – la cumbancha* (EGREM, 1998)

Orquesta Riverside y Tito Gómez en vivo (live on radio) (Discmedi)

Orquesta Típica and Rotterdam Conservatory, *Cuba: Contradanzas and Danzones* (Nimbus, 1996)

Peruchín, *The Incendiary* (GNP)

Guillermo Portables, *El carretero* (World Circuit, 1996)

Pérez Prado, *El rey del mambo* (Profono Records)

AArsenio Rodríguez, *Todos los barrios* (Harlequin, 1994)

Arsenio Rodríguez y su Magia, *La musica Afro-Cubana* (Caliente Records, 1973); *Quindembo/Afro-Magic* (Sony Tropical, 1995)

Tito Rodríguez and Louie Ramírez, *With Love* (Algo Nuevo, TR)

Armando Sánchez and Son de la Loma, *Regalo del ciego* (Ryko Latino, 1997)

Septeto Nacional de Ignacio Pineiro, *Clásicos del son* (EGREM, 1994)

La Sonora Matancera with Myrta Silva and Daniel Santos, *Live on the Radio, 1952–1958* (Interstate Music, 1996); *50 Years* (Seeco)

Trío Matamoros, *Ecos de Cuba* (Kubaney); *La China de la rumba* (Tumbao)

Bebo Valdés and His Havana All Stars, *Descargas calientes* (Caney)

Vieja Trova Santiaguera, *Hotel Asturias* (NubeNegra, 1997)

Various artists, *Cuban Jam Sessions Vols 1–5* (Panart)

— , *Son de Cuba* (original pioneering son groups) (EGREM, 1992)

— , *Cuba, I Am Time* (4-CD box set) (Blue Jackal, 1997)

— , *Tribute to Maria Teresa Vera* (Nubenegra/ Intuition, 1998)

— , *Hot Dance Music from Cuba, 1907–36* (Miguel Matamoros, Sexteto Habanero, Antonio Machín, Sexteto Nacional de Ignacio Pineiro) (Harlequin/Interstate, 1986)

— , *El Manisero* (25 versions of The Peanut Vendor) (Tumbao Cuban Classics/Blue Moon, Spain, 1997)

Chapter 2 New York: The immigrants' tale

Canario y su Grupo, *Plenas* (Ansonia)

César Concepción y Joe Valle, *Plenas favoritas* (Ansonia); *La plena y la bomba de Puerto Rico* (Carino)

José Curbelo and His Orchestra, *Rumba gallega* (Tumbao)

Rafael Hernández, *Cuarteto Victoria* (Ansonia, 1963); *El autentico* (Ansonia)

Ramito, *El cantor de la montana* (Ansonia)

Tito Rodríguez, *Tito, Tito, Tito* (WS Latino); *Tito Rodríguez and Noro Morales Orquesta* (Tropical); *The Best of Tito Rodríguez and His Orchestra* (RCA Tropical, 1992–94); *Xavier Cugat and His Orchestra (featuring Tito Rodríguez)* (Tumbao, 1991); *Legendary Sessions* (with leading bandleaders) (Tumbao, 1992); *With José Curbelo* (Tumbao, 1995)

Daniel Santos, *Con La Sonora Matancera* (Panart, 1974)

La Sonora Matancera with Celia Cruz, Daniel Santos, Miguelito Valdés, *65th Anniversary* (TH–Rodven, 1989)

Various artists, *Hot Music From Puerto Rico 1929–46* (Harlequin/Interstate)

Chapter 3 Salsa in the USA

José Alberto (El Canario), *Dance with Me* (with Sergio Vargas) (RMM, 1991); *Llegó la hora* (RMM, 1992); *Back to the Mambo – Tribute to Machito* (RMM, 1997)

Johnny Almendra y Los Jovénes del Barrio with Jillian, *Reconfirmando* (RMM, 1997)

Joe Bataan, *Subway Joe* (Fania, 1968); *Afro-Filipino* (SalSoul, 1975)

Rubén Blades, *Siembra* (with Willie Colón) (Fania, 1998); *Buscando América* (Elektra, 1984); *Poetry – The Greatest Hits* (Fania/Caliente/Charly Records, 1990); *La rosa de los vientos* (Sony, 1996)

Willie Bobo, *Latin Beat* (Trip Records, 1964)

Bongo Logic, *Tipiqueros* (Ryko Latino, 1996)

Jimmy Bosch, *Sonando Trombon* (Ryko Latino, 1998)

Cachao, *Master Sessions Vol I and Vol II* (Crescent Moon/Sony, 1994); *Cachao y su descarga '86* (Tania, 1986)

Willie Colón, *Grandes exitos* (Fania); *El malo* (with Héctor Lavoe) (Fania, 1967); *El juicio* (Fania, 1972); *Criollo* (RCA 1984); *Hecho en Puerto Rico* (CBS, 1993); *Tras la tormenta* (with Rubén Blades) (Sony Tropical, 1995)

Conjunto Cespedes, *Flores* (Xenophile, 1998)

Conjunto Clásico, *Si no bailan con ellos, no bailan con nadie* (Lo Mejor, 1981)

Celia Cruz, *Queen of Cuban Rhythm – The Legendary Seeco Recordings, 1959–1965*; *Celia y Johnny* (Vaya, 1974), *La incomparable* (Vaya); *Azucar negra* (RMM, 1993); *Mi vida es cantar* (RMM, 1998)

Cruz Control, *Cruz Control* (EVA Records, 1997)

Joe Cuba Sextet, *Lo Mejor/The Best of Joe Cuba* (Tico); *Hanging Out* (Caliente/Charly, 1989)

Oscar D'León *Una dimensión de exitos* (with Dimensión Latina) (TH–Rodven, 1994); *El Oscar de la salsa* (TH–Rodven, 1977); *Riquiti* (TH–Rodven, 1987); *El sonero del mundo* (RMM, 1996)

Luis Enrique, *Amor y alegria* (CBS, 1988)

Pete Escovedo with Sheila E, *Yesterday's Memories, Tomorrow's Dreams* (Crossover/Concorde Jazz)

José Fajardo, *José Fajardo y Sus Estrellas* (MPI); *Fajardo and Pacheco* (Fania)

Fania All Stars, *Live at Yankee Stadium, Vols I and II* (Fania/Charly, 1994)

Henry Fiol, *Sonero* (Earthworks/Virgin, 1990)

Wayne Gorbea, *Salsa Picante* (Wayne Go Records, 1998)

Larry Harlow, *Larry Harlow's Latin Legends Band, 1998* (Jerry Masucci Music/Sony, 1998)

Héctor Lavoe, *Comedia* (Fania, 1978); *El sabio* (Fania, 1980); *Fania Legends of Salsa, Vol I: Héctor Lavoe* (Fania, 1993); *Strikes Back – with Willie Colón* (Fania, 1987)

Lebron Brothers, *Salsa Lebron* (Caiman, 1986)

La Lupe, *Too Much* (Caliente/Charly, 1989)

Los Mangual, *Una diniastia* (Caiman, 1986)

Rebeca Mauleon and Rumbeca, *Roundtrip* (Rumbeca, 1998)

Hermanos Moreno, *Together* (RMM)

Tito Nieves, *The Classic* (RMM, 1988); *Yo quiero cantar* (RMM, 1989); *Un tipo commun* (RMM, 1995); *I Like It Like That* (RMM, 1997)

Manny Oquendo y Conjunto Libre, *Increible* (SalSoul, 1994); *Ritmo, Sonido, Estilo* (Montuno); *Libre* (Montuno 1983)

Orquesta Broadway, *El dengue* (Gema, 1966); *Lo mejor de Roberto Torres con la original Orquesta Broadway* (West Side Latino)

Orquesta de la Luz, *Salsa caliente de Japon* (RMM, 1991)

Johnny Pacheco, *Johnny Pacheco y su charanga* (Fania, 1960); *Pacheco and His Flute and Latin Jam* (Fania, 1965); *Canta 'El Conde' Pete Rodríguez, tres de café y dos de azucar* (Fania, 1973)

Charlie Palmieri, *Palmieri* (with Pacheco) (WS Latino, 1975); *A Giant Step* (Tropical Buddha, 1974); *Live from Studio A* (Mr Bongo, London, 1995)

Eddie Palmieri, *Eddie Palmieri and his Conjunto La Perfecta* (Alegre, 1962); *The History of Eddie Palmieri* (Tico, 1975); *Sun of Latin Music* (Coco, 1974); *Unfinished Masterpiece* (Coco, 1976); *El Rumbero del piano* (RMM, 1998)

Pucho and the Latin Soul Brothers, *The Best of* (BGP Records, 1993)

Louie Ramírez and Ray de la Paz, *Sabor con clase* (Caiman, 1986); *En algo nuevo* (with Tito Rodríguez) (TR, 1972); *Noche caliente* (with José Alberto) (Fania, 1992); *Con cache* (Caiman, 1984); *A Tribute to Cal Tjader* (Caiman, 1987)

Richie Ray y Bobby Cruz, *Lo mejor/The Best of* (Vaya/Fania, 1977); *El bestial sonido de Richie Ray y Bobby Cruz* (Vaya)

Al Santiago, *Al Santiago Presents Tambo with Johnny Almendra and Louie Bauzo* (Ryko Latino)

John Santos and the Machete Ensemble, *Ten Years on the Edge – Machetazo!* (Bembe Records, Redway California, 1998)

Típica 73 with José Alberto and Alfredo de la Fé, *Charangueando!* (Fania, 1980); *En Cuba – intercambio cultural* (Fania, 1989); *Charanga* (Charly, 1994)

Yomo Toro, *Funky Jíbaro* (Antilles/Island, 1987)

Various artists, *Yo soy de la son a la salsa* (soundtrack) (RMM, 1997)

— , *De la Habana a New York, Volumes I and II* (Familia RMM, 1996)

— , *Viva salsa!* (Fania/Charly)

— , *Mambo Kings Soundtrack* (with Tito Puente, Celia Cruz, Arturo Sandoval, Beny Moré, Linda Ronstadt) (Elektra, 1992)

— , *An Introduction to Latin Hip Hop* (Rhythm King, 1988)

— , (with Familia RMM), *La combinación perfecta* (RMM, 1993)

— , *Holding Up Half the Sky – Voices of Latin Women* (Shanachie, 1998)

Chapter 4 Cuba: Salsa in revolution

Jesús Alémany y Cubanismo, *Cubanismo* (Hannibal/Ryko, 1996); *Malembe* (Hannibal/Ryko, 1998)

Juan Carlos Alfonso y Los Dan Den, *Salsa en atare* (TUMI, 1989); *Mi cuerpo* (Fania, 1996)

Adalberto Alvarez y su Son, *A bailar el toca toca* (WEA Caribe, 1995); *Magistral!!!* (Milan Latino, 1997)

Asere, *Cuban Soul* (MCA, 1998)

Issac Delgado, *Otra idea* (RMM, 1997)

Candido Fabre, *Orquesta Original de Manzanillo* (Qbadisc, 1992); *Son de Cuba* (TUMI)

Juan Formell y Los Van Van, *Lo mejor/The Best of* (TUMI, 1996); *Ay, dios! aparame* (WEA Caribe, 1997)

Grupo Sierra Maestra, *Viaje a la semilla* (EGREM, 1994); *Tibiri tabara* (World Circuit, 1997)

Hanny, *The Voice of Cuba* (Mr Bongo, 1997)

Los Jovénes Clásicos del Son, *Fruta bomba* (TUMI, 1999)

Manolín (El Medico de la Salsa), *Una aventura loca* (Besame Mucho, 1984); *Para mi gente* (Ahi-Na-Ma, 1997)

Manolito y su Trabuco, *Contra todos los pronosticos* (Eurotropical, 1996)

N.G. La Banda, *En la calle* (Qbadisc, 1992); *José Luis Cortés y N.G. La Banda, Veneno* (WEA Caribe, 1998)

Orquesta Reve, *El explosión del momento* (Real World, 1989); *Suave suave plus 3* (EGREM)

Orquesta Ritmo Oriental, *Ritmo Oriental Is Calling You* (Ace/Globestyle/EGREM, 1988)

Paulito F.G., *El bueno soy yo* (Magic Music, 1996)

Giraldo Piloto and Klimax, *Juego de manos* (Eurotropical, 1997)

Son 14, *Son 14 with Adalberto Alvarez* (TUMI); *El Regreso de Maria* (Areito/EGREM, 1987)

Los Zafiros, *Bossa Cubana* (World Circuit, 1999)

Various artists, *Hasta siempre, Comandante* (TUMI, 1997)

— , *Buena Vista Social Club* (with Ry Cooder) (World Circuit); *A Toda Cuba le Gusta* (with Afro-Cuban All Stars) (World Circuit, 1997); *Introducing...Rubén González* (World Circuit, 1997); *Estrellas de arieto* (World Circuit, 1998); *Ibrahim Ferrer* (World Circuit, 1999)

— , *De New York a la Habana – Vol I* (Familia, 1997)

— , *40 Degrees Centigrade* (Milan Music/BMG, 1997)

— , *Ahi-Na-Ma Vols I and II* (Ahi-Na-Ma, 1996–1997)

— , *Rough Guide to Cuba* (Rough Guides, 1999)

Chapter 5 Puerto Rico: Salsa colony

Batacumbelé with Cachete and Giovanni Hidalgo, *Afro-Caribbean Jazz* (Montuno Records, 1987)

Descarga Boricua, *Esta, si ca!* (Tierrazo Records)

Jesús Cepeda y su Grupo ABC, *Pa' los Maestros* (Hi-Yield); *La historia se repite* (UP Records, 1988)

Rafael Cortijo y su Combo with Ismael Rivera and Los Originales, *El alma de un pueblo* (Seeco/Sonodisc); *Baile con Cortijo y su Combo* (Tropical/Sonodisc); *Maquina de tiempo* (Musical Productions, 1990)

El Gran Combo, *El Gran Combo de siembre* (Gema, 1962); *Y su pueblo* (Combo, 1986); *30 Aniversario: bailando con el mundo* (Combo, 1992); *35 Years Around the World* (Combo, 1997)

Cheo Feliciano, *Lo Mejor/The Best of* (Tico, 1974); *With a Little Help from My Friend* (with 'Tite' Curet Alonso) (Vaya/Fania, 1997); *Cheo* (Vaya/Fania, 1971); *Los feelings de Cheo* (RMM, 1990)

Frank Ferrer and 2013, *Puerto Rico 2013* (Telecumbre)

Grupo Afro-Boricua, *Bombazo* (Blue Jackal, 1998)

Raphy Leavitt, *Raphy Leavitt y Orquesta La Selecta* (Bronco, 1989)

Víctor Manuelle, *A pesar de todo* (Sony, 1997); *Ironias* (Sony, 1998)

Andy Montañez, *Andy Montañez* (TH–Rodven, 1981); *Canta sus exitos*; (TH–Rodven, 1989); *El Swing* (TH–Rodven); *De Regresso* (RMM, 1995)

Frankie Negrón, *Con amor se gana* (WEA Caribe, 1997)

Tommy Olivencia, *El jeque* (TH–Rodven, 1989)

Don Perignon, *...With Víctor Manuelle and Luisito Carrillon* (Top Hits, 1998)

Plena Libre, *Plena Libre* (Ryko Latino, 1998)

Los Pleneros de la 21 and Conjunto Melodia, *Puerto Rico, mi tierra natal* (Shanachie)

Puerto Rican All Stars, *Featuring Kako* (Gema, 1963); *Produccion Frankie Gregory* (Combo); *De Regresso* (RMM, 1995)

Ismael Rivera, *Maelo...el unico* (Sonido, 1992); *Y su cachimbos 'de colores'* (Tico)

Jerry Rivera, *De otra manera* (Sony, 1998)

Mon Rivera, *Mon y sus trombones* (Vaya/Fania, 1976)

Lalo Rodríguez, *Un nuevo despertar* (TH–Rodven, 1988); *Sexsacional* (TH–Rodven, 1989)

Roberto Roena's Apollo Sound, *Se pone bueno* (Tico); *Mi musica mil noviciento y siete* (MPI, 1996)

Willie Rosario, *The Salsa Legend* (Bronco, 1988)

Frankie Ruiz, *Historia musical de Frankie Ruiz* (TH–Rodven, 1987); *Nacimiento y recuerdos* (TH–Rodven/Polygram, 1998)

Gilberto Santarosa, *Keeping Cool* (Combo, 1987); *Perspectiva* (CBS, 1991); *Nace aqui* (Sony Tropical, 1993)

Eddie Santiago, *Sigo atrevido* (TH–Rodven, 1987); *Mi historia* (TH–Rodven/Polygram, 1997)

Marvin Santiago, *Caliente y explosivo* (TH–Rodven, 1980)

La Sonora Ponceña, *Determination* (Inca, 1982); *On the Right Track* (Inca, 1988); *Into the 90s* (Inca, 1990); *Soul of Puerto Rico* (Caliente/Charly, 1992)

Bobby Valentín, *Soy boricua* (Fania, 1972); *Presenta Cano Estremera* (Bronco Records, 1982); *En acción* (Bronco Records)

Various artists, *Salsa moderna* (including Tito Rojas, Roberto Roena, Willie Rosario, Orquesta Mulenze, Puerto Rican Power, Pedro Conga, Tito Allen) (Nascente, UK, 1998)

— , *Tribute to Roberto Clemente* (directed by Larry Harlow) (Ryko Latino, 1998)

— , *Los soneros de hoy* (including Gilberto Santarosa, Tony Vega, Van Lester, Víctor Manuelle, Domingo Quinones) (Sony, 1993)

— , *Juntos Pa'Gozar* (TH–Rodven, 1988)

DJ Vico C, *Aquel que habia muerto* (Casa de los Tapes, 1999)

Chapter 6 Santo Domingo: The merengue capital

Luis Alberti, *Trujillo, musica para la historia* (Remo Records)

Celínes, *La flor del merengue* (RMM/CBS, 1997)

Bonny Cepeda, *Freedom* (TH–Rodven, 1997); *Que canten los niños* (Combo, 1991)

Las Chicas del Can, *Pegando fuego* (Sonotone, 1986)

Fernando Echavarría and La Familia Andre, *Caribe 'Fusion'* (Kubaney, 1988)

Juan Luis Guerra y Grupo 4.40, *Ojalá que llueva café* (1989); *Bachata rosa* (Karen/BMG, 1990); *Areito* (Karen/BMG, 1992); *Fogarate* (Karen/BMG, 1994)

Alex Leon y su Orquesta, *Siempre pa'rriba* (TH–Rodven)

Alex Mansilla y Canaveral, *Un amor el nuestro* (WEA Latina, 1989)

Joseito Mateo y su Pericombo, *Abusadora – enllavadura II* (Quisqueya)

Kinito Méndez, *A caballo (homenaje a Johnny Ventura)* (Sony, 1998)

Millie, Jocelyn y Los Vecinos, *Flying Solo* (VQ Productions); Millie Queseda, *Millie...vive* (Sony, 1999)

The New York Band, *Nadie como tu* (RMM, 1989); *Dame vida...Always* (RMM/CBS, 1990)

Ramon Orlando, *Evolución* (Karen, 1997); *Toma! Toma!* (Oi, 1998)

Chichi Peralta, *Pa' otro la'o* (Caiman, 1997)

Pochi y su Coco Band, *Los cocotuces* (Kubaney, 1991)

Víctor Roque y La Gran Manzana, *Hanging Out II* (1989); *Donde estas vida mia* (Great Apple Ent, 1988)

Olga Tañón, *Llevame contigo* (WEA Latino, 1997)

Francisco Ulloa, *Merengue* (Kubaney/Ace Records, 1987)

Cuco Valoy y Los Virtuosos, *20 exitos de los ahijados* (Kubaney); *Tiza!* (Discolor Records, 1980); *Cuco Valoy y su Tribu* (Kubaney, 1984); *La gran obra musical de Cuco Valoy* (J&N/Fuga Records, 1991)

Sergio Vargas, *Y Los Hijos del Rey* (Karen, 1986); *Tiempo de amor* (BMG, 1997)

Wilfrido Vargas y su Orquesta, *Evolución* (Karen, 1979); *Wilfrido Vargas y Sandy Reyes* (Karen, 1982);

El jardinero (Karen, 1984); *Animation* (Sonotone, 1990); *Los años dorados* (hits) (TH–Rodven, 1993)

Johnny Ventura, *Asopao del pinguino* (South Eastern, 1973); *Un sueño* (Combo, 1982); *El señor del merengue* (CBS, 1986),

Various Artists, *Songs From The North – Music From The Dominican Republic Vol 4* (Ethnic Folkways)

— , *MerengFest (Round-Up) '98* (WEA Caribe)

— , *Aqui esta merengue* (annual greatest hits) (Karen)

Chapter 7 Miami: 90 miles to Cuba

Albita, *No se parece a nada* (Crescent Moon/Sony, 1995); *Una mujer como yo* (Crescent Moon/Sony, 1990)

Arabella, *Mas alla de sabor* (Kubaney, 1990)

Willy Chirino, *Acuarela del Caribe* (CBS, 1989); *Oxigenio* (Sony, 1991); *Cuba libre* (with Celia Cruz, Roberto Torres, Paquito D'Rivera, Arturo Sandoval) (Sony, 1998)

Gloria Estefán, *Mi tierra* (Epic, 1993); *Abriendo puertas* (Epic, 1995)

Hansel y Raul, *Blanco y negro* (CBS, 1988)

Andy and Larry Harlow, *Salsa Brothers* (Songo, 1988)

La India de Oriente, *La reina de la guajira* (Caiman, 1985)

Alfonso Lobo, *Wolf and the Pack* (Space Wolf Productions, 1998)

Mangu, *Mangu* (Island, 1998)

Roberto Torres, *La charanga vallenata* (Guajiro, 1980); *Roberto Torres y su charanga vallenata* (Guajiro, 1981); *Elegantemente criollo* (SAR)

Walfredo de los Reyes, Paquito Hechavarría, Tany Gil and Cachao, *Wal-Pa-Ta-Ca* (Tania)

Chapter 8 Colombia: Continental connections

Joe Arroyo, *Rebelión* (World Circuit, 1988); *En acción* (Discos Fuentes/Mango/Island, 1990); *Grandes exitos* Discos Fuentes, 1993)

Binomio de Oro de América, *A su gusto* (Codiscos, 1998)

Canta Bovea y sus Vallenatos with Alberto Fernández, *La casa en el aire* (Tribute to Rafael Escalona) (World Music Network/Riverboat Records, 1998)

Alfredo de la Fé, *Para Africa con amor* (Sacodisc, 1979); *Made in Colombia* (Mercurio, 1985); *Salsa! – The Tropical Sound of Colombia* (Discos Fuente/Mango, 1989)

Fruko y sus Tesos, *Todos bailan salsa* (World Music Network/Riverboat Records/Discos Fuentes, 1999)

Grupo Gale, *Listo Medellin* (Codiscos); *Grandes hits* (Codiscos, 1998)

Grupo Niche, *Llegando al 100%* (Sony, 1991); *Grandes exitos* (Globo, 1997)

Alfredo Gutierrez, *Vallenato King* (Erde Records, Germany, 1998)

Kike Harvey, *Salsa pachanga y amor* (1993); *La Isla Bonita* (TUMI, 1995)

La India Meliyara, *La Sonora Meliyara* (Riverboat Records/Women of the World, 1992)

The Latin Brothers, *The Black Girl* (Mango/Island, 1990); *Send las olas* (World Music Network/Riverboat Records, 1999)

Lisandro Meza, *Cumbias Colombianas* (TUMI, 1994); *Lisandro's Cumbia* (World Circuit, 1991); *Soy Colombiano* (CBS, 1990)

La Misma Gente, *El loco* (TUMI, 1992)

Los Nemus del Pacífico, *Harder Than Before* (Discos Fuentes/Mango/Island, 1988); *Lo Mejor/The Best of* (Riverboat, 1998)

Calixto Ochoa y Las Vibraciones, *Salsa...cumbia... vallenato* (TUMI, 1993)

Orquesta Guayacan, *Com el corazón abierto* (RMM/ Sony, 1994); *14 exitos* (Sony)

Perego y su Combo Vacana, *Tropicalisimo* (World Circuit, 1989)

La Sonora Dinamita, *Cumbia Explosion* (Mango/Island, 1988); *A mover la colita* (World Music Network/Riverboat Records, 1999)

Los Titanes, *Amor y salsa* (Discos Fuentes, 1990)

Los Tupamaros, *Caribe alegre y tropical* (Discos Fuentes/Mango/Island, 1988)

Carlos Vives, *Clásicos de la Provincia* (Sonolux, 1995)

Various artists, *Cumbia Cumbia* (World Circuit, 1989); *Big Cumbia – The Essential Cumbia Collection* (Mango/Island, 1991)

— , *Tropical Extravaganza – Salsa/Cumbia* (TUMI, 1992)

— , *Fiesta vallenata* (Globestyle/Ace)

— , *Big Cumbia – The Essential Cumbia Collection* (Mango)

— , *América 500 años – y su expresión musical!* (Discos Fuentes)

Chapter 9 Salsa in London: From Edmundo Ros to Snowboy

Don Marino Barreto, *...And His Cuban Orchestra* (with Edmundo Ros) (Harlequin/Interstate, 1939)

Víctor Hugo con Picante, *Oye latino* (Latin Arts Society)

Lecuona Cuban Boys, *Vols 1–5* (Harlequin/Interstate)

Merengada, *Un Mensaje de London/No Woman No Cry* (Merengada Records, 1998)

Roberto Pla and His Latin Ensemble, *Right On Time!* (TUMI, 1995)

Raíces Cubanas, *Mi carro* (Raíces Cubanas, 1999)

Robin Jones Seven, *El maja/denga* (Apollo Sound, 1997)

Edmundo Ros, *The Early Years* (Double, Decca, 1978)

Salsasonica, *Al fin!* (Wild Indigo, 1999)

Side Stepper, *Logozo* (Apartment 22, 1998)

Snowboy and The Latin Section, *Descarga mambito* (Acid Jazz, 1998); *Mambo Rage* (Ubiquity, 1999)

Tumbaito, *Otros tiempos* (Deep South, 1998)

Various Artists, *Afro-Latino – Live from The Bass Clef London* and *Samba con salsa – Latin Music from The Bass Clef London* (Wave, 1987)

Chapter 10 Latin Jazz, Afro-Cuban Jazz

Alegre All Stars, *Perdido* (Alegre, 1977); *They Just Don't Makim Like Us Any More* (Alegre, 1977)

Ray Barretto and New World Spirit, *Ancestral Messages* (Concord Picante, 1993)

Mario Bauzá and His Afro-Cuban Jazz Orchestra, *The Legendary Mambo King* (Messidor, 1992)

Cachao y su Ritmo Caliente, *'Descargas': Cuban Jam Sessions In Miniature* (Panart, 1956); *...y su descarga '86* (Tania, 1986)

Michel Camilo, *Why Not* (Bellaphon, 1985); *One More Once* (Sony, 1994)

Bobby Carcasses, *A l'esquina del Afro jazz* (EGREM, 1989); *Jazz timbero* (TUMI, 1998)

Steve Coleman and The Mystic Rhythm Society, *The Sign and the Seal* (BMG, 1996)

Paquito D'Rivera, *Manhattan Burn* (CBS 1987); *90 Miles to Cuba* (with Bebo and Chucho Valdés) (Tropijazz/ RMM, 1993); *40 years of Cuban Jam Sessions with United Nations Orchestra* (Messidor, 1993)

Dizzy Gillespie and Machito with Chico O'Farrill, *Afro-Cuban Jazz Moods* (Pablo, 1976)

Jerry González's Fort Apache Band, *Ya yo me cure* (American Clave, 1985)

Graciela, Mario Bauzá and Friends, *Afro-Cuban Jazz* (Caiman, 1986)

Roy Hargrove's Crisol, *Habana* (Verve/Polygram, 1997)

Irakere, *Misa negra* (Messidor, 1987); *Bailando asi* (EGREM); *Live at Ronnie Scott's* (World Pacific/Capitol/EMI, 1993)

Machito and His Orchestra, *Latin Soul Plus Jazz* (Tico, 1973); *Afro-Cuban Jazz: Mambo in Jazz* (with various artists) (Saludos Amigos, 1992); *Mucho macho!* (Pablo, 1978)

Maraca (Orlando Valle) and his band Otra Vision, *Sonando* (Ahi-Na-Ma, 1998)

Charlie Palmieri, *A Giant Step* (Tropical Buddha)

Daniel Ponce, *Arawe* (Island, 1988); *Chango te llama* (Mango/Island, 1991)

Tito Puente and His Latin Ensemble, *Mambo diablo* (Concord Picante, 1985); *50 Years of Swing* (RMM, 1997)

Tito Rodríguez, *Live at Birdland* (West Side Latino, 1963); *Palladium Memories* (TR, 1971); *Tito Tito Tito* (West Side Latino, 1981)

Gonzalo Rubalcaba, *Live in Havana* (Messidor, 1987); *Live at Montreux* (Somethin' Else/EMI, 1991)

Hilton Ruiz, *El camino* (RCA); *Doin' It Right* (Novus/BMG, 1990)

Bobby Sanabria y Ascensión, *NYC Ache!* (with Tito Puente and Paquito D'Rivera) (Flying Fish, 1993)

David Sánchez, *Obsesión* (Columbia, 1998)

Poncho Sánchez, *El conguero* (Concord Picante, 1985); *Lo mejor* (Concord Picante, 1992)

Mongo Santamaría, *Mongo at Montreux* (Atlantic, 1971); *Watermelon Man* (Milestone, 1973); *Summertime – Digital at Montreux 1980* (with Dizzy Gillespie and Toots Thielemans) (Pablo, 1981); *Soy yo* (with Charlie Palmieri) (Concord Picante, 1987); *Our Man in Havana* (with Willie Bobo) (Prestige, 1993)

Los Terry, *From Africa to Camaguey – Afro-Cuban Jazz* (Round World Music, 1996)

Tico All Stars, *Descargas at the Village Gate – Live* (Tico)

Cal Tjader, *Soul Sauce* (Verve/Polygram, 1994); *Cal's Pals* (BGP); *Bamboleate* (with Eddie Palmieri) (Tico, 1967)

Steve Turre, *Right There* (Antilles, 1990)

Bebo Valdés, *Bebo Rides Again* (Messidor, 1995)

Chucho Valdés, *Solo Piano* (Blue Note, 1998)

Various artists, Grupo Folklorico y Experimental Nuevayorquino, *Concepts in Unity* (SalSoul, 1975)

— , *Havana Jam* (CBS); *The Mambo King – 100th LP* (RMM, 1991)

— , *NuYorican Soul* (including India, Roy Ayers, Jocelyn Brown, George Benson) (Mercury Records, London, 1997)

— , *Cuban Jam Sessions, Volumes 1–5* (Panart/TH-Rodven, 1957)

— , *The Best of Latin Jazz* (Verve, 1993)

— , *Latin New York 1980–1983 – Live From Soundscape* (DIW, 1997)

— , *Nuyorican Soul* (Mercury, 1997); *NuYorica 2 – Chango in the New World, 1976–1985* (Soul Jazz Records, 1997)

— , *50 Years of Swing* (RMM)

— , *Latin Jazz Live from Soundscape – 1980–1983* (Jazpac/DIW Records, Tokyo, 1997)

Chapter 11 Africando

Africando, *Volumes I–IV* (Stern's, 1993–98)

Franklin Boukaka, Ses Sanzas et Son Orchestre Congalais, *Survivance* (Gilles Sala/Sacem)

Cuarteto Patria and Manu Dibango, *Cubafrica* (Celluloid/Melodie, 1998)

Franco and OK Jazz, *Originalité* (Retroafric, 1999)

Ricardo Lemva and Macina Loca, *Mambo Yoyo* (Putamayo, 1998)

Orchestra Afro-Charanga, *Ochestra Afro-Charanga with Nestor Torres* (Thiokis Records, 1980)

Orchestra Baobab, *Bamba* (Stern's, 1993)

Gnonnas Pedro, *La Compilation* (Ledoux Records)

Ry-Co Jazz, *Rumba'round Africa, Congo/Latin Action from the 1960s* (Retroafric, 1999)

Maestro Laba Sosseh con L'Orquesta Aragón, *Akoguin Theresa* (Disco Stock)

Star Band de Dakar, *Featuring Youssou N'Dour* (Stern's, 1993)

Various Artists, *The Sound of Kinshasa – Guitar Classics from Zaire* (Original Music)

— , *African Salsa* (Stern's, 1998)

Chapter 12 From Here to Mañana

Marc Anthony, *Otra nota* (Soho Latino/Sony, 1993); *Todo a su tiempo* (RMM/Sony 1996); *Contra la corriente* (RMM, 1997)

Bamboleo, *Y no me parezco a nadie* (Ahi-Na-Ma Music, 1998)

Charanga Habanera, *Tremendo delirio* (Universal, 1997)

El Clan De La Furia, *Do It* (Karen Publishing, 1994)

Elvis Crespo, *Suavamente* (Sony, 1998); *Píntame* (Sony, 1999)

Dark Latin Groove, *Swing On* (Sony Discos, 1997); *Gotcha* (Sony Discos, 1999)

D'Mingo, *Wepa-Je* (H.O.L.A. Recordings, 1999)

Fulanito, *El hombre mas famoso en la tierra* (Cutting Records, 1997)

Grupo Mania, *The Dynasty* (featuring Elvis Crespo) (Sony, 1998)

Karis, *El poder del swing* (BMG, 1998)

Los Ilegales, *Rebotando* (BMG, 1997)

La India, *Llegó La India* (with Eddie Palmieri) (1992); *Sobre el fuego* (RMM, 1997)

Ricky Martin, *A medio vivir* (C2/Sony, 1998); *Livin la vida loca* (C2/Sony, 1999)

Proyecto Uno, *New Era* (H.O.L.A. Recordings, 1996)

Sancocho, *Rumba te tumba* (Cutting Records, 1998)

Roy Tavare, *Arrebatame* (Karen, 1997)

Thalia, *En extasis* (EMI Latin, 1995)

Various artists, *Lo nuestro y lo mejor* (Sony Records, 1997)

— , *Revolución en la casa – The Essential Latin House Collection* (Nascente, 1999)

Essential Eccentrics

David Byrne, *Rei Momo* (Luaka Bop/Warner Bros, 1989)

The Champs, *Tequila* (Ace, 1992)

Kid Creole and the Coconuts, *Strange Fruit in Foreign Places* (Island, 1981)

Paul Simon with Rubén Blades, Marc Anthony, Frankie Negrón and Ednita Nazaro, *Songs from 'The Capeman'* (Warner Brothers, 1997)

Ned Sublette, *Cowboy Rumba* (Qbadisc, 1999)

Yma Sumac, *Mambo! And More* (Creation/EMI, 1997)

Record Stores

Bate Records, 140 Delancey Street, New York (212) 677 3180

Casa Latina, 151 East 116th Street, New York (212) 427 6062

Esperanto, 1440 Lincoln Road, Miami Beach (305) 534 2003

Mr Bongo, 44 Poland Street, London W1V 3DA (171) 287 1887

Internet Salsa Shopping: www.descarga.com – for superlative reviews and features, archive discs and up-to-minute releases.

Bibliography

Alberti, Luis, *De musica y orquestas bailables Dominicanas 1910-1959*, Santo Domingo, 1975

Aparacio, Frances A., *Listening to Salsa: Gender, Latin Popular Music and Puerto Rican Cultures*, Hanover, New England, 1999

Arnaz, Desi, *A Book*, Waltham, Mass., 1976

Bergman, Billy with Isabelle Leymarie and Tony Sabournin, *Reggae and Latin Pop – Hot Sauces*, London, 1985

Bloch, Peter, *La-Le-Lo-Lai – Puerto Rican Music and Its Performers*, New York, 1973

Boggs, Vernon W., *Salsiology – Afro-Cuban Music and the Evolution of Salsa in New York City*, New York, 1992

Cabrera, Infante Guillermo, *Three Trapped Tigers*, London, 1980

— , *Mea Cuba*, London, 1994

Carpentier, Alejo, *La musica en Cuba*, Havana, 1984

Chediak, Nat, *Diccionario de jazz Latino*, Madrid, 1998

Child, John, Salsa entries in *The Penguin Encyclopaedia of Popular Music* (2nd ed.), Harmondsworth, Middx, 1999

Collazo, Bobby, *La ultima noche que pase contigo*, San Juan, 1987

Colón, Jesús, *A Puerto Rican in New York and Other Sketches*, New York, 1982

Fernández, Crispin, *Melodias de merengue* (Musicians' Guides to Playing Merengue), Santo Domingo, 1986

— , *Jaleos de merengue*, (Musicians' Guides to Playing Merengue), Santo Domingo, 1986

Figueroa, Frank M., *Encyclopaedia of Latin American Music in New York*, St Petersburg, Florida, 1994

Gasca, Luis, *Cugat*, Madrid, 1995

Gerard, Charley with Marty Sheller, *Salsa – The Rhythm of Latin Music*, New York, 1989

Gillespie, Dizzy, *Dizzy – To Be Or Not To Bop: The Autobiography*, London, 1982

Glasser, Ruth, *My Music Is My Flag – Puerto Rican Musicians and Their New York Communities 1917–1940*, Berkeley, Calif., 1995

González-Wippler, Migene, *Tales of the Orishas*, New York, 1985

Haydon, Geoffrey and Dennis Marks (eds), *Repercussions*, London, 1985

Julia, Edgardo Rodriguez, *El entirero de cortijo*, San Juan, 1985

Manuel, Peter, *Caribbean Currents: Caribbean Music from Rumba to Reggae*, New York, 1995

Marre, Jeremy and Hannah Charlton, *Beats of the Heart*, London, 1985

Montejo, Esteban, *The Autobiography of a Runaway Slave*, London, 1993

Murphy, Joseph M., *Santeria – An African Religion in America*, New York, 1988

Orovio, Helio, *Diccionario de la musica Cubana* (2nd ed.), Havana, 1998

Ospina, Hernando Calvo, *Havana Heat, Bronx Beat*, London, 1992

Pacini Hernández, Deborah, *Bachata: A Social History of Dominican Popular Music*, New York, 1995

Rieff, David, *The Exile – Cuba in the Heart of Miami*, London, 1993

Rius, *Cuba For Beginners*, London, 1997

Rondon, César Miguel, *El libro de la salsa*, Caracas, 1980

Rough Guides, *Rough Guide to World Music*, London, 1999

Storm Roberts, John, *The Latin Tinge*, Oxford, 1979

— , *Black Music of Two Worlds*, New York, 1974

Sweeney, Philip, *Dictionary of World Music*, London, 1991

Thomas, Piri, *Down These Mean Streets*, New York, 1967

Valverde, Umberto, *Reina rumba, Celia Cruz*, Bogotá, Colombia, 1981

— , *Bomba*, Bogotá, Colombia, 1982

MAGAZINES AND PUBLICATIONS

Havana: *Tropicana Internacional*

New York: *CENTRO* quarterly from the Centre for Puerto Rican Studies, Hunter College, New York; *Latin Rhythm; New York Latino*

San Francisco: *Latin Beat*

San Juan: *Farandula*

London: *Folk Roots; Latin London; Que Pasa?; Salsa Pa' Ti; Song Lines*

Acknowledgments

The Puerto Rican writer Bernardo Vega said, 'Siempre es mas interesante vivir que escribir' – It's always more interesting to live than to write. Researching this book was an unimagined life-changing experience. It was made possible through the limitless generosity and hospitality I received during my travels and the time my hosts and companions gave to share their stories, their music and culture with the blonde English woman who kept appearing, note-pad and cassette recorder in hand.

Sadly, many musicians at the centre of the story have passed away, particularly Mario Bauzá, Charlie Palmieri and Héctor Lavoe. Friends who died too soon, Brad Graves in New York, Mary Corcoran and Linda Webster in London.

There are numerous uncredited people to whom I owe a debt, including those who provided photographs and images for the book. Please forgive such omissions.

USA

To John Storm Roberts, author of the first book to take the subject seriously, *The Latin Tinge*; Max Salazar, salsa's pre-eminent historian; Verna Gillis, for loyal friendship; Janette Beckman and Patti Bates, great companions on my salsa adventures; Tony Sabournín, *the salsa writer par excellence*; Fernando Campos and Albert White, for the run of *Canales* magazine archives; Harriet Wasser, for the first guest pass; and particularly to Joe Dolce.

To Willie Colón and Rubén Blades, for bringing the politics to the dancefloor.

And to Nando Alvaricci; Joseph Blum; Sergio Bofil; Ginger Canzoneri; Nat Chediak; Bob Christgau and Carola Dibell; David Corio; Joe Cuba; Brian Cullman; Garth Eaglesfield; EMI Latin; José Flores and Victor Gallo at Fania Records; Andy González; Graciela; Steve Griffiths; Jerry Masucci; Ralph Mercado; Carlos Ortíz; Carlos Perez at Sony Discos; Jessie Ramírez; Ruby Rich; Ramón Rodríguez and Louie Bauzo at Boy's Harbour; Jonathan Ruddnick and the staff at SOB's; Izzy Sanabria; John Santos; Irena Sednova; Dita Sullivan; Roger Trilling; WEA Latina.

CUBA

To Mario Blanco; Corinna Chute; Nelson García; Helen Mitskus; Glyceria and Juan de Marcos González; Pedro Sarduy; Rosa Escandell, Gilberto Valdés; Nievares and Kennedy, Jesús O'Reilly; particularly to Eva Kirkhope.

PUERTO RICO

To Daniel Nina; Hector Vega at the University of Puerto Rico; Loretta Santos; Anibal 'Andy' Vasquez.

SANTO DOMINGO

To Crispín Fernández; the late Fradique Lazardo; above all, Cholo Brenes.

MIAMI

To Arabella; Eliseo Cardona; Michael and Margot Carlebach; José Curbelo; Gloria and Emilio Estefán; Frank Amadeo at Estefán Enterprises; Tany and Miriam Gil; Ish Ledesma; Joe and Nancy Galdo; Ronnie Goodrich; Jordan Levin; the MIDEM organization; Tom Moon; Lisette Elguezabal at the *Miami Herald*; Paco de Onis; Tony Purino; James Quinlan; Laura Quinlan and the Rhythm Foundation.

To Caiman Records; Discos Fuentes; Epic Records; J&N Records; Karen Records; Kubaney Records; MPI Records; Sony Records; TH–Rodven Records.

LONDON

To Paul Bradshaw, Satchiko and Kathryn Wilgress at *Straight No Chaser*; Joanna Burns at Epic Records; Charlie Gillett; Lucy Duran; Pam Esterson; the K-Jazz and Starpoint radio pirates and Stuart Lyon; DJs John Armstrong, Dave Hucker, Paul Murphy, Luby Jovanovic, Gilles Peterson, Snowboy, Baz Fe Jaz, Dominique Roome; Chantal Bougnas, Sue Bowerman, Edna Crepaldi, Jan Fairley, Javier Farjé, Mike Frost and Jane Greening, Trevor Herman, Jumbo van Renen, Diana Mansfield, Jo Shinner, Richard Williams; photographers Adrian Boot, Julio Etchart, Karen Fuchs, Andrew Crowley, Cristina Piza and Laurie Sparham; salsa dance masters Nelson Batista and Elder Sánchez; salsa professors John Child and To'Mek; Dave Buttle and staff at Mr Bongo; Joe Boyd and staff at Ryko Latin; Mo Fini and Martin Morales at TUMI Music; Pete King at Ronnie Scott's Club; all at World Circuit.

To Sarah Crompton and Brenda Hayward at *The Daily Telegraph* for the generous leave which made the book possible.

To Sue Cheetham, Richard Edwards, Dorothy Judd and Joyce Vetterlein.

Most particularly, the book would not have been possible without the friendship and support of Shirley Bennett, Hannah Charlton, Suzanne Hodgart, Allan Jenkins, Paul Lashmar, Gerry Lyseight, Paul Marshall, Cherry Smyth, Neil Spencer, David Toop, Melissa Benn and Greg Neale.

Finally, to my mother, Jean Steward.

Sources of Illustrations

Abbreviations: a *above*, b *below*, c *centre*, l *left*, r *right*

1 Vinmag Archives Ltd 2–3 Mo Fini/TUMI Music 6a, 6b photos Karen Fuchs 7l, 7r photos Julio Etchart 8 Canales Archives 9 Mo Fini/TUMI Music 10l photo Mo Fini/TUMI Music 11 map Phil Green 12 photo Rolando Pujol/South American Pictures 13 photo Julio Etchart 14–15 photos Hugh Palmer, footsteps Paul Bevoir 16l Mo Fini/TUMI Music 16r Joy Gordon 17l photo James Bedding 17r photo Verna Gillis 18–19, 20 Biblioteca Nacional, Havana 21, 22 photos Julio Etchart 25 Courtesy Rene López, New York 26 photo Lucy Duran 28–29 photos Cristina Piza 30–31 Mercury Records 32 caricature Ñico, Havana 34 Carino Records, New York 35 photo Mike Dibb 36a Courtesy José Curbelo 36b Courtesy Blue Jackal Entertainment 37 Biblioteca Nacional, Havana 38 Bohemia 39 EGREM Records 41 Courtesy Blue Jackal Entertainment 42–43 photo Mike Dibb 43r Canales Archives 44–45 CENTRO Archives, Hunter College, CUNY, New York 46 The Jesús Colón Papers, CENTRO Archives, Hunter College, CUNY, New York: Benigno Giboyeaux for the Estate of Jesús Colón 47a BMI Archives 47b Max Salazar Archives 48a Author's collection 48b CENTRO Archives, Hunter College, CUNY, New York 49 Canales Archives 50l Ansonia Records 50–51 photo Janette Beckman 51b Canales Archives 52a Canales Archives 52b Philips Records 53a Max Salazar Archives 53b Courtesy José Curbelo 54a West Side Latino 54c Universal Records 54b Tropical Records 55a photo © Raymond Depardon, Magnum 55b RCA Victor 56–57 illustration Tony Wright/Fania Records 57 photo Janette Beckman 58a Canales Archives 58b Alegre Records 59al photo C. M.Guerrero 59ar Seeco Records 59c Rogelio Martínez Archive 59b photo Fran Vogel 61a photo Sue Steward 61b Fania Records 62 illustration Charlie Rosario 63a photo Jimmy Arauz/Fania Archives 64a Fania Records 64b, 65a photos Fran Vogel 65c Canales Archives 65b photo Fran Vogel

66a Canales Archives 66c TH–Rodven Records 66–67 photo Raul Melendez/Caiman Records 67a photo Ricardo Betancourt/RMM Records 67br RMM Records 68 photo Fran Vogel 69 PKO Records 70a photo Sue Steward 70b Rhythm King/Mute Records 71 RMM Records 72a photo David Belove 72b photo David Belove/Xenophile Records 73 Lo Mejor Records 74–75 photo Julio Etchart 76 EPA/AP Photo files 79 World Circuit Records 80 photo Cristina Piza 81 caricature David, Havana 82–83 photo Julio Etchart 83b photo Simon Broughton 84 photo Adrian Boot 86a Qbadisc Records 86c Caribe Music/EMI Spain 86b EGREM Records 87b Fania Records 88a Milan Latin Records 88b photo Cristina Piza 89 photo Carolina Salguero 90 clockwise from top photo Amanda Hobbs, photo Jon Mided/World Circuit Records, photo Geraint Lewis, photo Nick Gold 91a, 91c photos Hugh Palmer 91b Rolando Pujol/South American Pictures 92–93 Caribe Tourist Promotions 94–95a Cajiga Studios 96 photo Jeremy Marre 97 painting Cajiga Studios 99 background Tropical Records 100 Canales Archives 101a Combo Records 101c photo Rod Bristow/Fania Records 101b Inca Records 102a, 102b TH–Rodven Records 103a Sony Discos 103b TH–Rodven Records 104–05 photo Jimmy Arauz/*Latin NY* 106a Remo Records 106–08 photos Verna Gillis 109a Taller, Santo Domingo 109b Fradique Lazardo Archives 110a Oi Records 110b Kubaney Records 111 Cuco Valoy Records 112l Karen Records 112–13a photo Sue Steward 114a Karen Records 114b Julio Etchart 115 Caiman Records 116a photo Marian Balancer/J&N Records 116b photo Maracina Oliveira/Karen Records 117 photo Rafy Claudio/WEA Latina 119 poster Dina and Jeffrey Knapp Collection, Miami Beach

120 Courtesy José Curbelo 121 *Miami Herald* Archives 122a Epic Records 122b Estefán Enterprises/Epic Records 123 painting Esposito/courtesy Guajiro Records 124 *Miami Herald* Archives 125b Courtesy José Lobo 126 photo Sue Steward 127 Andrew Melick/Epic Records 128–29 photo Adrian Boot 130a Fuentes Records 130b photo Jeremy Marre 131a, 131b photos Adrian Boot 132 CBS Records 133 Mango/Island 134 photo Zeida/Codiscos 135 Globestyle/Ace Records 136–37 photo Hernan Diaz/Phillips/Sonolux 137r Adrian Boot 138 montage Darrel Rees at Heart Design 139 Pictorial Press 140–41a Vinmag Archives Ltd 142–43a photo David Redfern 142–43b Vinmag Archives Ltd 143 illustration Jevta 144 Acid Jazz Records 145a artwork Nina Jaffa/Merengada Records 145b photo Wendy Tomlinson 146–47 Ahi-Na-Ma Records 148 Canales Archive 149l, 149r photos David Redfern 150a Max Salazar Archive 150b BGP/Ace Records 151 Panart Records 152a photo Dah-Len/Talking Loud Records 152b Canales Archives 153a photo Fran Vogel 153b Courtesy *Straight No Chaser* magazine 154–55 photos David Redfern 156 Sony Jazz 157 photo © Malick Sidibé 158–59 photo Adrian Boot 159a All Art Records 159b Giles Sala Records 160 photo Graeme Ewens 161 Stern's Records 162–63 montage Darrel Rees at Heart Design 165a photo Felipe Cuevas/*Nuevo Herald* 165b photo Dah-Len/Talking Loud Records 166 all photos Sony

Index